The One Story

The One Story

Kenosis in Creation,
Redemption, and Discipleship

JOHN W. SIMPSON JR.

◆PICKWICK *Publications* • Eugene, Oregon

THE ONE STORY
Kenosis in Creation, Redemption, and Discipleship

Copyright © 2025 John W. Simpson Jr. All rights reserved. Except for brief quotations in critical publications or reviews, no part of this book may be reproduced in any manner without prior written permission from the publisher. Write: Permissions, Wipf and Stock Publishers, 199 W. 8th Ave., Suite 3, Eugene, OR 97401.

Pickwick Publications
An Imprint of Wipf and Stock Publishers
199 W. 8th Ave., Suite 3
Eugene, OR 97401

www.wipfandstock.com

PAPERBACK ISBN: 979-8-3852-2418-0
HARDCOVER ISBN: 979-8-3852-2419-7
EBOOK ISBN: 979-8-3852-2420-3

Cataloguing-in-Publication data:

Names: Simpson, John W., Jr., author.
Title: The one story : kenosis in creation, redemption, and discipleship / John W. Simpson Jr.
Description: Eugene, OR : Pickwick Publications, 2025 | Includes bibliographical references and index(es).
Identifiers: ISBN 979-8-3852-2418-0 (paperback) | ISBN 979-8-3852-2419-7 (hardcover) | ISBN 979-8-3852-2420-3 (ebook)
Subjects: LCSH: Incarnation.
Classification: BT220 .S43 2025 (print) | BT220 .S43 (ebook)

Contents

Preface ix

1. The Story 1
2. An Odd Thing about That Story 17
3. Freedom and Love 39
4. A Place for Us 53
5. Falling 68
6. The One Problem 90
7. Myths, Heroes, and Monsters 109
8. Redemption 132
9. How the Odd Story Converts Us 157
10. Following 173
11. Witness to Freedom 198

Bibliography 219

Index of Authors 231

Index of Biblical References 235

Preface

FOR THOSE WHO PRESENT and re-present the gospel of God to the people of God in preaching and teaching, reminders of the unity of their message are helpful—more than that, *needed* before the multiple claims of the liturgical calendar and other "church calendars," of different age groups and life transitions, and, as we all noticed in 2020, of unexpected events. That our responses to all these are directed by the unity of the gospel is itself part of the lesson to be conveyed in preaching and teaching.

"Kenosis" is one of the better candidates for a name for that unity. The extension of kenosis—the "emptying" of the Son of God in incarnation (Philippians 2:6–8)—into our understanding of creation, redemption, discipleship, and, indeed, the whole Trinity is not a new idea, but it is one that merits continued extension and celebration. That is the purpose of *The One Story*.

The One Story follows a progression of the topics named in its title and subtitle. Chapter 1 tells about "story," "*the* story," and indeed "the *one* story." Chapter 2 continues with the difference of that one story from typical stories, using and explaining the christological word "kenosis." Chapter 2 also begins the connection of "kenosis" with *creation*, which continues through chapters 3 and 4. With creation, the actions of the whole Trinity come into view, and chapters 2 and 3 in particular speak about the nature of God insofar as we can know God. Chapters 5, 6, and 7 depart from words in the book's title and subtitle to focus on *sin*, since there is no redemption without sin, and also because, after and during sin, God continues the human story by his method of kenosis. Indeed, were the subtitle not already unwieldy, it could have included "sustenance" or the like between "creation" and "redemption."

Chapters 8 and 9, then, turn to *redemption*, and there also God continues to operate by kenosis. "Faith" might also have found its way into the subtitle, and chapter 9 includes it as another place where kenosis is the method. In this way chapter 9 begins the turn toward *discipleship*, which is taken up more fully in chapters 10 and 11. "Church" (or "ecclesiology") is another word that could have edged into the subtitle, and chapter 11 speaks to how kenotic discipleship might shape the church's self-understanding and witness. Thus *The One Story* becomes a survey of some of the main loci of systematic theology under the heading "kenosis."

Another theme that travels alongside kenosis is *testimony and confession*. In chapters 1 and 9 those terms help us see how the story of creation and redemption becomes *my* story, that is, the story not only of humanity or the universe but also of the individual human. And "testimony" also plays a large role in explaining, in chapters 8 and 11, the believer's and the church's participation in Jesus's defeat of the powers.

Students of Christian theology can read this book alongside a comprehensive treatment of systematic theology as another voice that, while it does not cover the whole waterfront, approaches the whole from a different direction. One motive for the heavy footnoting in the pages ahead, alongside demonstration of my debts to others, is to supply beginning points for students who want to (or are assigned to) explore some points in greater detail or become further acquainted with the traditions and authors in the background of what I've written. For the same reason, some paragraphs have nearly become forests of Bible references. Other than for those purposes, it is reasonable to read this book with barely a glance at the footnotes.

Those whose task is (or will be) to preach and teach in churches will be led by *The One Story* to consider adding the kenotic perspective on a whole understanding of God and our salvation to their horizon—and to their teaching and preaching. And not just the broad perspective but also some of the many details along the way: I would be honored to hear some part of this book cribbed from a pulpit. Even more, I should be pleased by theology finding its home less in academia and more in church—in catechesis, witness, and action.

For that first audience, the students, it may be that *The One Story* should find its place in biblical studies rather than systematic theology. Indeed, there is plenty of exegetical discussion and synthesis herein. But I'm among those for whom the distinction between biblical studies and systematic theology is more historical than experienced. And I also slant a ways into ethics, at least in the last couple chapters. At any rate, this is not a textbook in the narrow sense for any course. As I look back over it,

I'm reminded just how personal it is. It comes out of my experiences as the child of my parents and as the student of certain teachers, even where I'm fighting against what I was raised to or taught. It is in many ways Mennonite (a more meaningful term than "Anabaptist," to my ears) and mildly Wesleyan, but also ecumenical. And *The One Story* does not so much survey any field as say what makes the most sense to me at the end of the day. So this is an opinionated book.

I use male pronouns for God in *The One Story*. I give my reasons for doing so in chapter 3, under "God Is Personal." Quotations from the Bible are ad hoc and not from any published version, though, with the numerous published English versions, it is inevitable that quotations here will often overlap with published versions. Quotations from patristic documents that are contained in the *Ante-Nicene Fathers* and *Nicene and Post-Nicene Fathers* series are adapted from the translations in those series of volumes except where noted otherwise. Quotations of works by Thomas Aquinas and John Calvin are adapted from multiple published translations.

1

The Story

STORIES AND THE STORY

Structure

People tell stories and listen to stories. A story is a series of more or less connected events, fictional or real, told of and understood according to a particular structure. There are two main components of that structure. First, a story centers around one character, though that character might be a multiplicity such as a nation or several generations of a family, and stories centered around more than one such character might be woven together into one story. Second, the events of a story proceed from a settled state through a challenge to a resolution, which is a new settled state. It begins with the central character in the first settled state, which is then interrupted, though the settled state might be in the past and already interrupted as the story begins. The interruption brings new possibilities and new threats. The story ends with a new settled state, the resolution of the questions raised by the interruption/challenge.[1]

For instance,

1. Cinderella has a happy life with her widowed father (initial settled state a), but then he remarries and dies, and her life becomes one of enslavement and misery (initial settled state b, the beginning of the story);

---

1. This structure is described with an emphasis on the interruption and the middle of the story in Aristotle, *Poetics* 18.

2. the prince enters the story and becomes an issue that threatens to upset the settled state in some way (and does upset marriageable women for miles around); and

3. the fairy godmother shows up and takes things through, aided by the prince's persistent love for Cinderella, to Cinderella's happily-ever-after with the prince (the final settled state).

The same structure applies where the story is a tragedy, where the final settled state is not happily-ever-after but something far different.[2]

We know that stories are structured this way without thinking about it because telling and hearing stories is part of being human.[3] We see this structure even in stories (most stories, in fact) that contain false appearances of settled states or resolutions. The story structure thus applies to parts of stories, just as to the whole story, but is fulfilled incompletely in the parts, thus setting in bold relief for our understanding the falseness of the false endings those parts lead to. There are many cycles and false endings on the way from the beginning to the end of, say, *Oliver Twist*. Story structure is the assumption on which Dickens was able to build such a collection of false endings leading to the definitive path out of the dangers faced by Oliver. We all share that assumption: it sets our expectations for what we will find in a story. And if Dickens, for instance, did not tell us how things "came out" for his character Oliver, he would be violating story structure.

Life

Humans are story-telling and story-listening creatures. We tell stories and listen to them because they organize life and depict it to us as leading through unsettled states—crises of opportunity and danger—to settled ends.

A story can be told of events that have actually happened, but, even so, the telling is not a mere recital of the events but is guided by the story shape. That is, such a telling of what has happened interprets those events as a story. Furthermore, we give coherence to a life by giving it,

---

2. For a helpful introduction to the field of narratology, see Jahn, "Narratology"; Hühn et al., "Living Handbook." On narrative structure, see Jahn, "Narratology," 58–61.

3. Such that listening to stories is fundamental to both anthropology and clinical psychology. See, e.g., Holstein and Gubrium, *Self We Live By*; Flanagan, *Consciousness Reconsidered*; Brown and Augusta-Scott, *Narrative Therapy*.

or parts of it, the structure of a story.[4] Circumstances were stable, then something happened to unsettle them. Then somebody did something that established a new settled state. Stories are thus a way we have of understanding, structuring, and accounting for what has happened to us and to others. They are thus a useful tool, even though they are not one-for-one representations of life. We tell and hear even fictional stories as a way of confirming to ourselves the belief that life does have this kind of structure, that things do get resolved.

But life is not like stories. In life, we do not reach settled states, because life goes on.[5] We might reach Dickens's last page and close the book with satisfaction, but real-life Olivers must grow up and keep facing new challenges. There can be no fixed happily-ever-after because life continues and changes and then eventually comes to an end whether all the issues have been settled or not. And the changes along the way are generally continuations of preceding changes. Life does not tidy up before the next issue comes along. Cinderella and the prince still have to sort out toothpaste etiquette, hair loss, and death. Charming might be crabby before his second cup of coffee. His bride might lose her girlish figure. She might have years of life after he has died, or vice versa. "Love is more pleasing than marriage for the same reason that novels are more entertaining than history."[6]

> All tragedies are finish'd by a death,
> All comedies are ended by a marriage;
> The future states of both are left to faith,
> For authors fear description might disparage
> The worlds to come of both . . .
> So . . . they say no more of Death or of the Lady.[7]

---

4. "Narrative inquiry rests on the epistemological assumption that we as human beings make sense of random experience by the imposition of story structures. That is, we select those elements of experience to which we will attend, and we pattern those chosen elements in ways that reflect the stories available to us" (Duff and Bell, "Narrative Inquiry," 207).

5. "The narrative form of historical discourse also presents a fundamental paradox to the historian: its order, coherence, and completeness are appealing and intelligible, but are imaginary. Reality does not present itself in the form of ready-made stories that come to a logical conclusion. Events occur in a sequence that often has no beginning or end, that lacks coherence, and surely does not exclude extraneous facts. The realism of narrative historical representation is a dream" (Mieroop, *Cuneiform Texts*, 79). See also Morson, *Narrative and Freedom*, 19–20.

6. Chamfort, *Maximes*, 100.

7. Lord Byron, *Don Juan* 3.9.

Few things in life find complete resolution. Stories express or fulfill our wish that things would reach resolution or our sense that they should. So, while it is a trait of humanness to use story-creation as a means for understanding life, story is not life but form, a mapping of reality, not the raw reality itself. To take the map metaphor a step further and carry it back from story to life, we can say that life is where rivers are more varied, surprising, and uncertain than the map's printed blue lines of equal width.

The Story behind All Stories

It is because we easily think in story form that we can understand in broadest terms our experience as humanity:

1. The original settled state is that of humankind with God in the paradise of Eden.
2. Complication comes in the form of sin and suffering.
3. The resolution, the final settled state, is promised for the future, which means not only that this story is *our* story but that we are now still in the midst of it, not at the end.[8]

Story is thus a means for understanding the relation between God and humanity. It is not that the course from creation to redemption *is* a story. A story is a telling, a mapping, or a structuring—interpretation of events, not the events themselves. But the story form is how we understand our creation and redemption because we are human and because creation and redemption are, irreducibly, events.

But it is more true the other way around: not that we understand creation and redemption as a story because we are storytelling creatures but that we are storytelling creatures because we live inside the story of creation and redemption. We are each born into the middle of the unfinished story of humanity, and we carry an awareness of that tension (though not of its origin or solution, unless we are told). We tell stories to enable our understanding of parts of life because our existence is really story-shaped. The invitation, as it were, to tell stories for that purpose—in order to make sense of ourselves—comes from our existence within

---

8. See Middleton, "New Heaven and New Earth," 80–82.

that biggest of all stories. We are the ones who tell stories, but the story structure is something our very existence calls for.[9]

That structure exists because we live within that big story of creation and redemption, but when we apply story structure to life understood other than within that big story, we might be mistaking false endings for the true ending. We might be putting something less complete in place of what God is doing among us. Applying story structure outside the creation-redemption story can sometimes, that is, be idolatry.

"Happily ever after" is eschatology (an understanding of end-times completion) with Prince Charming but not God, and it is debunked if we set that notion of "ever after" over against the realities of life, change, and death. Story structure tells the truth about us, but it is a truth that we try, but fail, to understand fully when we use stories to structure experiences smaller than the big story of creation and redemption. Prince Charming can represent truths, but he is not truth. "Ever after" with him is not the completion of the kingdom of God.

THE STORY IN OUR TIMES

What We Have against Stories and What to Do about It

So thinking of life in story form can be disillusioning. Marriage for "happily ever after" has to deal with what comes after. Disillusionment that comes from the failure of life to be like or to measure up to story, even to tragic story, can cause us to believe that story form is fundamentally deceptive and so cannot tell the truth about us. Day-to-day life is not like a story, and our intellectual heritage has expanded on our realization that it is not. The very notion that truth can be conveyed in story form—much more, that some truth *must* be conveyed in story form—runs up against a fundamental prejudice of modernity, that disillusioned sense

---

9. Ludwig Feuerbach and others saw religion as a projection into mythology of how the human mind works; e.g., Bakunin, *God and the State*, 23: "Heaven is nothing but a mirage in which man, exalted by ignorance and faith, discovers his own image, but enlarged and reversed—that is, *divinized*." What I am saying here about humans as storytelling creatures is a version of the apologetics (defense of the credibility of Christian faith) that works by a reversal of Feuerbach's direction, taking the human mind not as the explanation for faith in God (so Feuerbach and Bakunin) but as that which itself needs to be explained, which many have learned from C. S. Lewis and G. K. Chesterton. See further chapter 6 below, under "The Argument from Our Dividedness," especially note 18.

that story-telling is deceptive or is at least a long route to truth that is more easily arrived at and more directly expressed by those who have left story-telling behind. In other words, we prefer truth in forms that abandon part of our essential humanness.

The modern dislike for stories did begin to wear out during the twentieth century, which is one reason that we now speak of ourselves as "*post*modern." But it can have plenty of life left in it in how Christians sometimes prefer to express and understand their faith. I once preached, in good narrative form,[10] about the children who offended Jesus's disciples (Luke 18:15–17), and I received a response over coffee in the foyer that began with "So your *point* is . . ." I was asked, that is, to affirm a denarrativized or unstoried version of that Gospel story. But in becoming "like little children" we can find ourselves in the story and be changed by it rather than seeking a way around it to something more in accord with our modernity.

The modern intellectual heritage generally regards stories as harmless in their place but not for depicting things as they really are. Within this way of thinking, whatever is of value in a story is discoverable or at least said better when we take away the story, reducing whatever it offers to a more modern and abstract form. Otherwise, if we keep the story, we might be deceived by focusing on the container of truth—the story—in place of the truth itself. So what is true is better understood without the story. That elimination of the story is the meaning of "reductionism."[11]

The gospel gives us a way out of the dilemma brought by the modern "discovery" that truth is better understood and communicated after our separation of truth from that essentially human thing—telling and hearing stories. Understanding life by means of story-telling falls short for us because we apply it to the micro-experiences that make up our lives (however macro- they may seem at the time) and not to the overall experience of existing as God's human creatures. It is in understanding our relationship to God that story-telling has its most natural place and greatest validity. We know that humans use story form to understand

---

10. Having read, alongside many other seminary students, Lowry, *Homiletical Plot*.

11. Similarly, and not coincidentally, the large scale of anything involving a government or other bureaucracy forces us to understand individual narratives by classifying them. Have you ever had to make a complaint by checking boxes on a form? Or perhaps your narrative, spoken or written out, was later dealt with by such pigeon-holing: "We know how to respond to your concerns because they fit into a category we have already defined. Hence this very relevant form letter." More about this later, in chapter 10, under "Personalism."

things. But it is as we acknowledge that biggest story, the story of creation and redemption, and our embeddedness in it that we most clearly see why humans use story form.

Narrative Theology

Christian faith is irreducibly expressed in narrative, that is, in accounts of connected events. Our culture cannot fully understand the gospel without looking beyond its sense that truth is inadequately communicated in stories. Storylessness is how people in our times believe the best thinking is done, and that is what is confronted by theology that seeks to preserve the faith's original narrative expression.

Even as brief a statement as the Apostles' Creed contains a narrative of events without which there could be no Christian faith: Jesus was

> conceived by the Holy Spirit,
> born of the Virgin Mary,
> suffered under Pontius Pilate,
> was crucified, died, and was buried;
> he descended to the dead.
> On the third day he rose again;
> he ascended into heaven.

These essential connected events cannot be boiled down to any sort of philosophical or moral system of thought or teaching, no matter how profound that system might be or how much it might be based on Christian cultural traditions. What we believe in is not a system or a collection of ideals but a person, one who is described, like all of us, in terms of events, that is, in terms of his history and our history with him.[12] We do not extract any sort of fundamental principles or ideas from those events. Rather, we understand those events and that person as decisive in our lives, we interpret ourselves in terms of those events, and we take our places in that history.

Because we each thus become part of the story of Jesus, our faith is narratively expressed at another level besides that of Jesus's history: in terms of the life and experiences of each of us who believes and of the communities of those who believe. Just as the Bible communicates most

---

12. The difference between the biblical (and therefore narrative) base of Christian faith and the abstraction that has been typical of systematic theology was described well in Goldingay, "Biblical Narrative and Systematic Theology."

of its truth in terms of the life experiences of people—whether individuals or part of the whole of people of God—so also truth is not what a Christian knows abstractly but what he or she incorporates into life by experiencing and living the redemption given by God in Christ.

Hence the importance of testimony in Christian faith, whether we think of the centrality of eyewitness testimony to the resurrection of Jesus at the beginning of the spread of the gospel (Acts 1:8, 22; 2:24, 32; 1 Cor 9:1; 15:3–8, 12–14) or of personal testimonies given at baptism[13] or in the informal "testimony meetings" of some Christian traditions: "This was the state of my life as an unredeemed sinner, this is how Christ came into my life, and this is how he set things right."[14] The long historical prologue to the covenant renewal in Joshua 24 is a model, saying, in effect, "We are the people defined by God's great works among us and for us, specifically. . . ." The primary place where we answer the question "What is Christianity?" and give evidence for our answer is not in doctrinal exposition or apologetics but in the credibility of that testimony about what God has done.[15] God values our testimony enough that he calls on it to assert his uniqueness over against those who testify on behalf of idols (Isa 44:8–9).

Events do not redeem; God does. But we appropriate redemption as we see it in the events, as, that is, we adopt the interpretation of the events that identifies them as our redemption. Our appropriation is, then, part of that train of events, and is affirmed by narration, that is, in our testimonies.

Accounts of Christian theology have historically often focused much of their beginning attention on abstract questions of the nature, possibility, and coherence of religious knowledge, but, generally speaking, the trend through the twentieth century and especially since the 1970s has been toward beginning with the narrative basis of our faith, that is, with the Bible and especially the work of Jesus.[16] "Narrative theology" is used

---

13. E.g., the questions asked of candidates for baptism in *The Discipline of the Wesleyan Church 2012* begin with, "In order that we may hear your testimony of what God has done for you . . ." (Wesleyan Church, *Discipline* §5515).

14. On the genre of such testimonies, see Jacobs, *Looking Before and After*, 20–23.

15. On explorations of this distinction, see Ward, *Introducing Practical Theology*, 55–68.

16. This change is clearly and briefly defined in Barton, "Disclosing Human Possibilities," 53–54; Coakley, "Kenosis and Subversion." "There was something broadly similar in the orientations of eighteenth- and nineteenth-century Catholic neo-scholasticism, Calvinist orthodoxy of the same period, and nineteenth-century Protestant liberalism.

of a group of particularly conscious and deliberate attempts to ground theology in a narrative base, that is, in Scripture read with particular attention to narrative aims and structures.[17] It has been four decades since it was asked "whether narrative theology is only another fad in theological discussion or . . . a substantive contribution to the task of making Christian faith intelligible in the modern world."[18] Whichever it is, we still need the narrative expression of our faith—which has existed from the beginning, from Exodus 20:2 and Joshua 24 through the Gospels and the Apostles' Creed—to woo us from the anti-story prejudices of the modern era.

The Problem of Particularity

The people living in an isolated valley and not watching television or accessing online maps might well have a big story, a story that with its beginning accounts for the existence and relationships of everything and the end of which is a universal eschatology that resolves all the issues that have been left unresolved along the way and clears the way for whatever new state of existence (or nonexistence) there is to be. This story can include everything that exists, all gods, all humans and their ways of life, other beings, and all the furniture of the universe. And it certainly includes the people who tell and listen to the story, who are, as they speak and hear, in the middle of the story. The big story sets their lives in

---

All of them took the first stage of theology as philosophical, as an apologetic which is intended to speak the same language or share the same ground with non-Christians. . . . Barth is rejecting this when he affirms that the biblical story covers *all* of the ground and the only ground on which our faith in Jesus Christ rests" (Coakley, "Kenosis and Subversion," 100). So Francesca Aran Murphy: "The desire of early modern Christians for 'elaborate apologetics sprang from rejecting the overarching story, for now the biblical stories had to be fitted into other frameworks of meaning'" ("What Is Narrative Theology," in Murphy, *God Is Not a Story* §1.3, quoting George Lindbeck). Similarly, see Frei, *Eclipse of Biblical Narrative*.

17. See particularly Green, *Scriptural Authority and Narrative Interpretation*; Jones, "Narrative Theology." On the relationship of narrative interpretation to theology, see, e.g., Thiemann, *Revelation and Theology*, 112–40. "The ultimate canon within the canon must . . . be the person of Jesus and . . . the narration of the saving acts of God. This follows from the fact that the Bible as a whole corpus of literature is narrative in its framework. . . . That framework itself dictates the priority of the historical quality over levels of interpretation which would be less historical by being more abstract (such as ontology and systematic dogma) or individualistic" (Yoder, *To Hear the Word*, 77–78). See also Yoder, *To Hear the Word*, 80, 88.

18. Stroup, *Promise of Narrative Theology*, 6.

context and gives them their place in the universe and in its development and/or decay.

But the people in another valley on the other side of the mountain might have a different story, one that puts *them* in the center of things. That stage of modernism called postmodernism observes this and allows it, because

- neither story is true at the expense of the other or false to the benefit of the other,
- each story has uses—that is, it carries out functions for its own tellers and hearers,
- neither story, viewed from the perspective of the modern person who has been in both valleys and several other places, can uphold its claim to be universal, that is, normative everywhere, even outside its own valley (at the expense of other stories), and
- one can break down either story or both of them into parts, use some parts in creating another story, and disregard other parts.

The Bible story of creation and redemption is one such story, and it, too, claims universality. This story, like some others, makes no sense, in fact, unless it is the story of all of us, even of those people several mountain ranges away. It is possible to tell this story as if it were valid only in our valley, but then it is altered. The gospel story as it presents itself assumes that it describes the atmosphere in which all humanity lives and moves. This is the "stumbling block of particularity," the odd (in our time) belief that one man named Jesus, far more circumscribed geographically and temporally than most of us are today, makes all the difference, not just for those who ascribe that importance to him but also for every human being.[19]

One can use parts of the one story of creation and redemption and exclude other parts, but the result can only be another story, not the gospel story. What is more, to do so would be to judge the gospel by some standard or other from outside itself—by setting up criteria for selection or rejection of its parts. In that one story, taken as a whole (as it

---

19. It is not that we all have the *same* place in the story or that Jesus makes the *same* difference for all of us. In other words, the story's universality does not require universalism, which is the conclusion that, if anyone is saved by Jesus, then everyone is saved. The gospel is a universal challenge to response, and all do not respond in the same way. See further the discussion of faith in chapter 9 below.

demands), there is nothing to disregard, not because we want to protect a pretty story but because it is the story we and all people are born into, not one we have chosen. It cannot be ignored, negotiated with, or analyzed. Accepting it for what it is thus puts us out of step with our time.

Saying all that is very much like preaching, perhaps even with hellfire and brimstone. If it were heard in a time that believed in the possibility of universal truth, then it could be directed to the choir, but that is not the time in which we live. We have exalted minute choice so highly that the law of noncontradiction has become an affront (or choice is exalted for us such that ordering salad rather than soup introduces another menu of options: croutons? parmesan? which of six dressings and on the side or dump it on? and be ready with an answer when the pepper grinder is hovering over). If we hear any voices from that choir or its preacher, we reassure ourselves by perceiving the exception as an amusing or dangerous affirmation of our anti-universal rules.

To some extent, the postmodern dislike for claims to universal relevance gives way to modernity and becomes a preference for *particular* stories. If, for instance, my big story is like that of some indigenous Australians in claiming that human life began in my valley ("*we are the original people, and all of you come from us*"), that story (or that part of it) is rejecting, along with *its* claim to universal truth, the story told by genome science. Science claims to be non-story, that is, a properly modern expression of truth, and only as such does it make its own claim to be universal. Still, it is a story in direct competition with those indigenous Australians' story. We might say that the two stories answer different questions and have their places in separate contexts, but that would be to pass over their conflicting claims to universality. They give more than just answers to separable questions, and therefore they do compete.[20]

The gospel story must be a universal story because its God is the creator of all things. Some theologians have perhaps overestimated the

---

20. This is analogous to the Bible and evolution. "Theistic evolution" is certainly possible (there are, after all, people who teach it), but we cannot simply say, as I learned it in college, that there need be no problem because two separate compartments of knowledge are involved. Rather, those who do "theistic evolution" best are those who acknowledge that the conflicts of the Bible story and the science story cannot be sorted out by sending them to different corners, that those stories must be interwoven for a complete "theistic evolution" to be possible. Incidentally, the encounter of the indigenous Australians with the genome researcher was part of a televised presentation of how genome research contributes to understanding of human origins. I have not been able to track it down several years after seeing it, and the issues go much deeper. See Kowal et al., "Indigenous Genomics."

degree to which it is in competition with stories told by modern science and have reacted by discarding more of the story than they needed to. I think particularly here of Rudolf Bultmann.[21] The issue is not only, even not principally, how much the gospel can afford to claim but how much the stories told by modern science should claim, on which there is a large range of opinions, from scientists who claim that belief in God has become impossible (which is not far from the set of premises that Bultmann worked from) to scientists who believe in God. Christians might allow science to help in separating the gospel story from temporary cultural trimmings, but before that they begin by believing the story, and they recognize that temporary cultural trimmings include not just those of Bible times and the gospel but also those of our own times and cultures, including those of scientists.

The Story Matters

Understanding human existence before God in terms of story structure helps us to preserve the substance and significance of events rather than subjecting that substance to reductionistic interpretation. Time can be glossed over by other understandings, by timeless philosophy. Story structure, the temporality of anything presented in narrative genres, guards us from thinking that for something to be true it must be true outside and regardless of any particular events. It affirms that our existence and God's action among us take place in time. Story structure thus enables us to wait rather than wondering why the end was not created right away, just as we understand why Cinderella and Charming were not wed before birth, that is, why we do not throw away all the story except the last page.

Story also helps us to permit ourselves to attach importance to details, even to events that seem to pass without changing anything. Nothing is valueless: it is all bread on the water. And traveling along with those details is no less than the significance of our selves to ourselves. This is a way of saying that we have value because God has created us and is redeeming us. In this way this importance of details such as you and me is like the incarnation—God's coming among us as the man Jesus—which is God's clear affirmation of the worth of humanness because human is what God becomes in incarnation. The details of your testimony matter

---

21. E.g., Bultmann et al., *Kerygma and Myth*, 1–44.

because you are one for whom Jesus died. Because creation-and-redemption is a story, we can take seriously both our attempts to find structure by telling stories and our sense, expressed in that story-telling activity, that there is a meaning to our existence and our lives.[22]

Just as the story about Jesus and the children cannot be reduced to a "point" and remain effective, so also even a story with a clear moral lesson cannot be reduced to a moral principle. King David was changed, not by a propositional sermon but by a narrative sermon—when, that is, he realized that the prophet Nathan's story of the murderously greedy rich man was about David himself (2 Sam 12). The story became effective in that way, not by being reduced to a point or a principle.

But David's identification with the rich man connects us with the "point" of the prophet's story in another way. The point, from this other perspective, is not what the story can be reduced to but the *turning* point in how the king hears the story or in how any listener might hear a story. It is the point at which the story becomes a story *for* the listener or *about* the listener. "Having got 'the point' of the narrative, we do not then ignore the narrative and think simply about the point; on the contrary, we go back to the narrative better equipped to read it."[23] "Getting the point" in this sense is the beginning of conversion if the story is the whole or a part of that story behind all stories, the story of creation and redemption. Jesus's parables work in the same way as Nathan's parable: it is as a parable takes on the specificity of a story about me, that is, when its "point" is discovered, that it can disclose possibilities and call for repentance (a negative example is in Matt 21:45). Repentance begins when the proscenium is crossed and the hearer takes the responsibility of having a place in the story, when, that is, the hearer begins to exercise faith.[24]

THE UNITY OF THE STORY

We learn about the story of our creation and redemption from the Bible, though the Bible's mixed bag of stories, histories, poetry, propaganda, sage advice, and whatnot does not hand us the story on a platter. We are

---

22. Hence the apologetics described in note 9 above suggests that we seek meaning because there is meaning.

23. Barton, "Disclosing Human Possibilities," 56. Barton's article is the basis for most of what I say in this paragraph.

24. See further chapter 9 below, under "Faith Comes by Hearing."

faced with the task of discerning a unity in the Bible, and that unity is the one story of creation and redemption.[25]

Use of the story form gives us a framework for understanding the continuity of creation and redemption. For Irenaeus, writing in the latter half of the second Christian century, the unity of creation and redemption was an essential part of his response to the different story told by Christian Gnostics.[26] For them, creation, not sin, was the complication that made the rest of the story necessary. Their story was brought to blessed resolution for those who realized that their created bodies were prisons that held their souls and that subjected them to suffering. Irenaeus responded that the creator of the physical world and the redeemer are one and the same God, that redemption does not save us from the creator's sin or mistake but completes the creator's purpose.[27]

Christians have sometimes needed to hear that response again, not necessarily because of any doubt on our part about the identity of the creator but because in other ways we find it easy to separate our bodies from what we really are, what we wish we were, or what we will be as redeemed, or God's purposes in creation from his purposes in redemption, or our lives here and now from movement toward our goal and our blessing. The solution is to see how redemption continues and brings to its close the story that began with creation and continues even now.

That the God of Israel is the creator is presented as a reason for faith in God's future vindication of his people Israel:

---

25. And perhaps the very diversity of the Scriptures is an important part of how God is revealed. "The narratives of this God who eschews brute force [more about that later!] were not edited with the brute force necessary to impose a single, clear framework" (Placher, *Narratives*, 88). Thus God encourages both our acceptance of diversity in his people and our use of non-coercive rhetoric. I recognize the challenge here to my emphasis on "the unity of the story." Indeed, Placher goes on to a critique of "many of those who talk these days about the use of biblical narrative in theology [who] also emphasize the unity of the (singular!) story," naming—in particular—Hans Frei, George Lindbeck, Gabriel Fackre, and Stanley Hauerwas (89). The non-coercive diversity of the Bible, if we can call it that, points Placher in a different direction than it does me. I remain impressed by the unity of the scriptural story.

26. See further chapter 8 below, under "The New Beginning."

27. See Ratzinger, *In the Beginning*, 96–100, on the opposition between the strain of modern thought he calls "Gnosticism" and "the Christian option," according to which "the doctrine of creation is . . . inseparably included within the doctrine of redemption. The doctrine of redemption is based on the doctrine of creation, on an irrevocable Yes to creation" (Ratzinger, *In the Beginning*, 99).

> Why do you talk, Jacob,
> and say, Israel,
> "My path is hid from the Lord,
> and God disregards justice for me"?
> Don't you know?
> Haven't you heard?
> The Lord is the everlasting God,
> the creator of every part of the earth. (Isa 40:27–28; cf. the rest of Isa 40 and Ps 121:2)

This association of creation and redemption continues when redemption is understood as what God is accomplishing through Jesus.[28] The God revealed in Christ is the creator: "The God who said 'let light shine out of darkness' has shone in our hearts to bring the light of the knowledge of the glory of God in the face of Christ" (2 Cor 4:6). It is for this reason that Christ can be known as the one through whom creation happened (1 Cor 8:6; Col 1:16; Heb 1:2). "We are dealing with no other God in the event of reconciliation than we are in the event of creation."[29] So the purpose of God that existed before the fall or sin or suffering is still being carried out. The story of creation and redemption can be called a "mystery" that could only be revealed at the right time, but it was always God's purpose, from the beginning (Eph 1:9–11; 3:2–5, 8–11).

So creation and redemption are one story.[30] Since they are, we do not exalt creation or regard it as complete, nor do we regard it as setting a standard to which redemption must move back toward or by which our lives or our morality should be shaped: creation must always be viewed through its continuation in redemption. That is the flipside of saying that redemption is not a plan B. Redemption is the original plan.[31]

---

28. Note how creation, covenant, and redemption come together in Romans 4:16–17.

29. Weber, *Foundations of Dogmatics*, 1:465.

30. Jewett brings out two possible objections to regarding creation and redemption as sharing one purpose in his *God, Creation, and Revelation*, 494–95. First, if "the new creation in Christ is the ultimate purpose of the first creation, the transgression of the creature (the Fall [of humankind into sin, Genesis 3]) must have been necessary." Second, some believe—and Jewett apparently agrees—that a supralapsarian (pre-fall) purpose must mean that God's will for salvation must take the form of double predestination of individuals. A will that must be obeyed, like that of Rumpole's wife, crowds out the exercise of any other will. We will deal with both objections later (in chapter 5, under "The Fall Is Part of the Creation-Redemption Story," and in chapter 4, under "For Other Wills," respectively). For now, suffice it to say that the "mystery" passages in Ephesians, just referred to, require us to say that redemption does fulfill the one purpose of God.

31. "The whole temporal dispensation was made by divine providence for our

That creation and redemption belong together in one story means that Jesus matters from the beginning. "In the beginning was the Word" (John 1:1), and the incarnation of the Word did not occur as a solution to an unforeseen bump in the road. The crucifixion did not just meet some prerequisite for our forgiveness. Rather, Jesus's incarnation, crucifixion, and resurrection show us God's eternal intention and method in relation to humankind as they were from the beginning.

---

salvation" (Augustine, *On Christian Doctrine* 1.35). Another way of saying all this is that the actions *ad extra* of the persons of the Trinity are all conjoint. Perhaps the greatest challenges to this now are popular sayings that set the Son over against the Father in atonement (see chapter 8 below, under "Theories"). Or bits of popular Marcionism (a Christian heresy that dispensed with the Old Testament), against which we must say that the Old Testament is altogether about grace. The one story also draws us away from any vestige of an understanding of the creator as simply a "first cause" who exists to explain material existence, a deity congenial to deism (belief in a creator god who has no further involvement with what he has created once he has created it). See further Weber, *Foundations of Dogmatics*, 1:467–68.

2

An Odd Thing about That Story

JESUS, HUMAN GOD

God the Impassible

DEFENDERS OF CHRISTIAN FAITH in the second and third centuries did not have to face polytheism, plain and simple, but were able to assume and make use of a philosophical monotheism that had long been in place among intellectual elites in Greco-Roman culture. It was a simple matter to demonstrate that "we [Christians] are not alone in confining the notion of God to unity."[1] The traditional Jewish contrast between the God of Israel and idols (e.g., Deut 4:15–17; Isa 44:6–20; Jer 10:2–16; Ps 96:5; Wis 13–14; and in the background of 1 Thess 1:9–10)—played a part for these Christian writers,[2] but common ground already existed between Christians and non-Jewish non-Christians in the understanding of the one supreme God.[3] Later assessments of the effects of this identification

---

1. Athenagoras, *Legatio pro Christianis* 6, referring to Plato, Aristotle, and the broader philosophical tradition. See also John of Damascus, *Exposition of the Orthodox Faith* 1.3: "That there is a God, then, is no matter of doubt to those who receive the Holy Scriptures . . . nor indeed to most of the Greeks," "Greeks" meaning the intellectual elite. See further Mitchell and Nuffelen, *One God*, esp. Frede, "Case for Pagan Monotheism."

2. *Letter to Diognetus* 2; Justin Martyr, *I Apology* 9; cf. Irenaeus, *Against Heresies* 3.6.

3. Cf. the argument of Celsus, a Gentile non-Christian, against worship of images, in Origen, *Contra Celsum* 1.5: "Those who draw near to lifeless images as if they were gods act like those who would enter into conversation with houses."

of the Christian God with the supreme deity of the philosophers and poets have been both positive[4] and negative.[5]

Fundamental to this shared understanding was a "sharp division between the soul (or spirit) and the body" and "between God and the world."[6] This exclusion of the divine and the human/earthly from each other and the understanding of God as necessarily impassible and immutable, that is, never suffering or experiencing emotion, change, or movement, were shared broadly in Greco-Roman culture, going back as far as Xenophanes in the sixth to fifth centuries BC:

> There is one god, the greatest among gods and men, neither in
> form nor thought like unto mortals.
> He sees all over, thinks all over, and hears all over.
> But without toil he sways all things by the thought of his mind.
> And he abideth ever in the same place, moving not at all.[7]

Much the same might be heard later from Christians: God is "unchangeable, because he is immortal."[8] Origen, a Christian writer of the first half of the third century, quoted, as "an article of faith," apart from any context, Mal 3:6: "I the Lord do not change."[9]

---

4. Calvin in the sixteenth century reported positively on the second-century Apologists' use of philosophical monotheism as a basis for their work (*Institutes* 1.10.3). The effect of beginning with a shared concept of God takes on a new significance with "natural theology" (see note 22 below), which attempts to say as much as can be said about God apart from revelation (as in, e.g., *Institutes* 1). In response to Harnack (see the next two notes) this early "Hellenization" of Christian faith has been regarded as a necessary or positive development by, e.g., Williams, *Arius*.

5. "Christianity borrowed the very idea of theology, its methods and principles, from paganism.... Not only was Christianity contaminated by the pagan idea of theology, but the ancient Christian idea of hierarchical monotheism, so central to early Christianity, could be found within the evolution of paganism itself, especially under the influence of the imperial ideology." So Arnold I. Davidson in the introduction to Hadot, *Philosophy as a Way of Life*, 4–5. Most prominently, Adolf von Harnack regarded this "Hellenization" of Christian theology negatively. So also Ellul, *Subversion*, 22–26, who speaks of the Christian adoption of Hellenistic thought as the "transition ... from history to philosophy" (23).

6. Harnack, *Mission and Expansion of Christianity*, 31–32.

7. Burnet, *Early Greek Philosophy*, 115.

8. Theophilus, *Ad Autolycum* 1.4.

9. Origen, *Contra Celsum* 1.21. There was, though, nothing like a simple unanimity of Christian theologians in this understanding of God as remote and unaffected by change. Such an understanding was taken to extremes in the complications of Christian Gnostic systems, which were attempts to take the supreme God farther out of contact and involvement with the world than a sympathetic Christian reader of the Hebrew Scriptures such as Irenaeus (e.g., *Against Heresies* 4.2.3) could tolerate.

This understanding of God has continued through most of subsequent Christian theology. For example, God is immovable, "distinct from the world in existence and essence, blissful in Himself and from Himself, ineffably exalted above all things that exist or that can be conceived besides Himself."[10] Or "Naturally, we experience God as being sometimes more gracious than at other times, sometimes angry, sometimes distant, sometimes loving and attentive. But none of these ways of speaking is an accurate way of describing God in Himself."[11]

Recent decades have seen the growth of a reaction against such understandings of God, which are often lumped together and stigmatized as "classical theism." A major trend during the theologically busy twentieth century, and it is still with us, is away from the distant and unchanging deity the Christian God was for so long. It has become, in fact, de rigueur to say that the impassible and immovable God of "classical theism" is not like the God of the Hebrew Bible, who is moved by his passions, including his love for Israel and his wrath toward sin, or like the God revealed to us in Jesus.[12] This more passionate God is also the suffering God—God more identified with Jesus's sufferings.[13] This reaction is certainly necessary in view of the Bible's frank description of the acts and, dare we say, the emotions of God, his deep love and (resultant) wild wrath.[14] We

---

10. Quoting, just as an example that could be paralleled in many Christian traditions, First Vatican Council, *Dei Filius* 1, as translated in Neuner and Dupuis, *Christian Faith*, 109.

11. Smit and Fowl, *Judges and Ruth*, on Judg 2:6–3:6.

12. "Contemporary theology is presently occupied with the separation of the original Christian statement about God from all the general religious ideas which have clustered about it" (Weber, *Foundations of Dogmatics*, 1:398). "General religious ideas" means ideas of an abstract *divinitas* to which Christian teaching is, in effect, added. Also describing this development positively is Bauckham, "Only the Suffering God Can Help."

13. This turn to the "suffering God" has been seen as a turn to patripassianism, a version of the ancient heresy known as Sabellianism according to which the one God, not just the second person of a "Trinity," suffered on the cross (Goetz, "Suffering God"). Indeed, the third- and fourth-century context in which patripassianism was labeled a "heresy" included a view of God as "impassible," that is, without passions or suffering. In understandings of the atonement, therefore, assignment of different roles to the first and second persons of the Trinity, the Father and the Son, is less likely to be a feature than it was in the past. The suffering of Jesus is not what the Father demands of the Son but the suffering of the one God. See, e.g., Heim, *Saved from Sacrifice*, 4.

14. So Barth, *Church Dogmatics* 2/1:257: "God is who He is in the act of His revelation." That is, there is no impassive core of God's being behind what we see as God acts. Here "revelation" can sound too narrow, but for Barth, with his emphasis on God's initiative, "revelation" can be a term for the whole divine-human relationship.

always need to return to the events, to *what God has done*, in order to understand why we can talk about God at all. In this way we understand God's immovability as that of a faithful one who loves rather than that of a fixed object. Emphasis on divine action, love, and response is necessary and is a return to the Bible.[15]

Jesus the Impossible

Because of the traditional understanding of God as immovable, Jesus, the one who is divine and human, came in the early Christian centuries to be somewhat like a blend of oil and water.[16] God is impassible, but Jesus did, of course, suffer as other humans do. Indeed, suffering is a prominent and key feature of what he did.

The problem was posed already by the non-Christian philosopher Celsus, who argued in the second century against Christianity that it posits an impossible blending of human and divine in Jesus, given the distinction between God and anything earthly.[17] Origen's christological response did not attempt to think of God differently but, accepting Celsus's view on that point, sought to explain how Jesus could be both divine and human: Christ possesses *two natures*, one human and one divine.[18] This terminology of "two natures," already in place in the writings of Tertullian as well as Origen in the first half of the third century, came to be central in the fourth- and fifth-century church's christological solutions, in which

---

15. This return is why, in theology at least, the twentieth century was a time for gradually moving away from distrust of stories. Robert W. Jenson gives examples, among them Peter Brunner: "Antiquity's mode of thought read into God a fixed, unmovable, and abstract perfection" and thus made "talk of new judgments, new reactions, new deeds, and new words in God" sound like "naive anthropomorphism" (Brunner quoted in translation in Braaten and Jenson, *Christian Dogmatics*, 1:166).

16. E.g., Drown speaks of "an inability to conceive that God and man could actually be united. It was a part of the Greek dualism, which believed that God and man could come together only if God ceased to be God or man ceased to be man. The thought was that if God came into human life it must be at cost of human limitations. All these must disappear at the influx of divinity. But if we believe that God and man can really come together, that God can be manifested in human life, then we shall get rid of this antagonism. We shall believe that God's life can be manifested even in the limitations of humanity. We shall not begin with a premise that prevents us from reading the New Testament as it stands, and that dehumanizes the Christ" (Drown, "Growth of the Incarnation," 511).

17. Origen, *Contra Celsum* 5.2.

18. Most clearly in Origen, *De Principiis* 1.2.1.

- the two natures were asserted against understandings of Christ that excluded either divinity or humanity and
- the unity of the two natures was asserted against understandings that made such a radical distinction between human and divine in Jesus that he became two distinct beings, or nearly so.[19]

So, for instance, from the Council of Chalcedon (451):

> This one and the same Jesus Christ, the only-begotten Son [of God] must be confessed to be in two natures, unconfusedly, immutably, indivisibly, inseparably, and that without the distinction of natures being taken away by such union, but rather the peculiar property of each nature being preserved and united in one person and one subsistence; not parted or divided into two persons but one and the same Son, and only begotten, God, the Word, the Lord Jesus Christ.

Difficulties arose, and divided Christians, from how the unity and duality were to be given expression (and a contributing factor was the diversity of languages involved, mainly Greek and Latin). The unity of Jesus was axiomatic, but the two natures were necessary because of the understanding of God as that which does not change and is free from passions. In the equation known as Jesus, God was the most constant constant.

Beginning with Jesus

The picture changes if, instead of beginning with an understanding of God and then asking how the man Jesus can be that God, we look at the man Jesus and ask what kind of God he incarnates.[20] Rather than referring to a shared general concept of "God" so that, when we say "Jesus is God," we can apply that concept to the man Jesus, and then everybody will know what we mean, instead we know Jesus and derive our understanding of God from who Jesus is.[21] This means that we still work from

---

19. Such a radical distinction—the duality of the natures—was particularly insisted on in the Nestorian camp, e.g., by Theodoret, who regarded it as necessary in view of the immutability and impassibility of God and the suffering of the man Jesus (*Dialogues*; *Demonstrations by Syllogisms*).

20. With regard to Phil 2:6–11, see, e.g., Wright, *Climax of the Covenant*, 90. See further Hill, *Paul and the Trinity*, 88–99.

21. This is an extension of the Bible's presentation of God as the one who reveals himself, that is, who does not await or encourage our figuring him out but who reveals himself and expects that our understanding of him will come from his self-revelation.

the axiom that Jesus is a unitary being, God and human, but also that we do not assign parts of that being or aspects of his experience to either his divine or his human "nature." It means, rather, that whatever he is and does he is and does as God and as human. We set aside any prior understanding of God in favor of hearing and observing our teacher Jesus.

For some this might require a (perhaps only theoretical) atheistic moment as they move through not-knowing to hearing.[22] And it might be taken as a similar move—but in the opposite direction—to the *via negativa* of pseudo-Dionysius, for whom God begins to be known once we have negated any possible name for God or description of God.[23] But, beginning from Jesus, we do not know God (the new negative) until, except, and as we know Jesus as God. We believe in God not because of philosophical argument or social custom or habit, but because we know Jesus.[24]

On that, see Jüngel, *God as the Mystery of the World*, 13. As with calling Jesus "God," so also with calling him "the Word"; the author of the Gospel of John "had no intention of honouring Jesus by investing Him with the title of Logos, but rather . . . he honoured the title itself by applying it . . . as a predicate of Jesus" (Barth, *Church Dogmatics* 2/2:97).

22. Weber speaks of the necessity of paying heed to Feuerbach and Nietzsche on our way to an understanding of God (*Foundations of Dogmatics*, 1:398). David Ford speaks of "the sustained attack on 'religion'" in Karl Barth's *Römerbrief* making the word "God" itself problematic. "'God' is no longer someone Christians can assume they have in common with other religious people, even (or especially) within the Church. Since the crucifixion is seen to have an epistemological role in rebutting all claims to knowing God except paradoxically through itself and the resurrection, there is no longer any connection between the Gospel and religion or natural theology. This means that God is to be described only through that story" (Ford, *Barth and God's Story*, 21). "Natural theology" is the attempt to identify what can be said about God apart from revelation. For Thomas Aquinas, as one prominent example, this was always accompanied by the caution that we do still need revelation for our understanding to get to the God of the Bible. But for the eighteenth-century Deists, the point was to ignore or deny the possibility of, and certainly the need for, revelation.

23. Pseudo-Dionysius was a Christian theologian of the late fifth or early sixth century. The *via negativa* begins from the assumption that everything we might think of as earthly human experience is what God is not and goes on to describe God in terms of characteristics of created things, mainly of humans, that God does not possess, so that several of the traditional "attributes of God" are expressed in words beginning with negating prefixes—for example, *im*passible and *im*mutable.

24. Again, on the distinction between history and philosophy, see Ellul, *Subversion of Christianity*, 23. "Jesus believed in God" shows how "beginning from Jesus" is a trinitarian exercise: "Christians come to know God precisely as triune: the Logos incarnate in Jesus, the one whom Jesus called Father, and the Holy Spirit" (Placher, *Narratives of a Vulnerable God*, 55).

This also means that we believe not in a universal or abstract "God" waiting to be attached to specifically Christian content but in the God of the people of Israel, because Jesus did so. We believe in this God only because (and after) we have heard Jesus. In that way we are like the Thessalonian Christians, who, at least as Paul portrayed them to themselves, learned about "God Father" and "Lord Jesus Christ" (1 Thess 1:1, 3; 3:11, 13) simultaneously. Indeed (and again, as Paul portrayed them to themselves), because the gospel of Christ was the starting point of their experience of the one God, they understood God the Father only from the narrative of Jesus.[25]

Our "beginning with Jesus" also connects with language found in the Gospel of John and elsewhere in the New Testament about the relation of Jesus the Son and God the Father, especially as it touches on "knowledge." For example, John 14:6-7: "If you knew me, you would know my Father as well. From now on, you do know him and have seen him." In knowing Jesus, and only in knowing Jesus, we know God (cf. 8:19; 14:9-10; 1 John 2:13, 23; 2 John 9; 2 Cor 4:6). Similarly, Matthew 11:27 and Luke 10:22: "No one knows the Son except the Father or the Father except the Son and anyone the Son chooses to reveal him to" (cf. John 8:18). And, similar also in thought though not words, Paul tells us that we exist *for* God the Father and do so *through* the Lord Jesus Christ (1 Cor 8:6; cf. "life," "live" in John 5:26, 39-40; 14:19; 1 John 4:9).

Something that travels along with "beginning with Jesus" is also a more positive assessment of humanness, our humanness as well as his. The incarnation is "inconceivable" to theology on any other basis: apart from it having happened, we would not and do not think of it happening.[26] But, for Jesus, revealing God, even *being* God, is, in fact, apparently compatible with being human, with human limitations, sin excepted, but sin is not an essential part of the definition of humanness.[27]

---

25. So Paul seems to portray them to themselves, which seems to contradict the synagogue basis of the Thessalonian congregation according to Acts 17:1-4. See further my "Shaped by the Stories." "In a Christian confession of faith, faith in God is really a function of faith in Christ" (Cullmann, *Earliest Christian Confessions*, 39).

26. So Barth, *Church Dogmatics* 1/2:173; cf. 177. Barth argued for letting "fact," that is, Christ as God's actual self-revelation, precede "interpretation," which includes both christological doctrine and any premise one might bring to formulation of that doctrine, such as the nature of God (*Church Dogmatics* 1/2:3-6, 16-17, 26-27).

27. See below, chapter 5, under "What Sin Is" and "Life Goes On," and chapter 8, under "Jesus Does It Right" and "Staying on the Human Course."

KENOSIS

The Kenosis of Christ

Because we begin with Jesus, any sort of question about what kind of story the story of creation and redemption is would have to be answered by understanding him as the originator of the story. He gives shape to the story, and, because of him, it is an oddly-shaped story. He is the means of our knowledge of God, the depicter of God, and the description of God, so his incarnation and cross are at the center of our understanding of God. For this reason we focus on the kenosis of Christ as the key to our understanding of God in his relationship to us.

"Kenosis" as a term in Christian theology is derived from the use of *ekenōen*, often translated "emptied," in Phil 2:7.[28] It has been a fruitful concept in christological discussion for centuries and has also come to be, within the last century, a key term in reorientations of "theology proper," in, that is, our understanding of all of God as we know him. This extended use of the term has to some extent been based on the broader semantic range of the verb *kenoun* outside Philippians, but here I will keep it in close connection to the meaning of the verb in Philippians.

Christ's kenosis has been taken to mean that he "emptied himself" of possession of the "distinctively divine attributes," or something along that line, with this understanding intended to protect the humanity of Christ.[29] In response, some have moderated this to Christ setting aside "independent use" of the divine attributes, of "the exercise of the powers of Lordship," or the like.[30] But "he emptied himself,"[31] is not an abstract concept needing to be explained or filled out by christological discussion

---

28. The same could not be said about the origin of all uses of "kenosis" in Russian spiritual writings.

29. The kenosis was "a depotentiation of the divine nature, so that in the incarnate Logos remained only the bare essence of Deity stripped of its metaphysical attributes of omnipotence, omniscience, and omnipresence" (Bruce, *Humiliation of Christ*, 9 [not referring to his own view]).

30. E.g., Collange, *Philippians*, 100–103, quoting 101. Barth insisted that the incarnation involves no alteration of or departure from the divine nature. So *Church Dogmatics* 4/1:180–83. Incarnation/kenosis is Christ's condescending "concealment of his Godhead" without any loss or decrease thereof (180). Similarly, Baillie, *God Was in Christ*, 94–98. It has become standard practice in commentaries on Philippians to say that there is nothing of which Christ has been "emptied." See, e.g., Hawthorne, *Philippians*, 85–86.

31. I am not approving of the translation "he emptied himself" so much as using it as a placeholder for *heauton ekenōsen*. See the next note.

subsequent to Paul. It serves, rather, as part of a description of the incarnation of God in Christ as *self-enslavement*.[32]

The first half (vv. 6-8) of the hymn about Christ in Philippians 2:6-11[33] can be divided into four couplets:[34]

    1.a. Existing in the form of God,
       b. he did not consider being equal with God a thing to be used.[35]
    2.a. Rather, he emptied himself,
       b. taking the form of a slave.
    3.a. Being made in human likeness
       b. and being found in appearance as a human,
    4.a. he humbled himself,
       b. being (or "becoming") obedient.

The first and third couplets are brought together by the contrast of two repeated words, "God" in the middle of clause 1.a. and at the end of clause 1.b. (in the Greek word order) and "human" in the middle of clause 3.a. and at the end of clause 3.b. The second and fourth couplets, on the other

---

32. This was particularly urged by Warfield in "Person of Christ" (which was reprinted as "The Person of Christ according to the New Testament" in a couple collections of Warfield's essays). Because of this understanding of *kenoun* in this context, he regarded the KJV translation "made himself of no repute" as more to the point than that of RV/ASV (and later RSV), which is "emptied himself."

33. I would not insist on the term "hymn," but (against Fee, "Philippians 2:5-11"; *Paul's Letter to the Philippians*, 192-94) it certainly seems that 2:6-11 must be understood as poetic.

34. Other views of the structure arise if the articular infinitive "being equal with God" is treated as a separate clause. See, e.g., Wright, *Climax of the Covenant*, 56. One possible weakness of my understanding of the structure is the location of the central break (at 3.a.) before rather than at *kai* ("and" in 3.b.). But I find the arrangement of clauses compelling:

    1. participle, indicative
    2. indicative, participle
    3. participle, participle
    4. indicative, participle

35. "A thing to be used" is a clumsy representation of the understanding of *harpagmos* that has become dominant in scholarship (e.g., Wright, *Climax of the Covenant*, 83) since Roy Hoover ("Harpagmos Enigma") identified *harpagmon hēgēsato* as an idiom (*harpagmon*, predicate accusative with certain verbs): "[Jesus] did not regard (being equal with God) as something to use for his own advantage." Also reflecting this understanding is NRSV's "did not regard equality with God as something to be exploited." What comes to mind here are, first, Jesus's rejection of temptations based on "if you are the Son of God . . ." (Luke 4:3, 9; see chapter 8 below, under "Jesus the Warrior and Son"), and, second, understandings of Phil 2:6-8 as a deliberate reversal of a myth of a Prometheus or Adam figure, of one who *did* grasp at being equal to the gods (see chapter 8 below, under "Jesus Does It Right").

hand, are each an indicative clause with a reflexive pronoun (2.a. and 4.a.) followed by a participial clause (in 2.b. and 4.b.): "emptied–taking," "humbled–being." "Emptied–slave–humbled–obedient" in the second and fourth couplets, interwoven with the "God–human" movement of the first and third couplets, makes this first half of the hymn an invitation to consider the incarnation in terms of a move into a sociological category, that is, in a narrative metaphor of *self-enslavement*, not in terms of the exercise or non-exercise of divine attributes. Here again a problem arises if we try to account for the incarnation of an unmoving God. But if we begin from the incarnation and think of God as the incarnate one, that is, as one who did not sit still in the past and will not do so in the future, things look differently.

This use of *kenoun* for a change in social standing is not only readable from the context but is also in accord with usage of related words elsewhere. *Kenōs*, "empty," and its cognates were used of persons to characterize them as foolish—for example, an arrogant and self-seeking pseudo-prophet and his audience, an "empty vessel among empty vessels"—or as having suffered a sudden loss of status—for example, the same prophet embarrassed into silence in "an assembly full of righteous men," or as arrogant people ruined in final judgment.[36] The reflexive use of the verb in Phil 2:7 denotes, then, a surrender of position, privilege, or reputation. In the context of the hymn about Christ, what is involved in this divestiture is made clear by what is, conversely, "taken," namely, "the form of a slave."[37]

"Slave" is a metaphor inasmuch as Jesus was not a bondservant in society, but realizing the potency of that metaphor is difficult within the circumstances of most of us. *Doulos* was the general term for all non-free persons, whether temporarily or permanently enslaved and apart from education, occupation, nationality, or status within the mass of *douloi*. "Servant" and "slave" both have to be retained as translations to represent in our context the range of positions among *douloi* (in its simplest sense) in that time, as long as we remember that such a "servant" was not free to walk away from the job. *Doulos* could be used in an extended sense of those who were not slaves but clients, even client kings, of a "master,"

---

36. The quotations are from Hermas, *Shepherd* 43 (= *Mandates* 11).13, 14; 99 (= *Similitudes* 9.22).3. The same passages are quoted in interpretation of Phil 2:7 by Decker, "Philippians 2:5–11."

37. 2 Cor 8:9 speaks of the same motion as *kenoun* in different language, again in a hortatory context with Christ to be imitated.

such as the emperor. But the word always carried the notion of responding not to one's own will but to the command of another and, if the class relationships were working properly, of receiving that command with humility and obedience, as the fourth couplet of the Christ hymn says explicitly.[38]

So the "emptied" Son of God is one who is not directed by his own will. Indeed, in the first-century Mediterranean world, what he has become (metaphorically), a slave, is not acknowledged to have a will that can be exercised in any significant way.[39] The reflexive "emptied *himself*" makes Christ's kenosis a matter of *self*-enslavement, a decision of the will not to assert the will. The metaphor thus makes *will* the key issue in incarnation.

Incarnation is a scandal as that which places God and human together—hence a scandal to Judaism and Islam (1 Cor 1:23–24). The narrative metaphor of self-enslavement sharpens the scandal. It also, along with the added "as far as death, death on a cross," pulls us toward the "servant" christology of the Synoptic Gospels. There, Jesus the servant follows the servant identity all the way to death (Mark 10:45). He is accused but not vindicated, at least not vindicated before his society. He offers no defense and brings no counter-accusation (1 Pet 2:22–23; the silence in Matt 26:63; 27:12, 14). He takes on the role of the ritual victim, the powerless "scapegoat" in Girardian terms, the opposite of what humans normally seek to be.[40]

---

38. "Slave" echoes the Isaianic servant passages, in which "servant" is an honorific title (so Hawthorne, *Philippians*, 86–87; Collange, *Philippians*, 101–2). But if it is indeed an honorific in Isaiah, none of that characteristic seems to enter Philippians 2. For "slave" to be an honorific title seems to require an answer to "slave of whom?" But no such question or answer is given or assumed in Philippians 2. On that question see chapter 9 below, under "Divine Kenosis."

39. Any number of statements in ancient literature and law codes could be cited here. Sufficient examples are found throughout Wiedemann, *Greek and Roman Slavery*.

40. Caiphas's statement in John 11:50 is as good an example of the scapegoat mechanism as one could hope for. The priest says nothing about any guilt on the part of Jesus, and what he fears is not just Rome (v. 48) but (and more fundamentally) disorder among the people. Order is to be restored by the sacrifice of the scapegoat. James G. Williams's foreword to Girard, *I Saw Satan Fall*, is a handy summary of Girard's mimetic theory, which includes the scapegoat mechanism.

The Kenosis of the Trinity

The extension of kenosis to "theology proper," to the other persons of the Trinity or to the Godhead as a whole, cannot be as directly read from the Bible as the kenosis of God the Son can, but it has been fruitful in theological discourse of the last few decades.[41] The key point at which kenosis has been extended beyond christology is creation.[42] For Jürgen Moltmann, for example, kenotic creation refers to God's decision that there would come to be something other than himself.[43] Similarly Emil Brunner: "The idea of the divine self-limitation is included in that of the creation of a world which is not God." "God does not wish to occupy the whole of Space Himself, but . . . wills to make room for other forms of existence. In doing so He limits Himself. . . . The κένωσις, which reaches its paradoxical climax in the Cross of Christ, begins with the creation of the world."[44] One might also say "some*one* other than himself" or "other wills" in place of "something other than himself" or "other forms of existence," thus putting the focus on will, on created beings that possess and exercise will, rather than on "space" or whatever might be represented by the word "something."

This understanding of creation takes us in quite a different direction from what we find in some writers of the patristic period. For an especially clear example, John of Damascus attached the characteristic of changeableness to having been created. And, vice versa, the creator of everything else must be unchangeable:

---

41. The term "person" is traditional and used as such here. It has been increasingly problematic and misleading in trinitarian theology through most of its history and has become more a placeholder than a significant term. See, e.g., Calvin, *Institutes* 1.13.2–5. A helpful summary of "kenotic conceptions of God" is Murphy and Ellis, *On the Moral Nature of the Universe*, 174–76.

42. Creation, particularly *ex nihilo*, has normally been linked with divine sovereignty and has therefore been problematic for some process theologians, for whom the existence of other wills argues against a strict dependence of all things on God for their beginning and continued existence—dependence, that is, on creation and providence. But if kenosis is taken not as a static characteristic of God (an "attribute"?) but narratively as God's surrender to other wills, then, instead of jettisoning creation, kenosis allows us to see creation as the basis for a full acknowledgement of the freedom of wills other than God's.

43. Moltmann, *God in Creation*, 76, 80, 86–87.

44. Brunner, *Dogmatics* 2:173, 19. But taking the cross as "paradoxical" suggests that the a priori of a non-suffering God is still at work for Brunner.

> If things are created, it follows that they are also changeable. For things whose existence originated in change must also be subject to change, whether it be that they perish or that they become other than they are by act of will. But if things are uncreated they must in all consistency be also wholly immutable. . . . The Creator, then, being uncreated, is also wholly immutable. And what could this be other than Deity?[45]

But with the kenotic understanding of creation we see that God is himself affected by his decision to create. Since creation, God has been in passionate and self-giving relationship with humanity (and more specifically with Israel) such that God experiences his judgment of humans as regret and grief.[46] Any qualification of God's self-limitation and his entry into this relationship will likely amount to saying that there is a "core" or some such to God that is not involved in or affected by his relationship with us. But taking kenosis as the starting point—and remembering that what we know of God is limited to his relationship to us—has, in fact, redirected how we think of God in relation to change.

Even beyond God's relationship with humankind, God is present in relation to all creation kenotically.[47] Chapter 4 below will focus on some aspects of this. Suffice it now to say that God affirms his act of creation by continuing to allow what he has created to carry on its existence according to its own patterns, what we call "natural laws," and usually restricts his own actions in the world to the agency of those patterns. For this reason, science is able to proceed—indeed, must proceed—*etsi deus non daretur,* as if there were no God. God is thus hidden, hidden in plain sight as it were, hidden from and in creation by his kenosis in relation to creation and the integrity of its existence. For this reason, the apologetic suggested by Psalm 19:1–4 and Romans 1:19–20 does not really work.[48]

---

45. *Exposition of the Orthodox Faith* 1.3. Also essential to John's "Proof that there is a God" is the requirement that the world's existence be sustained, despite the tensions among its elements (or, one might say, its tendency toward entropy), by one who does not have such tensions within himself and is therefore not subject to change. One, that is, who is the "first mover, put in motion by no other" (Aquinas, *Summa Theologiae* I.2.3).

46. Gen 6:6; Ps 78:40; Isa 54:6; 63:10; Mark 3:5; Eph 4:30; cf. Prov 17:25; Isa 53:3. The psalms of lament can thus be heard as messianic *and* as the words of God, e.g., Ps 35. With all this, it should be remembered, however, that Hebrew and Greek words for emotions do not draw the same distinctions as English words for emotions: "grief" and "anger" can sometimes be possible translations in the same context.

47. This paragraph is based partly on Bonhoeffer, *Letters and Papers,* 360–61.

48. Indeed, "their voice is not heard" (Ps 19:3), and those who might have heard that voice "have become stupid" (Rom 1:22).

Jesus's incarnation and subjection to death, where this all began in Philippians 2, is, indeed, a logical outcome of this kenotic (and God-initiated) hiddenness of God in creation:[49] even in the key divine intervention, the incarnation, the overall structure of God's action is placed within the normal operations of the universe.[50]

But divine kenosis did not begin at creation. There was an intertrinitarian precedent. For Sergei Bulgakov, the kenosis of love in the incarnation is already present in the mutual love and surrender to each other of all three persons of the Trinity. God's self-abnegation is not represented solely ("exhausted") in the incarnation.[51] In kenosis God is present, but not in full power, because to be present in full power would destroy, not sanctify. As Christ in his kenosis does not lose "His Divinity and His place in the Holy Trinity; but, personally, for Himself, He depotentializes this Divinity to such an extent that He 'becomes flesh,'"[52] so also the loving kenosis of the Trinity is seen in creation, in the upholding of creation, in the covenant, and in the Holy Spirit's indwelling and sanctification.[53] In regard specifically to creation, "The kenosis of creation in God Who is in the Holy Trinity signifies His self-diminution with respect to His absoluteness."[54]

Kenosis thus moves beyond incarnation and creation into Bulgakov's understanding of God's continuing provision for and covenant with creation, in terms of the Holy Spirit's relation to creation: creation continues to exist despite the human rejection of God.

---

49. Though the incarnation might be said to be logically prior in that it is from the incarnation that we know that God acts kenotically.

50. Hence the cry of dereliction from the cross (Mark 15:34): at the key point in time, kenotically considered, God is hidden from God himself. The qualification "overall structure" is necessary because of the virgin conception of Jesus and the outbreakings of miracle in his ministry.

51. See Rawls, "Bulgakov on the Incarnation"; cf. Barth according to McDermott, *Word Become Flesh*, 186: "For Barth, God's self-emptying in the incarnation is rooted in the eternal self-emptying that occurs in the Godhead in the threefold personal self-gift. The three divine persons are described not as standing in themselves but as centered outside themselves." See further Gunton, "Barth, the Trinity"; Barth, *Church Dogmatics* 3/3:139.

52. Bulgakov, *Comforter*, 350.

53. Bulgakov, *Comforter*, e.g., 206–7, 219–20. See also Valliere, *Modern Russian Theology*, 331–32.

54. Bulgakov, *Comforter*, 219. In all of this, part of Bulgakov's context is the long history of use of "kenosis" as a term for the abasement and poverty of Jesus and of those who imitate him.

> The *kenosis* of the Holy Spirit . . . consists not only in the illumination of creation in general, but also in the acceptance of the *measure* of creation and of the fact that it is not very receptive to the revelation of the Spirit. This poor receptivity and even opposition of creation do not lead the Spirit to abandon it to the fate of its original vanity; rather, He abides in creation and sustains its being.[55]

The creator bends to the will of his human creation as he maintains the covenant of provision (Gen 1:29–30; 2:16) in the altered post-fall circumstances through the early chapters of Genesis.[56]

> After the deluge God concluded a new covenant with man, where He said that He would not destroy creation again (Gen. 8:21–22; 9:9–16). And this long-suffering patience of God, by virtue of which the whole cycle of earthly life and all its phenomena "shall not cease" (8:22), is God's kenosis with respect to creation, precisely the kenosis of the Holy Spirit.[57]

Kenosis and the Creation-Redemption Story

Following Bulgakov's understanding of Genesis, we can see God's role in the story of Adam and Eve and their progeny as paralleled in the father of the prodigal (Luke 15:11–32). Much like God in Rom 1:24, 26, 28, the father gives up the son (humanity in Romans 1) to the degrading and self-destructive consequences of his rebellion (Luke 15:11–16). Then he welcomes his son back, more than absorbing the losses and gladly and grandly providing for his son (vv. 22–24).

The prodigal's brother represents sense, propriety, justice, and a story governed by logical outcomes (vv. 25–30). If his views were followed by his father and by God, then his brother might as well not go home, and for us there would be no redemption to complete the creation-redemption story. But in saving us, in maintaining covenant with human creation, God violates that logic, in redemption as in creation and

---

55. Bulgakov, *Comforter*, 206.

56. Also seen in those chapters is the growth of the contradictory human sense that the human will must be protected from God. This effort to protect the human will and to establish human independence reshapes human life completely. This will be explored more fully in chapter 5 below.

57. Bulgakov, *Comforter*, 206–7. Similarly, in the eighteenth century Johann Georg Hamann spoke of God's self-abasement in creation, incarnation, cross, and inspiration of Scripture. See Bayer, *Contemporary in Dissent*, 55.

provision, using means and following a pattern that appear paradoxical to us:

In *creation*

1. God placed limits on the exercise of his sovereignty,
2. (though he still had all his sovereignty),
3. to create those who could love him.
4. He thus exercised his sovereignty over the eschatological end of the story.

God's *sustaining, providing, and covenant* follow the same pattern:

1. God serves those who have rejected him—
2. even while he is the sovereign God—
3. still with the creation goal of loving relationship with us,
4. a goal that will be fulfilled.

Similarly, in *redemption* (Phil 2:6–11)

1. God in Christ "emptied himself"
2. (though he still possessed all that he had before),
3. to restore our freedom to love him.
4. Jesus will therefore be recognized eschatologically as Lord by all.

Thus God continues to accomplish his goals by means that allow the exercise of human freedom to reject him and even to kill him.

JESUS IS OUR GOD

The Oddness of the Story

Christ's kenosis does not hide but reveal "the form of God."[58] Some interpreters see this already in the Christ hymn, taking the first (participial) "God" clause in Phil 2:6 as causal rather than (or as well as) concessive: not "even though he was in the form of God" but "*because* he was in the form of God." In this way "a kenotic Son reveal[s] a kenotic Father, a

---

58. Cf. Moltmann, *Crucified God*, esp. 297.

kenotic Christ image[s] a kenotic God."[59] It is precisely *as God* that Christ "emptied himself." But that can be done without ascribing to Paul or to the author of the Christ hymn a causal meaning in that first "God" clause. This is still the God of Israel, and ascribing incarnation to that God is still an "offense" (1 Cor 1:23–24).[60] For Jews unpersuaded by the gospel, "God" and "human" remain mutually exclusive, which means at least that Paul could not count on "existing in the form of God" being heard as causal.

Nonetheless, as Christ takes on the form of a servant, he moves into a role God has been in before. It is precisely as kenotic, as a servant, that Christ does not step away from being God or even from displaying God's "attributes," but reveals God.[61] If we say, for instance, that Christ "renounces the exercise of the power of God,"[62] we also have to say that that is also how God has acted other than in the incarnation. Christological kenosis is appropriate because it is God making the same kind of motion as in creation and in his continuing covenants with humankind and with Israel. Incarnation is not a unique act of divine self-limitation,[63] but it is for us humans the key historical instance of the trinitarian dialectic. Nothing is said in the hymn about Jesus to make him one who only plays the part of a servant, knowing all the while that he is the king's son (or the king). His self-enslavement is not a disguise. As a servant, he is in his natural place. He is, in fact, in God's place, thus showing us what God is. Acknowledged lordship comes later (Phil 2:9–11). Jesus is "the one who is to rule all the nations with a rod of iron" (Rev 12:5), but he is so as the bleeding lamb (v. 11).

In incarnation God does not change, but this is so because God has always been as he is in Christ.[64] Much of the fourth- and fifth-century

59. So Crossan and Reed, *In Search of Paul*, 290 (worded as a question there). Gorman, *Inhabiting the Cruciform God*, 9–10, 20–21, and throughout, makes use of this understanding of the "God" clause and mentions a number of authors who have supported it.

60. Skipping, of course, past the large amount written in recent decades about the state of monotheism in Second Temple Judaism as possible background to what Paul says there.

61. So Hooker, "Letter to the Philippians," 508; Fee, *Philippians*, 196; Jüngel, *God as the Mystery of the World*, 13.

62. Collange, *Philippians*, 101, though this goes more against the "kenotic christology" that Collange rejects.

63. In agreement with, e.g., Forsyth, *Creative Theology*, 72. Pages 71–74 are from Forsyth, *Person and Place of Jesus Christ*, 269–73.

64. So Forsyth, *Creative Theology*, 77–78. Pages 76–78 are from Forsyth, *Person and Place of Jesus Christ*, 318–20.

christological disputes were necessitated, as we have seen, by a belief in the basic incompatibility of the divine and the human, which, to their credit, the fathers did not entirely succumb to, though their efforts to distinguish the "two natures" of Christ can seem strained.[65] Incarnation is, indeed, both a scandal to Jews (and Muslims) and foolishness to Greeks (and Gnostics) because it means that Christ fully manifests God by being fully human.

> Christ's earthly humiliation had to have its foundation laid in heaven, and to be viewed but as the working out of a renunciation before the world was. The awful volume and power of the willwarfare in which He here redeemed the world, and turned for eternity the history of the race, was but the exercise in historic conditions of an eternal resolve taken in heavenly places. . . . The Cross was the reflection (or say, rather, the historic pole) of an act within Godhead.[66]

The terms "kenosis" and "setting aside" suggest that in incarnation God steps away from what is normal for God, namely, exercise of power. Kenosis might thus be understood as an interruption of God's true nature, a conflict between God's nature and God's action, or a movement on God's part away from power and coercion toward service and covenant. But there is no "from" and "to" of that kind in God. The problem is not just the word "kenosis" but human understanding and language as a whole. Exercise of power is what we understand. It is what makes sense to us, so it is what determines the resolution of human stories, even where it is not apparent, as in trickster stories, magic stories, and sports underdog movies. Power wins.

Therefore, what God does in creation and incarnation only looks like a departure from what is normal, a reversal, an upside-down way of doing things. It is just plain odd, a departure from the normal, but only in relation to our world, in which sin has made the exercise of power normative. Kenosis is a departure from *our* normal. Exercise of power is how our thinking is structured this side of the fall.[67] But for God, what

---

65. E.g., "inconfusedly, unchangeably, indivisibly, inseparably," in the Symbol of Chalcedon.

66. Forsyth, *Creative Theology*, 72.

67. Some would connect exercise of power particularly with Western, Europe-based cultural norms. I would be more willing to concede that any account *I* give of this aspect of humanness will have to be in terms of the Western tradition. I do not know firsthand, for instance, how much of a departure, if any, from what sort of normative Buddhism is needed for Buddhism to be the more-or-less official religion of Sri Lanka or Myanmar.

we (including the apostle Paul) try to understand with terms like "kenosis" is the norm. The divine economy reaches its goals without any either explicit or hidden exercise of power.[68] The lamb defeats the dragon by shedding his own blood.[69]

Kenosis is how God acts. Better yet, it is no act, in two senses. First, it is not a disguise or incognito. Second, the kenosis of Christ is not a temporal process or event. There is no before, during, or after in his kenosis because it defines or displays what he is as God.[70] True, there was kenotic action he had to carry out in first-century Galilee and Judea, but he carried it out as the one he had always been, the God who created in self-giving.

There is therefore in this kenotic understanding of God no need to speak of God "becoming."[71] The movement of kenosis is how God acts, and we know God only as the one who acts.[72] We know God in motion, so to speak, or as motion, and that motion is kenotic.[73] This may bring us close to an understanding of the incarnation as occurring throughout God's eternity,[74] but, again, we know God only as one who acts, not in

---

68. Charles Gore wrote of a new idea of "a self-limited God" in contrast to God understood as "the great unfettered monarch of all worlds" and particularly in relation to natural law and what we might call "spiritual patience" (Gore, *Incarnation of the Son of God*, 129). The "unfettered monarch" is mainly "due to the tendency always present in the vulgar imagination, to see the Divine rather in what is portentous and unaccountable than in what is orderly and tranquil; to think of power, not as what works through law, but as what triumphs over it. Thus it is that God's omnipotence has been understood to mean, not His universal power in and over all things which works patiently and unerringly in the slow-moving process to the far-off event, but rather the unfettered despot's freedom to do anything anyhow" (130).

69. More about that in chapter 8 below.

70. Similarly, Abe, "Kenotic God and Dynamic Sunyata," 10.

71. The "becoming" denied here is not quite what Jüngel speaks of in *Doctrine of the Trinity* but more that of process theology.

72. Bulgakov would not limit this to human knowledge of God but speaks, as we have seen, of kenosis as characterizing intra-trinitarian relations.

73. So we come to a middle ground between the God of process theology who is "becoming" and the God of "classical theism," characterized by *apatheia*, unable to move, and therefore a model for those seeking Stoic perfection. Rahner, "On the Theology of the Incarnation," refers to a similar middle position in regard to the incarnation of the Word, in which becoming (the economic Word) and unchangingness (the immanent Word) are held together.

74. Luther's "semper nascitur" and "Filius principium non habet temporis," both in "Promotionsdisputation von Georg Major und Johannes Faber"; cf. Forsyth, *Creative Theology*, 72–73.

the same way that God knows God.⁷⁵ Incarnation is only an instance of kenosis, but for us it is the normative instance, the one that gives us the model and the vocabulary to understand God's actions as kenotic.

It is, therefore, from the perspective of the middle of the story, that is, from the cross, that we best know what God is like. And it is only from the perspective of the middle and end of the story, from cross and resurrection, that we can understand it as a story. Without God's continuing kenosis, no story would be possible.⁷⁶

Kenosis Is Not an Attribute⁷⁷

In the incarnation, God came as one specific person, not as whatever sort of person we would like him to be or as what the *Zeitgeist* might prefer. He did not become part of *our* history. Rather, as a brashly speaking Jew, he upset our history. God exercised sovereignty in and over his condescension. This paradox, if that is what it is, works throughout kenosis. In creation as well God did not ask our advice (Job 38–39). If we associate God's means with an ideology,⁷⁸ then we set up expectations that God in his freedom, which is his sovereignty, will surely disappoint.

Understanding God as defined by kenosis might be akin to what some have meant by calling God "nonviolent."⁷⁹ But, first, there is considerable difference between nonviolence and kenosis.⁸⁰ And, second,

---

75. God has not told us everything, and our knowledge of him is limited to what he has told us (John of Damascus, *Exposition of the Orthodox Faith* 1.1–2 is helpful in explaining that). If I know someone only as a church attender, I might think that she is the same every day as she is on Sunday morning. But still, I do have knowledge of her. Our knowledge of God, arising from revelation and limited to revelation, is really knowledge of God. See Barth, *Church Dogmatics* 2/1:331–32.

76. Cf. Barth's insistence that creation is a creedal statement and that it is not visible as creation except through the cross. See, e.g., *Church Dogmatics* 3/1:3, 13, 38.

77. Masao Abe used the same words in an argument going the opposite direction: "Kenosis or emptying is not an *attribute* . . . of God, but the fundamental *nature* of God" ("Kenotic God and Dynamic Sunyata," 16). Here I use "attribute" and "nature" together to represent any abstracted description of God that could become an a priori ruling out God's freedom, which could, indeed, be called "the fundamental *nature* of God."

78. I almost wrote "a human ideology," but the point is really that there is no non-human, i.e., *divine*, ideology that we could recognize as such.

79. God is consistently nonviolent according to, e.g., Weaver, "Peace Church as Worship"; *Nonviolent God*.

80. "Nonviolence" is a problematic term in ethics (see further chapter 10 below) and therefore here.

the "nonviolent God" is another instance of a characteristic attributed to God that can stand over God, blocking his self-definition, freedom, and action.

Talk about God's "attributes" or "nature" can become a threat to appreciation of God's freedom.[81] God's actions are freely chosen. In the same way, we cannot absolutize kenosis as a complete description of God's *actions*, as if we knew them all, and on that basis create a rule about God's *nature* that determines the choices made by God's *will*. If we did so, and added to it an understanding of kenotic love as absorption into the beloved, then we would have to mourn or celebrate the disappearance of God on our behalf.[82]

This takes us back to what was said above about the kenosis of incarnation: understanding it as a sociological metaphor removes from us any need to talk about divine "natures," "attributes," or "modes of being." In the same way, understanding the kenosis of God allows us to look toward divine actions and divine freedom rather than toward abstract divine nature or attributes. Kenosis is, in fact, misunderstood unless we regard it as action. Furthermore, the evidence is not in hand to fashion such a rule (especially if stated as a negation: "*non*violent") about the nature of God because we know God only in his actions as they impinge on us.[83] Theology must deal with our knowledge of God, not with any speculation about God's self-knowledge.

In the Bible God does, in fact, do violent things. Kenosis, understood as a rule about how God acts, cannot account for everything God has done. To those who are offended by the biblical God because he (with emphasis on the gendered pronoun) bashes people's heads, so to speak, we have to begin by acknowledging that God does, indeed, do so. Or, to give their argument greater depth, we could say that God does punish people and harden people's hearts. We cannot easily account for that by way of kenosis, God's self-enslavement. Searching in the accounts of God's violent actions in the Old Testament or in eschatological texts for some detail or key that takes the edge off, so to speak, is a method that

---

81. See further chapter 3 below.

82. As in Abe, "Kenotic God and Dynamic Sunyata," 14–19. In saying that this is not pantheistic, he protests a bit too loudly.

83. The response by Snyder Belousek, "God, Jesus, and Nonviolence," identifies correctly the circularity that must be part of an argument from the Bible that God is consistently nonviolent. For the distinction between God "as he is in himself" and as he is "in relation to us," see, e.g., Calvin, *Institutes* 1.10.2.

guarantees that the center of the text will not be found. Apparently, kenosis is not all. The reason for that is that kenosis is *human* language, *our* attempt to understand. It cannot, therefore, set any limit on God, nor can it comprehend, in both senses of that word, God's actions.

3

Freedom and Love

GOD

GOD CREATED FREELY, NOT in order to meet some need or because he was subject to some compulsion. There is not and never has been a standard for what a god should be that was applicable to the one God of the universe and that might require some components or attributes that the one God might be lacking.[1] So he did not create in order to meet such a standard. Neither is there, or ever has been, anything that could stand before or over against God that could tell him what to do or give him a plan to fulfill or characteristics to live up to.[2]

Therefore, the universe that God created could have been otherwise or might not have come into existence at all.[3] God was not improved by

---

1. See Oden, *Living God*, 27–28, on the impossibility of defining God, with patristic references.

2. For this point and for this section as a whole, the most important exposition is that of Barth in *Church Dogmatics* 3/1:272–97 (§28.2, "The Being of God as the One Who Loves").

3. This can be characterized as a difference in perspective between Anselm and Aquinas. Anselm speaks easily of God acting in certain ways because of "necessity" (e.g., *Cur Deus Homo* 1.1; 2.4–5, 17), meaning that God does what is necessary in order for him not to violate his own nature, including create (see Rogers, "Anselm on God's Perfect Freedom," 1–2). Creation is "the necessarily perfect divine action" (3). Aquinas, on the other hand, asks "Whether Whatever God Wills He Wills Necessarily" (*Summa Theologiae* I.19.3) and answers No: the necessity lies only in the divine will itself; God has no "cause prior to Himself" (objection 5 and reply). "What we [or God] work according to the counsel of the will, we [or God] do not will necessarily," and "since the goodness of God is perfect, and can exist without other things inasmuch as no perfection can accrue to Him from them, it follows that His willing things apart from Himself

having created something rather than nothing. It was solely because of his will and love that he created. Therefore, our existence and the existence of everything else are dependent on God's grace and are thus like our redemption from sin. Indeed, the attitude of the worshiper can be surprise that God created anything:

> The truth is, that all genuine appreciation rests on a certain mystery of humility and almost of darkness. The man who said, "Blessed is he that expecteth nothing, for he shall not be disappointed," put the eulogy quite inadequately and even falsely. The truth "Blessed is he that expecteth nothing, for he shall be gloriously surprised." The man who expects nothing sees redder roses than common men can see, and greener grass, and a more startling sun. Blessed is he that expecteth nothing, for he shall possess the cities and the mountains; blessed is the meek, for he shall inherit the earth. Until we realize that things might not be we cannot realize that things are. Until we see the background of darkness we cannot admire the light as a single and created thing. As soon as we have seen that darkness, all light is lightening, sudden, blinding, and divine. Until we picture nonentity we underrate the victory of God, and can realize none of the trophies of His ancient war. It is one of the million wild jests of truth that we know nothing until we know nothing.[4]

To some extent this takes the side of "will" in discussion of what comes first, the divine "nature" or God's will: Does God create because he chooses to do so or because his very nature demands it?[5] But we can, indeed must, hold the two together: we speak in one breath of God's freedom (will) and God's love (his nature) because his love is freely chosen. Either freedom or love thought of without the other might become absolutized. Divine freedom might become simple caprice or arbitrary exercise of power closed to our understanding.[6] Or God's love might become a force or principle outside God that makes creation necessary.[7]

---

is not absolutely necessary. Yet it can be necessary by supposition, for supposing that He wills a thing, then He is unable not to will it, as His will cannot change" (reply).

4. Chesterton, *Heretics*, 65.

5. See again Aquinas in note 3 above.

6. As, perhaps, with William of Ockham. Aquinas and Barth held that God's free choice to create is inscrutable because it is not necessary (*Summa Theologiae* I.46.2 answer; *Church Dogmatics* 3/1:4-5), but they certainly knew how to hold love and freedom together. See further under "Freedom and Commitment" below.

7. Otto Weber aligns God's love and God's freedom with other dualities: condescension-transcendence, revealed-hidden, communicable versus incommunicable

God "wills and posits the creature neither out of caprice nor necessity, but because He has loved it from eternity, because He wills to demonstrate His love for it."[8]

Seeing freedom and love together in this way enables us to avoid the problems of some understandings of God. For instance, focus on the traditional "attributes of God"—omniscience, omnipresence, omnipotence, eternity, aseity, immutability, holiness, goodness, and the like—as used to be de rigueur in systematic theologies,[9] puts us in danger of setting up principles outside God to which he must consistently conform in order to be, by our definition, God.[10] Freedom and love are more basic. Because we know that God's free love is central to what we can know about God, we are not compelled to explain away apparent deviations from conformity to the "attributes." We can know that God is still God when he does not, at least to our comprehension, properly display some "attribute" or other.

Rather than providing a standard for an adequate God, the Bible provides us with a God who is often shocking to our refined sensibilities, a God who speaks, moves, reacts, relates, and thus appears to depart from the self-consistency and immovability of the classical "attributes" in favor of his own action and self-definition. When God speaks directly about how he wishes to be known or named by his people, he tells them to remember his "mighty acts" (e.g., Ps 145:4–7).[11] In the same way we speak not about an idea of "the absolute God," but about the revealed God, God as he wishes to be known, and therefore, as far as human knowledge goes,

---

attributes. The result is that love and freedom become the rubrics under which the divine attributes are discussed. See Weber, *Foundations of Dogmatics*, 1:401–8, 420–60. With what I am saying here, on the other hand, it is always important to press toward the unity of freedom and love and to understand both as what God has revealed himself to be in his actions.

8. Barth, *Church Dogmatics* 3/1:95. Moltmann, *God in Creation*, 82–83, is similar, but Moltmann is concerned that Barth's understanding overemphasizes God's choosing, implying a "before" and an "after," to the detriment of God's eternal nature. He cites in this regard, with some caution, Tillich's identification of "divine life" and "divine creativity" (Moltmann, *God in Creation*, 83–85).

9. E.g., Strong, *Systematic Theology*, 243–303.

10. A greater problem in the tradition of "attributes" talk is its rootedness in talk of God apart from revelation, in derivation of attributes by means of logic games and metaphysics games. One continuing result of this wish to derive knowledge of God by thought free of revelation (which ipso facto must fail to reach truth about God) is categorization of the attributes according to the "three ways" of pseudo-Dionysius, namely eminence, negation, and causality. See, e.g., Schmid, *Doctrinal Theology*, 117–18.

11. See, e.g., Wright, *God Who Acts*, 13.

the only God.[12] God's freedom and action, rather than the attributes, are central to both how we come to understand God and the understanding we have of him. God in himself may be entirely consistent and completely characterized by the attributes, but that is not how we know him.

THE UNIVERSE

God created in order to love. "He did not create the world to be empty but formed it to be inhabited" (Isa 45:18). For us that should be made more specific: God created *us* in order to love *us*. But we need not regard the universe as existing only to be the location of God's human project,[13] and now more than in past centuries the universe does not seem to wait on any humanity-centered purpose to be existing and changing. Our faith does not require of the universe that it all ultimately serve us. We can tolerate gaps in our knowledge of meanings or purposes of things and still understand humanity in relation to God and celebrate what God has done in creating and redeeming *us*.

We do know that God created us in order to love us and that nothing God created violates that purpose in any final sense. God created that which he could love (us) and which could return his love. Because that love is kenotic, then "*kenosis* is the underlying law of the cosmos."[14] How we experience the universe and fellow humans and what we find to be the center of our nature can both be set within that mutual love: the universe becomes, more than anything else, a place where love happens. Knowing that it is is not a privilege reserved for a self-reflective elite: understanding oneself as created for this mutual love is not some sort of esoteric doctrine unreachable by those who are underfed, uneducated, busy, or unintelligent since all such human conditions make no one any the less human. (The phrase "understanding oneself" is problematic in this context if it implies otherwise, but more on that will have to wait for the discussion of faith in chapter 9.) Whatever else we might think defines us takes its place within that basic circumstance of love.

---

12. Luther distinguished between *deus nudus*, "the absolute God," and, on the other hand, God as we know him, "not naked but clothed and revealed in his Word" (commentary on Psalm 51 in Luther, *Selections from the Psalms*, 312).

13. As in, e.g., *Pseudo-Clementine Homilies* 3.36; John Chrysostom, *Homilies on Genesis* 8.4; Catholic Church, *Catechism* 299: "Destined for and addressed to man."

14. Murphy and Ellis, *On the Moral Nature of the Universe*, 251.

Before the universe was created, relationship, love, and interaction existed in the mutual love of the three persons of the Trinity.[15] Before creation the Father loved the Son and shared his glory with the Son (John 17:5, 23–24). With the act of creation, the circle of mutual love was broadened to include more than the persons of the Trinity, namely us.[16]

> God is the One who, although wholly self-sufficient in His possession of all perfections, and absolutely glorious and blessed in His inner life, did not as such will to be alone, and has not actually remained alone, but in accordance with His own will, and under no other inward constraint than that of the freedom of His love, has, in an act of the overflowing of His inward glory, posited as such a reality which is distinct from Himself.[17]

Love and freedom are thus both basic to what exists. Conscious interaction, response, and love—that which we experience among ourselves—did not begin with us, and it exists far beyond us. Relationality thus defines the origin and nature of the universe as far as we can understand and experience it, and love is older than the universe. This is a shocking thing to say in our age, provided that it is expressed as something that matters rather than as a "private opinion." "The modern idea is that cosmic truth is so unimportant that it cannot matter what any one says." The modern person "may turn over and explore a million objects, but he must not find that strange object, the universe; for if he does he will have a religion, and be lost."[18]

For people who live in such an age, coming to a realization of the place of love in the universe and at the beginning of the universe reverses the restriction of personality to ourselves and perhaps some other material beings such as dogs, bunnies, and maybe residents of other planets.

---

15. On Trinity as the basis of love's centrality in the universe, see Wilken, "Resurrection of Jesus," 28.

16. So, e.g., Barth, *Church Dogmatics* 3/1:274. In John 17, the Father loves Jesus's disciples (and "those who will believe in me through their word," v. 20) "even as" he has loved the Son (v. 23; just as now Jesus shares with his disciples the glory he had with the Father before creation, v. 22), but the distinction there between Jesus's disciples and the rest of humanity is not operative at the level of creation. A "social trinity" as the basis for an understanding of creation was particularly developed by Moltmann, e.g., *God in Creation*, 1–2, 54–56.

17. Barth, *Church Dogmatics* 3/1:15; similarly, e.g., 29–31, 43, 257, 273.

18. Chesterton, *Heretics*, 14, 13. In the second quotation Chesterton is responding particularly to G. B. Shaw. Religion may fare better among intellectual elites now than in Chesterton's time, but still only as opinion.

And it is the reverse of an apologetic theology that makes use of whatever gaps are left after physics, the science of very big and very little things, has had its say.[19] It speaks, rather, of the vast totality, the universe characterized by love, within which physics is able to explore a few parts.

Realization of the place of love in the universe is like the so-called postmodern re-enchantment of the universe,[20] but it is also quite different from that: it is helped neither by physics admitting chance nor by a person pretending that ancient myths might be "true for me." It does not come from or center itself around that "me," but is, rather, like unexpectedly meeting a close friend in an empty desert or a strange city—not in a wishful vision but in what we used to reserve the term "reality" for. That picture might imply that a realization of the place of love in the universe is rare as well as unexpected, but the real rarity in view of the long experience of humankind is *not* having such insight. Our age's depersonalization of the universe, which we take so much for granted and which has an aura of permanence for us, is itself enough of a rarity in human experience that perhaps we should begin by suspecting that our age's understanding might be faulty. The universe has seldom needed to be "re-enchanted" as it seems to now. The depersonalization of the universe in our age is also called into question because it makes it hard to explain the origin of *human* personality or easy to engage in the contradiction of being persons who do not believe in personhood.

THE IMAGE OF GOD

Freedom is a prerequisite of love. Only as beings with free will could we ever return God's love. Forced or coerced love is not love, or at least is not the love God wants in return for his love. He wants love, not the simple compliance that one expects of a well-aimed stone. Our freedom is therefore neither a mere abstraction nor limited to one choice. It is analogous to God's freedom: just as the world could have been otherwise because God is free, so, because of human freedom, much of what I have done I could have done otherwise.[21] This analogy between human and divine

---

19. The deserved criticism of much "classical" apologetics, i.e., that of Paley, *Natural Theology*, is that it can support belief in only a "God of the gaps," of, that is, what science has not yet explained.

20. E.g., Wojcik, "Uses of Re-Enchantment"; Griffin, *Reenchantment of Science*, particularly Griffin's introduction.

21. For a more complete definition of human freedom, see Plantinga, "Free Will

points, in one direction, to theological discussion of humanity's creation "in the image of God,"[22] or, in the opposite direction, to a Feuerbachian critique of theism: in describing God we are actually just projecting an idealized humanity—what we wish we were but fail to be—onto an imagined suprahuman being.

There is good reason for associating the language of "image" with the analogy of divine and human relationality, that is, with freedom and love:[23] the alternation of singular and plural humanity in Genesis 1:26-27 stands alongside God's deliberation with himself in his plurality—"Let *us* make humanity" (v. 26). The latter has been understood in Christian theology as a reference to the plurality of the Trinity,[24] but one need not include that further step. The usual criticism, that the divine plural here in Genesis is *solely* deliberative,[25] passes over the prominence (prominent because it is unusual and absent otherwise from the creation accounts) of the divine deliberative plural. Its significance stands without reference to the Trinity.[26]

Defense," 29-30. See the defense of human free will as essential to understanding "image of God" language in Gregory of Nyssa, *Great Catechism* 5.

22. Clines, "Image of God in Man," 101, argued that b^e, "in," should be understood as "as," and that "*as* the image of God" indicates that the "image" speaks not so much of the manner or result of creation as of the human mandate to represent God to the world. This argument has been oft-repeated, but its basis in the sense of b^e was, I believe, successfully challenged by Barr, "Image of God," 16-17.

23. This despite Barr's main argument in "Image of God," which is that attempts to say in what human capacity or quality the "image of God" in humanity consists are wrong-headed: "The putting of the question in this form arises from a misunderstanding of the literary characteristics and the spiritual situation of the P writer. There is no reason to believe that this writer had in his mind any definite idea about the content or the location of the image of God. . . . His terminology, when seen within the context of his situation and his literary work, had been moulded by questions and concerns different in character from the problems which have generally been in the minds of those who have sought to identify the content and location of the image of God in man" (Barr, "Image of God," 13, 26).

24. E.g., generally against Arianism, Augustine, *On the Trinity* 1.7 (14); *City of God* 16.6; *Sermons on Selected Lessons of the New Testament* 2(52).18; 76(126); Athanasius, *On the Councils of Ariminum and Seleucia* 2.26; Hilary of Poitiers, *On the Councils* 38, 49; *On the Trinity* 4.17-18; Ambrose, *On the Duties of the Clergy* 1.50.

25. As if I were to say to myself, "What shall we do?" See, e.g., Sands, "*Imago Dei*," 35.

26. Barth argued that "in the image of God" (v. 27) is explained immediately by reference to the primary plurality of humanity: "Male and female he created them" (*Church Dogmatics* 3/1:95). This was "a particularly ill-judged and irresponsible piece of exegesis" (so Barr, *Biblical Faith and Natural Theology*, 156-73).

The context also places the creation of humanity "in the image of God" alongside the human task of subjection of creation and "dominion" over non-human animate life (1:28; cf. 2:19–20).²⁷ This would also accord with the ancient Near Eastern use of "the image of God," among other terms of deity or semi-deity, as a term for royal rulers.²⁸ In Genesis, humankind as a whole takes that role of ruler over against the rest of animate creation and in that way is like God and is in relationship with creation.²⁹

The upshot is that the full meaning of being human is not expressed or accomplished by the individual human but by all of us in our relationships.³⁰ It is in our diversity—ethnic, linguistic, and all the rest—that we represent God. Our individual self-descriptions always include relationships. I am a spouse, father, uncle, brother, son, coworker, fellow church member, etc., and to leave any of that out solipsistically is to fail to say who I am. Adam said "bone of my bones and flesh of my flesh" (2:23), and we can imagine a response from Eve that similarly named someone other than herself, Adam, whose name and relationship with her was essential to her self-identification, just as her name and relationship was to him.

---

27. "It was therefore as a ruler that [the man] bore God's image, or represented Him on earth" (Hodge, *Systematic Theology*, 2:102). So also Ephraim the Syrian, *On Genesis* 1.29.1; Holzinger, *Genesis Erklärt*, 11–12. Or, specifying that the image is not dominion itself but that which makes the dominion possible, see Skinner, *Genesis*, 32; Heppe, *Reformed Dogmatics*, 232. This is the mandate associated with Clines's argument regarding the meaning of b^e (see note 22 above). The connection of the image to dominion is denied by Calvin, *Institutes* 1.15.4.

28. Clines, "Image of God," 80–85; Wenham, *Genesis 1–15*, 30–31. Similarly, the king as God's son in Pss 2:7; 72:1. It is interesting, in the light of Matt 20:26 (on which much more in chapter 11 below), that human power/authority/rule *over humans* is not mentioned till after the fall (Gen 3:16; 9:25–27; 10:10).

29. How the fall into sin has affected our representation of God as his image will be taken up in chapter 6, under "The Argument from Our Dividedness." Christ as the image of God (Col 1:15, etc.) and the restoration of the image as an aspect of redemption (Col 3:10, etc.) will be taken up in chapter 10.

30. The assumption that the "image" had to be located in or identified with whatever was thought to distinguish the human from other animals was based on the old idea of a hierarchy of being and usually led to an identification of the image with something like rationality. So, e.g., Calvin, *Institutes* 1.15.1, 3, 4; Skinner, *Genesis*, 32; Driver, *Genesis*, 15. We have generally shed the understanding of *ratio*, rationality, as that which stands against passion and therefore against sin (and perhaps have also shed some of our self-congratulatory self-identification as "rational"), so such an identification of Godlikeness as rationality is less possible today.

The temptation to see the image question as an invitation to an implicit natural theology has been strong,[31] and the problem is the direction of the process. If, however, we move *from* what God is *to* what God's human image is rather than the reverse (i.e., beginning with ideal humanness and then imagining God), among divine qualities that we see most evident and most perverted in humankind are choosing, speaking, and ruling (or, in our case, attempting to rule). We still have dominion over creation, or at least partly over the part of it on the earth's surface (quite a limitation! and hardly anticipatable by the authors of Genesis). But we are finding that our attempt to live outside covenant with God—really, *against* God—means that our dominion, no longer as God's agent, is badly executed. We do not rule "because we do not know the world as God's creation and do not accept the dominion we have as God-given but seize hold of it for ourselves."[32] Similarly, we are still relational, but our relationality is bizarrely distorted. So it is only with an unhealthy dose of self-deception about "what is most significant" about humankind,[33] ignoring our very significant wickedness, that we can extrapolate from that human "most significant" to an understanding of God. It is as we know God that we come to understand ourselves, what we are as created—relational and ruling—and, conversely, what we are as fallen.[34]

GOD IS PERSONAL

God is like us, but not only like us. We can say, for instance, that "God is personal," meaning that, like us, God engages in relationship.[35] We pro-

---

31. See Barr, *Biblical Faith and Natural Theology*, 156–73. "Natural theology" is study of what can be inferred of theological truth from observation of the world apart from any explicit revelation—in this case from observation of what we humans are like.

32. Bonhoeffer, *Creation and Fall*, 67.

33. "But our definition of the image seems not to be complete until it appears more clearly what the faculties are in which man excels, and in which he is to be regarded as a mirror of the divine glory" (Calvin, *Institutes* 1.15.4). To Calvin's credit, he continues: "This, however, cannot be better known than from the remedy provided for the corruption of nature," that is, christologically.

34. There is a place here for a natural theology of sorts—a natural theological anthropology. A Christian response to the Feuerbachian critique of theism (see above) might begin with asking why we should project an idealized humanity onto an imagined suprahuman being, that is, why we should work so hard on conceiving an image of ourselves improved. See note 9 in chapter 1 above, and chapter 6, under "The Argument from Our Dividedness."

35. It also means that God knows his own existence. On the difficulties that arise

tect our understanding of the "like us" by using the same sort of language for God as for us, such as "knowledge," "relational," and the personal pronoun. But in calling God "personal" we do not mean only what we mean when we say that a human is a person. This is so, first, because God was personal before anyone else was. Because God is Trinity, he did not have to wait for us in order to be relational. He acted out of his will before our wills existed.

Second, that God is personal is not tied to anything physical and is therefore not threatened by illness or death. No one will ever have to say "I miss visiting God. He's so far gone that one can no longer have a real relationship with him." Our relationality can be broken, but God's relationality is unthreatened.

Third, God's relationality exists within God himself. Humans normally cannot quite conceive of their own deaths, that is (if this is what death is), of the cessation of their own personhood. Personhood seems to define us. The sight of a human body smeared across four lanes of highway or blown to bits on a battlefield can spook most of us because it seems to testify against what we wish we could believe about ourselves, namely that there is no cessation of our personal existence and no world without me in it. But only God is personal eternally in and of himself. If we are each personal eternally (and I would at least not put it that way), we are so only by resurrection, that is, by God's gracious act of new creation. The cessation of our personhood seems strange or counterintuitive to us,[36] which suggests that we have some sort of knowledge of the eternal personhood that does, in fact, exist, though not in us but in God. And it is that eternal personhood of God that will make possible our resurrection to new life.

"God is personal" cannot mean that God is a member of a class of things that are personal. No adjective that can be applied to both God and humans can be applied in quite the same way to both, since God originated whatever characteristic is spoken of and possesses it absolutely. It is

---

if we assume that being personal and being infinite are incompatible see, e.g., Joseph Rickaby in his translation of Aquinas's *Summa contra Gentiles*, 31n91. As with creation (see chapter 4 below), so also with relationality, whatever we have of God is by his kenotic grace.

36. Witness the placing of human immortality/persistence of consciousness after death within natural theology/apologetics by some nineteenth-century writers. See, e.g., Frazer, *Belief in Immortality*, 1:26–28; Adler, *Creed and Deed*, 1–36; Beecher, "Immortality." Of course, immortality was defended because it was attacked. See, e.g., in his usual frame of mind, Bierce, *Cynic Looks at Life*, under "Immortality."

for this reason that we might say that God does not exist in the sense in which other things exist; rather, he is being itself.[37] Or not "God is loving" but "God is love." Or "God is freedom" or "God is personality" or God is "*the Person*."[38] Whatever participation we have in these characteristics we have only as those created (by God's grace) in God's image.[39]

In the English language the personal pronoun is more than a placeholder: it is often our way of saying "this is not a scientific treatise but a communication about and within relationships among people (or people and their pets) in which the relationships set the tone and dominate the content and the manner of speaking." (It does not work in quite the same way in languages in which objects and concepts can be masculine or feminine in grammatical gender.) God is personal, like us in being capable of relationship, so referring to God with a personal pronoun seems essential to what I am saying here about God.

God has no gender. One cannot have gender without physiology, without, that is, DNA. So everything that is tied to either "female" or "male," excluding the other, can be attributed to God only metaphorically. Since we have no non-gendered third person singular personal pronoun[40] and since the traditional use of the masculine personal pronoun for God can be taken to make some sort of claim that God does have gender, we have a difficulty.

I follow that traditional usage because, it seems to me, the alternatives call too much attention to themselves. They add a message. I have worked as a copy editor of works in theology and biblical studies. One of the pieces of advice I have for authors, or would have if they asked, is that an author in their fields should control his or her agenda and should make that agenda explicit. Using non-gendered language of God (or trying to, or alternating genders), it seems to me, is either a way of recognizing an item on the agenda or a confusing intrusion that makes the reader wonder: Does this represent an item on the agenda or not? My explicit agenda here does include recalling the personhood of God again

37. In a modified echo of Paul Tillich.

38. The last of these is from Mozley, *Doctrine of God*, 53.

39. I think Victor Hugo meant something along the lines of *unless one believes in God one cannot believe in humans* by these words: "The infinite is. He is there. If the infinite had no person, person would be without limit; it would not be infinite; in other words, it would not exist. There is, then, an *I*. That *I* of the infinite is God" (*Les Misérables* 1.10).

40. Other than clumsy substitutes such as "he/she," "(s)he," "co," and "they," though the last has been with us for quite a while and appears to have the best chance of becoming standard.

and again, at every stage of the way, and a personal pronoun is needed for that.

There was good reason for the tradition, reasons within the biblical cultures, that mostly masculine metaphors were used for the God of Israel. Those reasons would not have the same force today, but I show my appreciation for, acceptance of, and submission to the people we are referring to when we speak of "the tradition" by following their usage. If my aim here were to challenge the tradition on points touching on the gender of the pronouns used of God, it would be better to do so explicitly and to be specific, not tucking that agenda between the lines of a document that has another purpose.

Feminist theology, like other contextual theologies, does make the challenge explicit and specific. Attention to the problem of our gendered personal pronouns has helped us to think about issues concerning God and gender, and feminist theology is correct in saying that our departures from the tradition can be made effective with the aid of changes in our uses of words. Other than that aside, that is not a point I am making here, while the use of a personal pronoun is essential to some points I am making.

FREEDOM AND COMMITMENT

Freedom is not contextless self-determination but choice among available options.[41] Warfield, for instance, regarded the Pelagian defense of free will as faulty: it "scarcely allows for the existence of a 'man'—only a willing machine is left." "In such a conception, there was no place for character," because freedom of choice had crowded it out.[42] Critics who have seen belief in God, or sometimes just some version of Christian

---

41. A primary victim of the postmodern critique has been the contextless freedom of the absolute (perhaps Stoic) subject. And the critique goes on to say that freedom "is constantly distilled from the complex strategies of power within which subjects are interpellated as unequal, mutually dependent persons. The protection of an equality of freedom therefore collapses into the promotion of the inequality of power" (Milbank, *Theology and Social Theory*, 279). All true, but not all that needs to be said. Milbank criticizes some "neo-Nietzscheans" for saying as much on the basis of a smuggled-in Kantian liberalism. But what I will argue later is that faith in God allows us to anticipate the end of the human game of power-plays and, indeed, the end of the power of the powers.

42. Warfield, "Augustine and the Pelagian Controversy."

theology,[43] as incompatible with belief in human autonomy have often thought that "the only autonomy worthy of the name is to be found in some kind of independent self-realization by the creature," freedom as "the law of our being, grounded in ourselves rather than in the grace of God," which is not the freedom we have.[44] There is a difference between free will as freedom from absolute determination by someone else and free will as absolute *self*-determination.[45]

Divine freedom is not and human freedom need not be capricious, indecisive, or flakey. Freedom is, rather, most clearly seen as exercised in commitment, in unrevoked decision, in free choice intended to be ingrained as habit and determinative for the future.[46] Character, whether of God or of a human person, is made up partially of the sum of commitments. God's love is such a commitment. If any love is a decision that might be reversed or weakened in a day, a year, or a decade, then it is therefore less deserving of the name "love."

Freedom and love are thus necessary to each other. If "commitment" sounds like a reduction, qualification, or surrender of freedom, then the freedom sought, whether in logic or in lifestyle, is that of serial one-night affairs in which love is impossible. A man who has given up such dalliances for marital commitment has been freed for love from his former so-called "freedom," which used to put love beyond his reach.[47] Thus it is that marriage can be an analogy for Christ's love for the church (Eph 5:25): in marriage the human image of the faithful divine lover is seen.

How we think of God's freedom thus determines how we think of human freedom. Barth's emphasis on the freedom of God, which I have drawn on several times here, can lead into a cul-de-sac in his ethical thinking. He emphasized that God's freedom is responsible and not capricious,[48] which is close to what I am saying here about "commit-

---

43. On critics of Barth, see Gunton, "Barth, the Trinity," 323–24.

44. Gunton, "Barth, the Trinity," 324.

45. Schmid, *Doctrinal Theology*, 257–68, though here the second definition comes down to ability to do good, which, after the fall, would be the ability to save oneself, which is impossible.

46. So, e.g., Yoder, *Karl Barth and the Problem of War* [2003], 129; Moltmann, *God in Creation*, 75–76, 82–83.

47. If this change is connected to a conversion to belief in God, then the man exemplifies what David Burrell has pointed out and explored in detail in "Can We Be Free without a Creator?": the free will one believes in is different depending on whether one also believes in God.

48. *Church Dogmatics* 3/1:95, quoted earlier.

ment." But Barth could also, in effect, posit unpredictability as evidence of that freedom, thus going off in the opposite direction: because God might at some time command what he has never commanded before, there can be no moral rules sufficient to direct us: we must always listen for God's command.[49] This is like Ockham's defense of God's freedom, which requires the possibility of God's reversal of his prior commands.[50] But if we regard God's freedom as most clearly demonstrated in his trustworthy love, in commitment, then we can also regard God's commands as permanent.[51] Thus God's character—or the fact that he *has* a consistent character—becomes the basis for human character, for regarding our freedom as compatible with adherence to moral absolutes.[52]

In redemption we are given freedom from the powers (about which more in chapters 7 and 8), freedom from their supposed authority, so as to obey (that is, to choose) God's command. Ultimately our freedom, in order to be genuine freedom, must be obedience.[53] It is for this reason that redemption, sanctification, and discipleship are all terms for the restoration of our freedom. Barth in particular distinguished between obedience to God, which frees, and the only alternative, obedience to "powers and dominions and authorities which restrict the freedom of man."[54] "There is no will that is a room, swept clear and uninhabited— at least, not for long."[55] In redemption as in creation, our freedom is grounded in God's grace.

---

49. E.g., Barth, *Church Dogmatics* 3/4:342–43. This is the most important point, in my opinion, that Yoder makes in his critique of Barth's ethics in *Karl Barth and the Problem of War* [1970], 66–67, 70–71, 78.

50. E.g., William of Ockham, *Opera philosophica et theologica*, 5:352.

51. With, of course, the qualification that attention must be given to whom the particular command was given to.

52. The meaning of "moral absolutes" here is subject to another point made by Yoder: Distinguishing ethical systems as "absolutist" versus "situationist" or the like somewhat misses the point since all moral decision-making must take account of conflict among moral *absolutes* in concrete *situations*. See Yoder, *Karl Barth and the Problem of War* [1970], 76–77n1.

53. See Gunton, "Barth, the Trinity," 320, on Barth's statements to this effect.

54. Barth, *Church Dogmatics* 2/2:585.

55. Gunton, "Barth, the Trinity," 324, referring to Matt 12:43–45.

4

A Place for Us

ALONGSIDE THE INFINITE

LOOK AT THE CONCEPT of infinity in three ways: First, if there were an infinite number of potatoes in the universe, nothing else could exist in that universe since all the available space would be taken up by potatoes. It would be an all-potato universe. Second, if there were an infinitely large potato, the result would be similar: the universe would be a potato. Third, if I attempt to stockpile an infinite number of potatoes, my goal would have to entail there being no potatoes outside my warehouse (which itself would have to be infinitely large), because any outside potatoes would imply that more could be added inside.

Of course, some statements of this kind must be ridiculous, because infinity is impossible (there can always be one more potato: infinity plus one) or at least inapplicable. But these are intended to be statements about the concept of infinity, which has been regarded as applicable to God.[1] Does divine infinitude exclude the possibility of anything else existing? Does it use up existence? Is God like a mythical chemical that dissolves or incorporates whatever it comes into contact with, that is, eventually, everything except itself?[2] "It seems that God does not exist; because if

---

1. E.g., Aquinas, *Summa contra Gentiles* 1.43; Strong, *Systematic Theology*, 254–56.
2. Or like the Borg (*Star Trek*). Cf. William James on "the lazy monism that idly haunts the region of God's name" and excludes consideration of any limitation of God, in James, *Pluralistic Universe*, 124–25. The same questions might be asked about absolute chaos, chaos that knows no bounds and must be complete and therefore preclude the existence of anything else, or about chaos-defeating order, which, if absolute, would mean no chaos could be left. See Milbank, *Theology and Social Theory*, e.g., xvii, 394–95.

54   THE ONE STORY

one of two contraries be infinite, the other would be altogether destroyed. But the word 'God' means that He is infinite goodness. If, therefore, God existed, there would be no evil discoverable," no room left for evil because of the infinitely large potato of goodness, "but there is evil in the world. Therefore God," that infinitely large thing, "does not exist."³ There would be no room for *us*. "Are we so sure that the creature—heaven and earth and we ourselves—forms a sphere which is even possible side by side with God? . . . What place is there for another when God is there? How can there be another being side by side with His being?"⁴

The answer is that we exist because of God's grace.⁵ Knowing that things other than God do exist, having been created by God, we understand nonetheless "the transience and therefore the impossibility of the creature before its Creator."⁶ But the impossibility is overcome by grace.⁷ If God had wanted to be all that existed, he would have reserved freedom to himself and love to the intratrinitarian relationships. But he did not do that. It is only through a miracle of love that we are able to exist alongside the infinite—to have been created and to continue in existence. For that reason our existence is not self-sustaining but dependent on the one in whom "all things are held together" (Col 1:17).⁸

Pantheism would be another solution: since nothing can exist alongside the infinite, only the infinite exists and creation is not separate from God. God and the universe are identical, or "God" includes the universe. Over against that, accepting the grace expressed in creation allows

---

3. Aquinas, *Summa Theologiae* I.2.3, objection 1.

4. Barth, *Church Dogmatics*, 3/1:6. A related question would be whether statements along the line of "God has quality *a* to an infinite degree" preclude anyone else having quality *a*. If God has infinite potatoness, then there are no other potatoes.

5. Paul Jewett denies the sensibleness of saying that creation is by grace (Jewett, *God, Creation, and Revelation*, 494). A different answer, one that focuses on the distinction between God and the universe and locates God's infinitude outside the universe, is given by Aquinas in *Summa contra Gentiles* 1.42. See the elaboration in Joseph Rickaby's translation (31n91). But the very existence of the universe, in view also of the completeness *in se* of God, points to an original act of grace.

6. Continuing in *Church Dogmatics* 3/1:6; see further 3/1:4–7. Similarly, Anselm, *Proslogion* 22: properly speaking, only God exists, since all other existence is derived, dependent, and temporary.

7. Similarly, the incarnation: the collocation of divine and human is impossible; the debasing of God is impossible (and hence is "an offense to Jews" and Muslims, 1 Cor 1:23) and so occurs only by impossible grace.

8. See again *Proslogion* 22. From this perspective, the ways in which creation's existence seems to be self-sustaining (natural laws) are actually ways in which God sustains creation's existence.

us to avoid pantheism and still in some way affirm divine infinitude.[9] Because God has allowed things other than himself to exist, creation is an act of divine self-limitation. Creation shows not only God acting with power and freedom but also God setting a limit on his own power and freedom.[10]

> In order to create a world "outside" himself, the infinite God must have made room beforehand for a finitude in himself. It is only a withdrawal by God into himself that can free the space into which God can act creatively. The *nihil* for his *creatio ex nihilo* only comes into being because—and in as far as—the omnipotent and omnipresent God withdraws his presence and restricts his power.[11]

The divine self-limitation for the sake of creation—for the sake of the existence of things other than God—was what God chose and carried out. The narrative aspect is essential here: part of the kenosis in creation is that God causes a change that occurred *in time*.[12] If matter had been eternal, that is, if the space for creation was always there, then we would, along with John Stuart Mill, have to give up all talk of divine infinitude,[13] since what now exists would set the standard for eternity. Rejecting pantheism does not require jettisoning divine "infinitude," but it does require that we see it as a characteristic of the God who loves freely that which he has created and allowed to exist in time.

BETWEEN THE WATERS

When God creates he not only causes things to exist. He also divides undifferentiated space into unlike regions. Before creatures of land, sea, and air come into existence (Gen 1:20-25), the primordial watery world (v. 2) is divided (vv. 6-7) and land and water are separated (vv. 9-10). Thus God makes a space for us.

---

9. Strong, *Systematic Theology*, 254-55. Perhaps we should specify here that after creation God's infinitude is potential but not actualized, or something like that.

10. Some consider it important here to say that God sets a limit on the *exercise* of his power (see note 33 below). To me, the difference is barely discernible.

11. Moltmann, *God in Creation*, 86-87.

12. It might also be said to have started or created or originated time.

13. On Mill, see James, *Pluralistic Universe*, 124. Creation is reordering of existent matter according to Mill, *Three Essays on Religion*, 178. On the limits to God's knowledge and power, see Mill, *Three Essays on Religion*, 183-84.

The issue is not just all that water. It is also the mysterious forces of chaos.[14] The tale of the defeat of Rahab (Job 9:13; 26:12) shows that, while Israelite monotheism produced creation accounts very different from those of Mesopotamia,[15] part of how that could be accomplished was through reference to the same chaos monsters: the Mesopotamian god Marduk defeated Tiamat/Rahab for the sake of an ordered cosmos, and the God of Israel could fill that role as well.

Indeed, the understanding of water as chaos was helped along by the Israelites not being a seagoing people. The sea was not distant, but it was foreign, mysterious, and dangerous. Furthermore, agriculture in the Israelites' land depended not on annual flooding, as in Egypt and Mesopotamia, but on rain (cf. Gen 2:5-6). Untamed water was evil, so the defeat of chaos is the taming of water. Furthermore, like creation, the salvation of the people from Egypt was accomplished by God exercising sovereignty over water and dividing it (Exod 14:21; 15:8). God creates by exercising power against water, Rahab, and God's enemies (Ps 89:9-10).

The description of the man overboard in book 2, chapter 8 ("Shadows") of *Les Misérables* is a metaphor for the "immensity of wretchedness" experienced by the outcast Jean Valjean. "He feels himself buried in those two infinities, the ocean and the sky, at one and the same time: the one is a tomb; the other is a shroud."[16] The nothingness above and below do not hear his shouting for life, for rescue, for justice. This same experience of being swept from the deck, the place where one can stand, into the watery sea can also portray the difference between existence, which is order, and chaos, which negates existence.

Our entertainments occasionally show that we still have the uneasy sense that chaos waits for an opportunity to invade the ordered universe. Perhaps a simple game will unleash wild beasts (*Jumanji*) or cause the house to get sucked into a black hole (*Zathura*). Devastating attacks by fictional space aliens are generally preceded by well-ordered life, sometimes symbolized by the small Midwestern town. Perhaps what is *really* in the back of the wardrobe is the abyss, so watch your step.

---

14. To say, with Tsumura, "Genesis and Ancient Near Eastern Stories," 33, that Gen 1:2 speaks of a world that is "unproductive and empty, uninhabitated," "not yet normal, that is to say, not yet productive or inhabited and without light," but not of a "primeval 'chaos,' in direct opposition to 'creation'" begs the question. "Normal" and "productive" are, indeed, the opposite of chaotic.

15. Pritchard, *Ancient Near Eastern Texts*, 3-4, 66-69.

16. Hugo, *Les Misérables*, from the translation by Isabel F. Hapgood.

Order is not self-sustaining. Only human hubris (deism, for instance) assumes otherwise and thus sets the stage for the worst possible surprise (1 Thess 5:3, etc.). But God is not surprised. The flood through which only those in Noah's ark survived resulted from God's act of suspending creation: the barriers that kept the waters down under the ground or up above the sky were opened (Gen 7:11; 8:2). The space between the waters could be invaded by the waters, but only because God explicitly called for that to happen, and he has promised that he will not do the same again (8:21-22; 9:11-16).[17] Apocalyptic visions tell of other invasions of the created order, but again only by God's bidding (e.g., Jer 4:23-26; Mark 13:24-25).

Perhaps an analogous way of thinking of the creation of space for us and our furry and scaly neighbors has come with quantum mechanics. Newtonian physics defines our world, but it no longer holds when we get to the level of electrons and their kin. Our ordered Newtonian world exists alongside—or is made up of or contradicted by—an existence in which Newton's rules do not hold, where language and arithmetic do not work, where physicists sometimes resort to poetry.[18] Perhaps God cleared a Newtonian space for us within the quantum soup. This Newtonian space is suspended, as it were, above the abyss of quantum undifferentiation.[19] Order is always threatened by chaos, but God sustains our existence and does so out of love, just as surely as he sustains the seasons for the sake of our nourishment (Gen 8:22).

FOR THEOLOGICAL SPEECH

Because of who *we* are, theology is analogous to Newtonian mechanics, which is sufficient at the level at which it operates. But alongside it there is the quantum level, that of God's existence, where the rules are different. We can speak of the location of a subatomic particle or of its motion, but not of both at the same time. If we speak of an electron in Newtonian terms, saying that it has both position and momentum, it defies us and

---

17. Because the natural tendency of water is to rise above land and sink below air (Aristotle), God maintains our place by actively and constantly holding back the waters above and the waters below. So Calvin, *Commentary on Psalms*, vol. 4, on Ps 104:5; *Institutes* 1.5.6.

18. See Taylor, *Luminous Web*, 33-56.

19. When a physicist suggests that only one electron exists, perhaps we are getting a glimpse of the collapse of differentiation.

says that by having both it has neither. It stretches itself beyond our ability to understand by making location and motion, space and time, into one thing or even nonexistent. Thus both location and motion are merely ways in which it allows itself to be known by limited creatures who live in a Newtonian world and for whom, therefore, space and time are two very real and distinct dimensions of existence.

A Newtonian mechanic stranded in our world, in which there is less and less that he or she can fix, might feel nostalgia for an earlier time. Space and time travel are not achieved by a wacky genius in a nineteenth-century novel but by large groups of well-funded specialists, each of whom need not understand the other's work. Theology also can be and has been divided, subdivided, and populated by sometimes arrogant academics. But theologians are at their best as Newtonian minds facing a God who is beyond even the quanta, facing him with gratitude for the rude tools he has given them for understanding not God himself but only the relationship between him and ourselves in the ways and to the degree he wishes us to. Revelation is the gracious mediation to us, not of God or interesting details about him or his daily habits, but of what we need to know for salvation and for being God's people (2 Tim 3:15–17), which is, therefore, what theological language is about. As God created a space for us between the waters or within the chaos or the quantum soup, so also he granted us a new creation and enabled us to come up with words by which to live in it.

Theology is a language game. It is not like entomology, which with a journey to the interior of New Guinea can add to its catalog some new creature who was there all along. God does exist, but all theologians have are words. Electrons elude definition by Newtonian minds; we do have language for them, though it is self-contradicting or poetic. Similarly, when we speak about God sometimes we have to contradict ourselves. Theologians go at least to the far edge of their discipline when they attempt to name something else as the object of their observations and thus stray into social psychology, speculative metaphysics, or mysticism.[20]

And little wonder that theologians are occasionally led out of their discipline if they have come to believe that there is no reality signified by its language. Quantum physics has led physicists into a realm where, sometimes, their discipline "is less concerned with what nature *is* than

---

20. Worse yet, so-called "creation science"'s pretense at linking God and the hard sciences.

with what can be *said* about nature,"[21] and so theology can come to be not about the living God but about what can be achieved by God-talk.

FOR SPACE AND TIME

The teeming multiplicity we see extending through time and space began from God's decision that there would be someone other than himself (than himself in Trinity, that is). In creating, God thus committed himself to multiplicity. What he created he called "good." Any philosophy or metaphysics that rejects multiplicity or extension in favor of some sort of single absolute principle must in some way reject or collapse the creation-redemption story.

One such monism, the favoring of a single thing or principle, is rejection of spatial extension, that is, materiality. In some forms of Gnosticism or Manicheism, what exists must be either immaterial or wholly evil, and blame for sin is shifted from the human decision not to love God to something prior, to the creation of materiality by a malevolent deity. Dislike for materiality has not been restricted to any particular era in Christian history because its source is at least partly that, at almost any time and place, we can dislike thinking of our imperfect, clumsy, and messy bodies as being what we really are.

Time, temporal extension, is materiality's companion. Neither of the two is the human problem: neither is the reason we must be redeemed, and neither is an enemy of our redemption. They are, rather, the arena in which our existence and our redemption take place. Without them we would not be what God created us for. Without time there could be no space for the exercise of human will and therefore no sin and no redemption.[22]

Christians have found a number of ways to denigrate time by collapsing creation or redemption. First, by saying that *God's perfection means that he has no involvement with time. Therefore, creation, at least considered as an act of God's will, was instantaneous.*[23] But creation was

---

21. Taylor, *Luminous Web*, 34. In this whole section I am indebted to chapter 3 of *Luminous Web*.

22. This acknowledgment of time cannot be reduced to existentialism. See Ratzinger, *In the Beginning*, x–xii, against existentialist reduction of time to stasis.

23. Augustine, *Confessions* 12.15(18). This understanding of creation arises ultimately from Plato's idea of a fixed and unchanging number of "forms"; so Gunton, *Triune Creator*, 185–86; Brunner, *Dogmatics* 1:266–67. Fundamentalist discomfort with

not complete from the first moment because human freedom had not yet been exercised. If creation had been immediately complete, the first humans' freedom and the Bible's whole tale of God's love, call, patience, and wrath would be a sham. God's close involvement in Israel's story on every page of the Old Testament would be merely something to be explained away, along with the seven days in Genesis 1 and the stages in time in Genesis 2, which, even if not "literal,"[24] indicate a closer involvement with creation and time than instantaneous creation would allow to God.

Second, by saying that *our actions take time because of our fall into sin.*[25] But what God created was all "good" (perfect in that sense) but not complete (that is, not perfect in that other sense). It was created in order to be eschatologically complete. "The perfection of beginning is not the perfection of the completed."[26] Human love for God was not complete at the first moment of human life: because it requires the exercise of human will, it requires time, change, and risk. If God had not accepted time, change, and risk, he could not have extended the circle of mutual love.

Third, by saying that *redemption is the remedy for the fallen creation's woes—in effect, God's "Plan B."* Or that *the age to come will be a return to conditions as they were before the fall.*[27] But redemption is God's original intention in creating, not a salvage operation. Sin is a step off course, but this does not mean that God was surprised by it. We can say that "redemption or salvation is that divine action which returns the creation to its proper direction, its orientation to its eschatological destiny, which is to be perfected in due course of time by God's enabling it to be that which it was created to be,"[28] but only if we also say that this redemption was intended in the original creation, that it is, and always was, how

---

biological evolution can be linked with such a view of creation (of fixed species, at least) as complete from the beginning; this is sometimes made explicit, as in, e.g., article IV of the doctrinal statement of Toronto Baptist Seminary and Bible College: "All animal and vegetable life was effected by special creation, and God's established law was that they should bring forth only 'after their kind.'" I do not know the prehistory of this statement or how widespread such statements are.

24. On that issue, see chapter 5 below, under "Truthfulness."

25. Augustine, *City of God* 11.6, 30. See further Gunton, *Triune Creator*, 16, 77, 83–84.

26. Gunton, *Triune Creator*, 183. See most of all Irenaeus, *Against Heresies* 4.38. See also Bulgakov, *Bride of the Lamb*, 149–50. Creation is originally imperfect (i.e., incomplete) and entrusted to humankind for its perfection (Gen 1:28; 2:5, 15).

27. "Recapitulation" as understood by Origen, not Irenaeus. See further chapter 8 below, under "The New Beginning."

28. Gunton, *Triune Creator*, 56.

creation reaches its goal. The eschaton (the end-times fulfillment) is the completion of creation: Adam and Eve were the perfect beginning, and Christ is the perfected goal (1 Cor 15:49).[29]

Fourth, by saying that *who is to be included in redemption is not based on any act of human freedom but on decisions made by God prior to or as a part of creation*. But predestination thus understood collapses redemption into creation (or into pre-creation decrees). Creation-redemption makes a good story because of its non-linear path toward its goal. The story must be non-linear simply because it includes wills other than God's. If, in accordance with such predestinarian soteriology, all the decisions regarding salvation were made before time existed, then we might have free will, but it would not be a freedom that matters in the long run, and there would be no story.

FOR OTHER WILLS

Will itself is, like materiality and time, an aspect of the multiplicity created by God. God made room for other wills.[30] A parable can unpack the spatial metaphor of "making room": If Joe is in a room (or a universe) by himself and then Bob enters, Joe has lost some of his freedom, simply because there is less of the room for him to occupy. This still holds even if Joe has invited Bob in. If Bob sits down and then Joe wants to sit in the same chair, then he will have to live without fulfillment of that desire or find a way of displacing Bob.[31] The problem did not exist until Bob entered the room. Before then, Joe had complete freedom of the will with regard to which chair to occupy. He was in the happy condition of one playing musical chairs solitaire. The addition of another will, Bob's, complicates Joe's world. And if Nancy comes in after Bob, then Joe's sovereignty over the chairs in the room is in even greater trouble.

If Joe is God, then what he has done is to *create* Bob and Nancy. And that is amazing.

---

29. This is somewhat like what Bulgakov says about creation still reaching toward its completion through the sustaining/indwelling and sanctification of the Spirit: "Creation is always the *future* too, not only *nata*, but also *natura*" (Bulgakov, *Comforter*, 220).

30. Moltmann's kenotic theism is a way of speaking of creation as God making room, though Moltmann does not bring will to the fore in his use of this spatial metaphor (e.g., *God in Creation*, 86–87). Even less so the kenotic theism of Bulgakov. This language of kenosis is useful, but I employ it in a different way.

31. Assuming chairs that can hold only one person each.

> It is only the heathen gods who envy man. The true God, who is unconditionally the Lord, allows him [humankind] to be the thing for which He created him. He is far too highly exalted to take it amiss or to prevent it. . . . There can be no doubt that with an autonomous reality God does give to man and to all His creatures the freedom of individual action.[32]

Determinism of any sort arises from a reduction of each possible factor in outcomes to either absolute decisiveness or absolute inconsequentiality. It arises, that is, from some sort of dislike, whether scientific or theological, of multiple causes (monism again). On the theological side, those who dislike multiplicity of causes can ascribe to God a sovereignty that cannot limit itself. If God's sovereignty were absolute and unlimitable, even by God himself, then there could be no creation of other wills. What is created would have to be a lifeless plaything or mere limb of the creator, not a living and changing returner of love to God.[33] This would be "that terrible theism which can imagine nothing else but deity, and which denies altogether the outlines of human personality and human will."[34] But we do not know God's sovereignty in the abstract but as his will to create and redeem this world, as, that is, love.

Consideration of such belief in a sovereignty that cannot limit itself brings the extension of time back into view. To say, for instance, "God is in control of everything" (in addition to saddling God with blame for "everything") can be taken as eliminating any need for the eschaton since anything the eschaton would achieve is already in force. But that bumper sticker slogan ("God is in control . . .") need not be taken as expressing complete determinism, and the only way it could be correct would be for it to mean that it is how the whole story of creation and redemption comes out that God is in control of. At any rate, an ultimately fatalist theology, the sort of thing Christian writers have identified with Stoicism or Islam,[35] has been regularly rejected by Christian theologians.[36] Apart

---

32. Barth, *Church Dogmatics* 3/3:87.

33. Aquinas distinguishes between God's absolute omnipotence and his actual use of his power (*Summa Theologiae* 1.25.5. ad 1).

34. Chesterton, *Heretics*, 106. Chesterton is writing here about Islam, as he viewed it. A few lines later Chesterton says about scientific determinism that the problem with "this scepticism" is "not in the least that [it] denies the existence of God; it is that it denies the existence of man" (107).

35. E.g., Barth, *Church Dogmatics* 3/3:113, and see previous note.

36. Regarding fatalism, Terrance Tiessen has written: "Unlike all the other models [of providence], this one has no Christian theologians who admit to holding it as a

from the extent to which this is fair to whichever variations of Islam, it does describe well a form of theism, locatable in variations of Christianity, that does away with humanity as we experience it.

But any serious attention given to popular expressions of theological determinism would have to focus first on rhetorical setting and function rather than on theological content. Such language of "God's will" assumes that God is "in the details" in ways the devil could only dream of. "It was God's will," spoken at a funeral, fortunately less often now than in generations past, makes God's presence decisive when, for instance, a drunk driver crosses the center line. And the practice of "seeking God's will," even if that will is thought to be resistible, assumes that God's planning includes many details that God is actually quite willing to leave up to us.

Things happen to us that are not "God's will" because God really did create a world that is separate from himself and because sin really has had drastic effects in that world.[37] One might refer such events to God's "*permissive* will," but only if we mean by that that God has *permitted* the existence of wills other than himself and events he has not initiated and does not control.[38] On at least a terminological level we are better off just rightly understanding God's sovereignty in creation. God is sovereign. But he freely and sovereignly chooses to give up some choices to others, to accomplish his purposes slowly, and to allow other free beings to determine some part of the story and its outcome (by, for instance, receiving or rejecting redemption). Because we believe in creation, we can know that what happens does not happen necessarily. Things could be other than as they are.[39] Like scientific determinism, any form of theological determinism is monism, a reductive rejection of multiplicity.

Competition for space for the effective exercise of one's will characterizes human behavior. Will colonizes. If I want to extend my capacity

---

biblical doctrine of providence. . . . No Christian theologian intentionally asserts fatalistic determinism" (Tiessen, *Providence and Prayer*, 272–73). But I asked a well-trained Christian theologian teaching at a well-known evangelical seminary what his understanding of providence was and, for clarification, whether "God *does* everything that happens," to which his answer was an unqualified Yes.

37. Furthermore, it can be argued that the logic of God's creation of other wills requires a world that includes gratuitous evil. See Peterson, "C. S. Lewis on the Necessity of Gratuitous Evil."

38. God's permission of evil is normally thought of in Reformed theology as involving more than permission of the existence of other wills. E.g., Heppe, *Reformed Dogmatics*, 274.

39. Barth, *Church Dogmatics* 3/1:38: there is real evil in the world.

to decide effectively so that it occupies the space presently occupied by someone else's will, the alternatives I have, assuming we do not agree, which will eventually be the case, are to deny my own desire and thus allow that space to that other will, or to use persuasion or coercion to accomplish my desire. This takes us back to the story of Joe, Bob, and the comfortable chair. Subject to my submission to some standards of how persuasion or coercion should be carried out (say, some pattern of respect for that other person or some rules of engagement), then the only thing that matters is the goal, which is to gain what I desire. This is the basis for violence among humans (Jas 4:1–2).

Creation is the prototypical act of nonviolent love. In it, God makes room for other wills.[40] Competitive humanity sets itself against the manner and the matter of creation. The violent person or community seeks to divinize itself by reversing creation.[41] As I evict another person's will from its space, I am, in effect, telling God that he was wrong to create and that I would be a better god, one that would not mess up things with all that multiplicity, one that would reserve the exercise of will to myself.

Behind what the more generous God has done is the fact of the Trinity. God's acceptance of differentiation within himself—the mutual acceptance of the persons of the Trinity[42]—enables his acceptance of the distinction of creation from God, for, that is, the existence of free creatures. Barth saw a necessary link between unitarianism and determinism: "The god who is abstractly single is the enemy of human freedom, for he is not the triune God who because he is differentiated in himself is the ground of true differentiation in the creature."[43]

FOR THE ONE STORY

Theodicy is the attempt to defend the goodness and justice of God, and it usually begins from a conundrum something like this: If God is both loving and all-powerful, there should be no evil or suffering in creation.

---

40. Hauerwas, "End Is in the Beginning," 21. Creation was "God's determinative act of peace" (Milbank, *Theology and Social Theory*, 5–6). This does not mean that we should try to speak of God as consistently "nonviolent" (see the last subsection of chapter 2 above).

41. See further chapter 5 below.

42. E.g., Bulgakov, *Comforter*, 65–67.

43. Gunton, "Barth, the Trinity," 323–26. Gunton cites Barth's *Church Dogmatics* 3/3:139 in this regard.

But there is evil and suffering. Therefore, either God fails to be loving, or he fails to be powerful, or both, or he does not exist. As mentioned earlier, talk of God's "attributes" sets up standards for God, and the questions that must be answered by any theodicy ask whether he does meet those standards.

The questions leading to theodicy typically collapse time by wanting everything to be okay now. A suicidal person might complain to his friends as they drive him to the hospital that death is the most sensible option, but it is so only under the assumption that there can be no change, or, in theological terms, no redemption. The theodicy questions require that everything be alright right now. It is no good to say that things will turn out right, because surely someone as good and powerful as God could have made things right to start with. But, rather than calling creation into question in this way, perhaps it would be better to wait and see how things play out before passing judgment. The creation-redemption story responds to the questions by asking for that kind of patience.

Theodicy has been fundamental to understandings of God in much recent theology. Process, open, or relational theologies can be examples of such theodicy-driven theologies.[44] But theodicy fails as a starting point for theology because of that fundamental collapsing of the creation-redemption story. The relationship between God the creator-redeemer and us is not timeless, always the same.[45]

Because of the time (story) factor, our response to the theodicy questions is to proclaim the gospel: we tell a story that places all questions in context, making them questions about God. Thus the *Heidelberg Catechism*'s answer: "Whatever evil he [God the Father] sends upon me in this vale of tears, he will turn to my good; for he is able to do it, being Almighty God, and willing also, being a faithful Father."[46] Heidelberg's

---

44. For example, "open theism" posits an incompleteness in the divine attributes over against "classical theism." E.g., Pinnock, "From Augustine to Arminius," 23–26. Refusing to go this direction links us up with a strain in theology that has existed at least since Søren Kierkegaard, who criticized apologetics, specifically attempts to shore up the authority of Scripture by demonstrating its adherence to historical facts. History does not provide certainty, and anyway certainty is not compatible with faith, that is, with passion. So Kierkegaard's *Concluding Unscientific Postscript*, 25–35. See also, e.g., Barth's emphasis on divine freedom and his reaction against what he regarded as natural theology. Yoder, "Trinity Versus Theodicy," continues Barth's viewpoint.

45. So Barth, *Church Dogmatics* 3/1:13. Granted that such theodicy-driven theologies come to the same conclusion, still they do so for quite different reasons, and "not timeless" means something quite different from one to the next.

46. *Heidelberg Catechism*, 26. An attentive reader will already know that I do not

statement acknowledges the theodicy questions: there is suffering and evil, but—with more assertion or proclamation than explanation—God is nonetheless loving and powerful. The answer to the questions comes after and within the confession of faith and will thus be *fides quaerens intellectam*.[47]

Heidelberg's answer need not be taken as encouraging the sort of piety that seeks to understand "my good" in any further detail or even to move "my good" out of the eschaton at all. That is, I need not be able to narrate how suffering has been instrumental to "my good" in the past in order to believe in this loving and powerful God. There is a broad middle ground between that sort of piety and the reaction of deism.[48] In that middle ground, faith seeks understanding, knows that understanding is not complete, and is not upset by that knowledge.

A theology that strives to be only natural theology, such as deism, cannot perceive the creation-redemption story. It starts outside the confession and stays there—where creation stands alone doctrinally—and so can eliminate any God-given meaning from the continuation of time. But starting within the confession, considering creation as part of the larger creation-redemption story, binding it together with soteriology, christology, and eschatology, makes something quite different of creation.[49]

We engage in something of a balancing act when we talk about God and time or God's involvement in events in our world. On the one hand, deism gives too simple an answer by placing God above it all, outside our affairs altogether. On the other hand, making the creation-redemption story a story about God, as process theology can do, is hardly necessary. That creation-redemption requires time does not mean that God requires time. It is God's story only in that he is the creator and redeemer. To have a story about oneself, one must have needs and must come into being in a world that already exists, neither of which God has done.[50]

---

agree with the ascription to God of sending "whatever evil."

47. "Faith seeking understanding," as opposed to faith premised on understanding, was an important slogan for Anselm in the twelfth century and Barth in the twentieth.

48. Deism is belief in a God who, having created us, now keeps his hands out of our affairs.

49. Cf. Moltmann on "the future of creation," *God in Creation*, 5.

50. So Augustine, *Confessions* 13.37. See further Mills, "Brief Theology of Time." God existing in time can also make the distinction of creation from God difficult, as pointed out by Moltmann, *God in Creation*, 78–79. Cf. Origen's insistence that time and creation began together (*De Principia* 3.5.4).

God is certainly "in time" insofar as we know him through his freely-chosen participation in the creation-redemption story. God identifies himself to his people by reciting a narrative about themselves—at the beginning of the Ten Commandments ("I am the God who brought you out . . . ," Exod 20:2) and, indeed, in Scripture as a whole. That is how we know God. Theology must deal with that kind of knowledge, not with any speculation about God's self-knowledge.[51] The creation-redemption story is not a story about God.[52] Setting God outside time does not necessarily result in determinism, even if God is held to have complete foreknowledge, because the transcendent God has created wills outside himself.

The theological or philosophical doctrine that complete divine foreknowledge necessarily makes human freedom impossible becomes a similar way of complaining against "classical theism."[53] If creation-redemption is a story, then, it might be said, there is a storyteller. Storytellers are normally sovereign in relation to their stories, and characters within the stories are not real people with freedom to choose. But that is not what we experience here in the midst of creation-redemption. So "story" is a *metaphor* for the course of humanity, and we must control the metaphor lest such implications be allowed to take over.

---

51. "Knowledge" might be a potentially misleading anthropomorphism here. See further chapter 7 below, under "Does It Do Any Good?"

52. Some theologians have wanted to place God more nearly *in time* than I have here because of God's involvement with humankind and faithfulness through time. For instance, "The God who is the subject of Christian theology is not timeless. The God of Israel and Jesus, the God we find in Scripture, is a storied God. That we learn of God, or more exactly, that we learn who God is through a narrative is not accidental but rather indicative of God's nature. God's storied character expresses, as Aquinas maintained, that 'God's act of being is constrained by no form other than itself.' Accordingly the biblical God's eternity is not immunity to time but faithfulness. 'God is not eternal in that he is faithful to his commitments with time. At the great turning, Israel's God is eternal in that he is faithful to the death, and then yet again faithful'" (Hauerwas, *Better Hope*, 121, quoting Jenson, *Systematic Theology*, 1:215, 217). Barth spoke of the divine spatiality and temporality in relation to the triunity of God (*Church Dogmatics* 2/1:468–70, 615). See further Gunton, "Barth, the Trinity," 317–18.

53. Older Reformed theology accepted the premise (e.g., Heppe, *Reformed Dogmatics*, 152), but it has also been accepted among recent theologians who use it to argue in quite a different direction, i.e., that God's foreknowledge cannot be complete (e.g., Rice, "Divine Foreknowledge and Free-Will Theism," 123). On the exclusion of human freedom by complete divine foreknowledge as a philosophical doctrine, see, e.g., Swartz, "Foreknowledge and Free Will"; Fischer "Foreknowledge, Freedom"; Mills, "Brief Theology of Time."

5

Falling

TALES OF REBELLION

The First Story

GOD'S ORIGINAL ARRANGEMENT FOR humans made one tree off-limits for food and included God's establishment of human sovereignty over all other animate life (Gen 1:26, 28; 2:19–20) and provision of a garden for human sustenance (1:29–30; 2:8–9).[1] The first people, Adam and Eve, were "naked and unashamed," having done nothing so far to be ashamed of (2:25).

If the humans had continued to rely on God to decide what they needed and to provide for those needs, they would have kept away from the fruit of that one forbidden tree. But the snake talked Eve into eating the fruit, and Adam followed her example (3:1–6).[2] Then they felt shame, improvised some clothing, and hid from God (vv. 7–8). God confronted them about eating the fruit (vv. 9–12), and everything changed (vv. 16–24). Since then, we have lived outside the garden, worn clothes, and experienced much shame.

The snake's argument had set Eve's mind outside the understandings provided by God. It first threw up some confusion about what God had actually prohibited (3:1) and then challenged God's prohibition head-on:

---

1. This way of putting it recognizes the canonical placement of the creation accounts, that is, that Genesis 1 counts in our reading of Genesis 2.
2. I use "snake" rather than "serpent" to avoid an archaic or "biblical" tone. The words are synonymous otherwise.

despite what God had threatened (2:17), the humans would *not* die after eating the fruit (3:4). God had simply lied about that because the tree would make them more "like gods" in ways that God wanted to reserve for himself (v. 5).

At the root of Eve and Adam's actions was a changed understanding of both God and themselves. They had come to see their creator and provider as their rival and had begun to desire for themselves something beyond what he provided for them. God had created those who could return his love, but he had not created reliable lovers. He took the risk of not being loved and made room for the human will, which then set aside relationship with God in favor of self-determination.[3] To establish their independence, to become "like gods," Adam and Eve had to free themselves from the original arrangement.[4] Only in that way could they rise above conformity to God's will and live by their own "knowledge of good and evil" (2:9; 3:5). They took that radical step because they correctly saw God as one who would seek to prevent their becoming "like gods" in that way (3:22).

What Sin Is

The story of Adam and Eve and the subsequent stories of Cain, the flood, and Babel together describe a decline in the relationship between God and humans. First, each of these stories includes humans seeking to define and meet their own needs apart from God's provision:

- Eve believes that the forbidden tree is "good for food" (Gen 3:6) despite God's prohibition.
- Cain needs to improve his religious standing, but figures out his own incorrect method (4:4b–8).

---

3. Though the story does not require that we imagine it as a completely informed and deliberate decision. We can imagine Adam and Eve foreseeing their action accomplishing an adjustment in their relationship with God that would lead to fewer consequences than actually followed. In later traditions it was said that they (or just Eve) were deceived (e.g., John 8:44; 2 Cor 11:3; 1 Tim 2:14), perhaps about what sort of decision they were making. The reading of the story represented here includes this element of deception only in a very small way and has Adam and Eve initiating broad changes in their relationship with God and therefore in their own nature by eating the fruit, but without understanding the consequences, particularly that nakedness would become an issue.

4. On the issue of whether to read the phrase in 3:5 (cf. v. 22) as "like God" or "like gods," see chapter 7 below, under "Myths of Knowledge and Goodness."

- Then, even after God has made provision for his protection (4:15–16), Cain builds a fortified city for the same purpose—to protect himself (v. 17).
- For their preservation and protection, the Babelites build a city and a tower (11:4).

A similar distrust of God's provision runs through the accounts of the exodus generation: the Israelites in the wilderness were sure that God had abandoned them there without provisions of water (Exod 15:24) and food (16:2–3).[5]

Second, in the Genesis 3–11 stories people also seek to make gods of themselves, sometimes at the expense of other people as well as of God:

- Eve believes the fruit of the forbidden tree will allow her and Adam to gain their own independent wisdom (3:6). All humanity, both Adam and Eve, eat the fruit in order to accomplish the development of a self-understanding different from the place given to them in creation.
- Lamech expands and monopolizes the law of retribution, placing himself above other humans (4:23–24).
- The people of Noah's time intermarry with divine beings (6:1–2) and begin to celebrate some of their number as heroes (v. 4).[6] Their time is characterized by violence (vv. 11 and 13), again humans attempting to place themselves above each other.
- The Babelites say "let us make a name for ourselves" (11:4), presumably to distinguish humanity among other kinds of beings. Or, we might say, they want the universe to take notice of them.

The precondition for these efforts to provide for self and to divinize self is distrust of God. God is not trusted to provide sustenance and protection, God's way of life for humanity—that is, what God has done in creating us—is not trusted to be the best for humanity, and God is perceived as a rival to the divine ambitions of humans. It is as if humanity went in a direction opposite to that of despairing Job—"Let that day on

---

5. See chapter 8 below, under "Staying on the Human Course," on how Jesus's response to temptation at the end of his forty-day fast reverses the response to temptation of both Adam and Eve in the garden and Israel in the wilderness.

6. An essential part of the foundation for polytheism is the blurred or nonexistent distinction between heroes and gods.

which I was born go away!" (Job 3:3)—and decided to rescue the human project from its creator/founder.

Distrust of God's plans and provision for the human project and the resulting desire to supplant or eliminate God (self-divinization) is, therefore, the definition of sin.[7] Augustine saw the anxiety of an infant as paradigmatic for the distrust that leads to sin: even as the loving parent is bringing food, the infant screams and flails about in fear that he has been abandoned to his own resources. He believes that he is being forced to take care of himself. "I grew indignant that my elders were not subject to me and that those on whom I had no claim did not wait on me, and I avenged myself on them by tears."[8] In the same way we regard God as one who cheats us by withholding from us what we regard as good (Gen 3:6) and perhaps as deserved (hence Cain's anger in 4:5). The human person is not complete in itself at any age, so the same distrust and self-centeredness continues. Humans consistently try to organize their own sustenance and growth, whether as individuals or as collectives.[9] That Adam and Eve did this and that we do so is the cause of all human distress, competition, greed, fear, and violence.

Behind this we can also see the route by which these stories have come to us. They came through Israel, the people that used the derogatory concept of "idolatry" to refer to worship practices of other peoples. Accounting for the existence of idolatry, of worship not directed to the God of Israel, is part of the aim of the Genesis stories. This is so even though they do not mention religious worship directed to anything other than the one God, though perhaps coming close by mentioning the heroes (6:4). There are altars and sacrifices (4:3–4; 8:20–21) but not images. The stories find the origin of idolatry in humanity's turn, not to external objects and imagined beings, but to humanity itself. Thus it is that *anthrōpos*, "humanity," is among the objects of human worship other than God mentioned by Paul (Rom 1:23). In the ultimate sense addressed by the Genesis stories, self becomes the fundamental object of human worship.

---

7. "Adam, by longing for more than was allotted him, manifested contempt for the great liberality with which God had enriched him" (Calvin, *Institutes* 2.1.4).

8. *Confessions* 1.6(8); similarly, 1.7(11).

9. I would not necessarily, with Augustine, regard the infant as more than an analogy—not because babies are cute or "don't know any better" but because their parents are not God. Learning to distrust one's parents is a sensible part of growing up.

Life Goes On

The astounding thing about life after the fall into sin is that there is life after the fall into sin. The penalty for eating fruit from the forbidden tree, "in that day you shall die" (Gen 2:17),[10] was not carried out. In Gen 3:16–19 God does not describe a progression of events that will culminate in fulfillment of the threat of death. He gives, rather, a description of life in the new, post-fall circumstances. That this life ends with death (v. 19) is not the point God makes. In fact, given how life is described in those verses, we are permitted to think of death as release from the hardship that continues "until you return to the ground."[11]

Along with that, God's provision for Adam and Eve continued after their rejection of his way for them,[12] though not in the garden and therefore with greater difficulty (vv. 17–19). They had to move out of Eden so that they would not carry their becoming "like gods" any further by eating from the tree of life and thus becoming able to live forever (vv. 22–24).

So here God both reverses the law that would have destroyed humanity (the penalty prescribed in 2:17)[13] and protects humanity from divinization in the form of unending life. The further stories in Genesis also tell of God's protection of humanity against self-divinization and (self)destruction).[14]

---

10. The emphasis in the threat is on the certainty of the death sentence. "Dying you shall die" (*môṯ tāmûṯ*, often translated "you shall surely die," 2:17) was a way of threatening death for a covenant violation (as in Gen 20:7; 1 Kgs 2:37; third person in Gen 26:11) or of announcing that such a threat will be carried out (as in 1 Sam 14:44; 22:16), not of specifying the death penalty for a named crime or to pronounce a death sentence. See Wenham, *Genesis 1–15*, 67, against Westermann, *Genesis 1–11*, 225. "In that day" also stresses the certainty of what is threatened.

11. So Westermann, *Genesis 1–11*, 267.

12. Beautifully stated in Calvin, *Institutes* 1.16.1, with reference to Pss 33 and 104:27–30.

13. So Tertullian, *On Repentance* 2: "After the condemnation of humanity," God "hurried back to his mercy and from that time on inaugurated repentance in himself by rescinding the sentence of his first wrath, engaging to grant pardon to his own work and image"; *Against Marcion* 3.25: God "did not actually curse Adam and Eve because they were candidates for restoration."

14. In the myths of non-Israelite ancient peoples, one often hears of gods taking action to prevent humans from becoming more like the gods, but not with the same connections with God's continuing care for and protection of humanity, or, indeed, with Israel's monotheism.

In the preface to the flood story, humankind is said to have become evil. God decides to undo creation, at least as far as animate life is concerned (6:5–7). The material in 6:1–4 probably originally had nothing to do with the flood, but by being placed between Noah's genealogy (chapter 5) and the flood story (beginning at 6:5), it has become another account of God's decision to destroy humanity by taking his own "spirit" (v. 3), that is, the "breath of life" (2:7; Ps 104:29–30), away from humanity.[15] As such, both parts of this preface (Gen 6:1–4, 5–7), like Gen 3:22, tell of a decision by God to forestall further self-divinization of humanity, which is happening at this point via intermarriage with divine beings and the growth of hero cults. In fact, God decides here that creation of humanity was a mistake, one that he will undo.

But then Noah catches God's eye and God changes his mind (6:8). The flood does occur, but it does not carry out the decision to destroy humanity or all animate life. It becomes, rather, the means by which God purifies the corrupted earth in order to give it back to a preserved and purified humanity. Verse 8 thus marks a strong transition-point in the story.[16] The flood was necessary for the preservation of humanity, not because of divine wrath but because corrupted humanity could not avoid self-destruction, destruction of God's human project, by self-divinization. With the flood, God, as with the reversal of the threat in 2:17, reverses a decision to destroy humanity and provides for the continuation of humanity, now by saving one family. Then the covenant is renewed in a form that places special emphasis on the acknowledgement of human rule over all other animate creation (9:2), that extends to all people the protection earlier given to Cain (vv. 4–6), and that reaffirms and strengthens God's reversal of the decision to drown all animate life (vv. 11, 15).

Then in Babel God again graciously protects humanity by breaking up the city (11:4, 8). The problem that God speaks of and acts against is neither the city nor the tower, which are not mentioned in vv. 6–7. It is, rather, the unity of the people in one place that threatens their humanness

---

15. A key interpretive issue in 6:3 is whether, as in 3:22, the prevention of self-divinization will be carried out by limiting the lifespans of humans, here to a maximum of 120 years, or by destroying humanity altogether after another 120 years has passed. The first may have been the case at some points earlier in the history of the story's tellings, but the latter certainly makes more sense in the text as it stands now, particularly in connection with 6:5–7.

16. The "But" often supplied at the beginning of v. 8 in English translations can be considered interpretive: it does not represent a strong adversative in either Hebrew or Greek.

and existence. Because they have achieved this unity of language, location, and purpose, they believe (wrongly, because they do not realize the threats facing a geographically concentrated species) that they can act to preserve and exalt themselves. The city and the tower are just expressions of this. But God sees city and tower as signs of evil to come: there will be no limit to the humans' future projects, so he must act to save them from themselves. "Nothing will be impossible" (v. 6) is a description of their potential at that point for future self-divinization. For God nothing *is* impossible (Job 42:2; Luke 1:37), but for humans to gain that capability would make them other than human.

Throughout these stories God's protection of humanity includes what the snake told Eve to regard as God's hidden agenda (Gen 3:5): God always works against human self-divinization, whether it is to be gained by access to the tree of life (3:22–24), by self-centered expansion of the law of retribution (4:23–24; "violence" in 6:11, 13), by intermarriage with semi-divine beings (6:1–4), or by unification, intended to be permanent, in one place (11:1–9). The snake told the truth, but did so to encourage rebellion against God.[17]

Cain's Misinterpretation

A third step in these stories, after the initial rebellion and God's continuing or renewed protection of humanity, can be human disbelief in God's protection. We see this most clearly in Cain's story, and it can become fundamental to an understanding of the development of our age's secularity.

---

17. This runs counter to what some parts of the New Testament and some noncanonical Jewish writings say, which is that the snake lied (John 8:44), deceiving Adam and Eve (2 Cor 11:3) or just Eve (1 Tim 2:14). But, along with this, the snake has been transformed into Satan (e.g., Rev 12:9; 20:2), the personification of evil, whose sole aim is to subvert God's purposes by drawing people into rebellion against God. All this makes the snake more important than he is in the Genesis 3 story, extending his role (not "*its* role" since he is now a personal being, not just a handy garden creature) beyond the garden and into the future. Even Satan, or, more properly, "the satan," that is, "the opponent," is in the Old Testament nothing like what he became as "the great dragon, the ancient snake, the one called devil and Satan, the whole world's deceiver" (Rev 12:9). The satan does things much like what the snake does, and he does so as a servant of God or member of the heavenly court (Job 1:6–12; 2:1–7; cf. 2 Sam 24:1 with 1 Chron 21:1).

At every point in God's dealings with Cain, God acts for Cain's welfare and protection, and Cain rejects God's path for him:[18]

1. Cain wants God's favor,
   but he misunderstands what is required of him, taking it in mechanistic rather than ethical terms (Gen 4:3–5).

2. God points out the issues involved in Cain's standing before God,[19]
   but Cain kills his brother as an alternative solution to the problem (vv. 6–8).

3. God confronts Cain with this new issue, murder, which is a continuation of the old issues,
   but Cain tries to lie his way out (v. 9).

4. God tells Cain that the human system of retribution will be against him,
   but Cain blames God and claims (wrongly) that God is withdrawing from him, thus interpreting his situation as total catastrophe (vv. 10–14).

5. God provides for Cain's protection with a law aiming to contain human violence,[20]
   but Cain abandons God and makes other arrangements for his own protection by building a city (vv. 15–17).

The last two pairs of statements here need some further explanation:

4. In vv. 11–12, God does not curse the ground, but merely tells Cain that his life as a settled farmer is over. As a fugitive, he will not be around to benefit from the harvest: he will be "banished from the land."[21] Furthermore, what Cain says in v. 14 about God—"you have

---

18. This idea is developed, though a bit differently, in Ellul, "Cain"; see also Ellul, *Meaning of the City*, 1–7. There is a tension in Cain's story between the outside and the inside of the story, between, that is, its placement in the second human generation and its assumption of an already numerous humanity with specialization into agriculturalists and pastoralists and traditions of sacrificial worship and retributive punishment of murderers. So we have to talk differently about Cain in his own story versus Cain in the development of Genesis 2–11.

19. As 1 John 3:12 says, the issue was not the different sacrifices of the two brothers, but that "Cain's deeds were evil and his brother's righteous."

20. This understanding of Gen 4:15 is from Girard, *I See Satan*, 84.

21. Vv. 11–12 "are not really a curse or a sentence but are saying something about

driven me from the land; I must hide from your face"—is Cain's incorrect perception of what has happened, not a mere report of events.[22]

5. A city is necessarily a walled city—a fortress. Such provision for one's own protection becomes the modus operandi of Cain's descendants (4:23–24), and retreat into a city is also the basis of the Babel story in chapter 11.[23] In this way Cain represents all humanity, much as his parents did, specifically as the one who rejects God's protection and takes steps to take care of his own protection.

Thus Cain misinterprets his situation as catastrophic. His mistake is paralleled, we might say, in interpretations commonly given to his story and to these other stories of humanity prior to Abraham—interpretations that take these stories not as demonstrating God's grace but as catastrophic, as showing only judgment and destruction:

- The expulsion from Eden is seen as punishment, not as gracious preservation of human life as human rather than divine.[24]
- Cain's understanding of his own situation, which takes God's words as curse and as withdrawal of God's presence and protection, is accepted as correct.

---

the consequence of the deed" (Westermann, *Genesis 1–11*, 306, though his interpretation goes in a different direction). Conversely, God's statements in these verses are taken as God's pronouncement of a curse either on Cain (e.g., Calvin, *Genesis*, 1:208–13, through the agency of the ground, as certainly suggested by Calvin's Latin translation of v. 11, *maledictus eris e terra*, in *Mosis libri*, 44; the Vulgate has *maledictus eris super terram*) or on the ground (e.g., Delitzsch, *Genesis*, 1:186). Some commentators refer to the rule in Num 35:33 that the land is polluted by bloodguilt until the murderer is executed, but that might not be relevant because God does not treat the murder of Abel as a capital offense and in fact stands in the way of (not judicial execution, but) revenge-killing of Cain.

22. Contrast, e.g., the reference to Cain's loss of relationship with God in Wenham, *Genesis 1–15*, 108. On v. 14: "Alienation from God leads to fear of other men" (109). Like Cain, his parents hid from both each other and God at their own initiative, not because of anything God said or did (3:7–11).

23. Cf. the connection of city-founding with conquest and empire-building in 10:8–12.

24. As eviction by "a landlord dissatisfied with his tenants" or as exile. McKeown, *Genesis*, 37–38.

- The flood is seen not as God's gracious preservation of humanity, a reversal of his earlier decision to destroy creation, but as destructive judgment.[25]
- And the scattering of the people of Babel is seen not as gracious preservation of human life, but as vindictive, fearful, and selfish destruction of what humans want to accomplish.[26]

Such interpretations arise, in a fundamental way, from our continuing assumption, which long ago became, as it were, part of our very nature, that God is against us. Despair like that of Cain is one possible response to this assumption, but not the only possible response. In fact, we are now more accustomed to regard this (false) realization that we cannot depend on God as liberating knowledge, as enlightenment. We have come to rely on ourselves and gladly leave God out of the life equation.

Did God preserve the people of Genesis before Abraham only to destroy them, and in the meantime show what he thought of them by being stingy and unresponsive? No, they and we have been preserved for redemption and are constantly the recipients of God's gracious and kenotic protection and provision.[27] At every point, a step forward for humanity toward autonomy, power, life, and knowledge, that is, toward divinization, is actually a step toward self-destruction. And at every point God intervenes to save humanity.

The people of Babel thought they were really something, but they would not be able to comprehend even a fraction of a percent of our accomplishments. Hubris rebooted after their project was thwarted, and it has done quite well for itself since. But new technologies—say, the use of fossil fuels or nuclear energy—cause new problems, and we continue to rely on yet newer technologies or refinements of the old to solve the newest problems. That is, we rely on yet more exaltation of human power and knowledge to solve the problems created by earlier exaltations of our power and knowledge.[28]

---

25. And with that, too little is made of the radical change in direction that begins in 6:8.

26. God stops the tower project because it is "a threat to the divine will and rule." So Hamilton, *Genesis 1–17*, 355. One could add to this list that the words of hungover Noah (9:25) are taken as God's decree.

27. Kenotic because God serves us even though we reject him and do not believe in his provision. On Bulgakov's understanding of God's sustaining of creation, see chapter 2 above, under "The Kenosis of the Trinity."

28. This paragraph should not be too hastily taken as supporting some sort of

Despite these self-destructive ways, we are still here. Perhaps God is at every point saving us from ourselves. Perhaps another Genesis 1–11 tale is being written about us without our knowing it. Perhaps, but the idea of God intervening in this way in our times might be so presumptuous and potentially dangerous that I will leave it be.[29]

But there is a less specific way in which we can affirm it. A pattern is established in Genesis that God still follows. The covenant with Noah still stands. We look forward—perhaps to a fiery apocalypse—but certainly to the new heaven and earth, which will still include humanity and will thus affirm that the original creation was a good idea. Noah still finds favor in God's sight.

At every stage and in every circumstance, our need for bread is answered more fundamentally by God's creative word than by any number of grain fields (Deut 8:3). But the temptation is always there: "take care of it yourself!" (Matt 4:3). God's protection was and still is an affirmation that God still regards the kenosis of creating, his making room for us, as the right choice.[30] But it is also what humans seldom believe in. We accept our supposed abandonment by God, whether as a cause for fear, so that we seek to appease God, or as a cause for celebration.[31]

Truthfulness

G. K. Chesterton said of William Morris,

> He has the supreme credit of showing that the fairy-tales contain the deepest truth of the earth, the real record of men's feeling

---

anti-technology viewpoint. But if implications are drawn in the direction of thought about the anti-spirituality of capitalism, that would be a better guess.

29. I remember hearing "God would never allow a nuclear war to happen," and this, of course, well after the bombing of Hiroshima and Nagasaki.

30. God's continuing commitment to the covenant in the face of human sin is, of course, central in Karl Barth's theology, e.g., *Church Dogmatics* 3/2:33–34.

31. The latter, to speak briefly of what could take up volumes, was part of Kant's expression of the Enlightenment sense of religion as that which restricts and from which humans must be freed. Bakunin takes the rebellion back to the garden, though as a myth representing the modern revolt against religion: "[God] expressly forbade them from touching the fruit of the tree of knowledge. He wished, therefore, that man, destitute of all understanding of himself, should remain an eternal beast, ever on all-fours before the eternal God, his creator and his master. But here steps in Satan, the eternal rebel, the first freethinker and the emancipator of worlds. He makes man ashamed of his bestial ignorance and obedience; he emancipates him, stamps upon his brow the seal of liberty and humanity, in urging him to disobey and eat of the fruit of knowledge" (Bakunin, *God and the State*, 10).

for things. Trifling details may be inaccurate, Jack may not have climbed up so tall a beanstalk, or killed so tall a giant; but it is not such things that make a story false; it is a far different class of things that makes every modern book of history as false as the father of lies: ingenuity, self-consciousness, hypocritical impartiality.

And to make it clear that he was not condescending to the quaint old stories, Chesterton went on to describe the truth of *Beauty and the Beast*.[32] Elsewhere he described *Jane Eyre*, particularly in comparison with the novels of Jane Austen, as, while filled with illusion and improbability,

> perhaps the truest book that was ever written. Its essential truth to life sometimes makes one catch one's breath.[33] For it is not true to manners, which are constantly false, or to facts, which are almost always false; it is true to the only existing thing which is true, emotion, the irreducible minimum, the indestructible germ. It would not matter a single straw if a Brontë story were a hundred times more moonstruck and improbable than "Jane Eyre," or a hundred times more moonstruck and improbable than "Wuthering Heights." It would not matter if George Read stood on his head, and Mrs Read rode on a dragon, if Fairfax Rochester had four eyes and St John Rivers three legs, the story would still remain the truest story in the world. The typical Brontë character is, indeed, a kind of monster. Everything in him except the essential is dislocated. His hands are on his legs and his feet on his arms, his nose is above his eyes, but his heart is in the right place.[34]

To affirm the truthfulness of a biblical story in the same way sounds to us like condescension only because we have for so long given so much value to the concerns and works of modern historians. Two ends of a theological spectrum have agreed that those historians' concerns are nearly all-important, with one concluding that the Bible does not serve our needs well (our needs *as historians*, though that need not be specified) and the other that it does serve our needs well, that the biblical stories must have happened exactly as narrated, that they must be true in the sense sought by our historians.[35]

32. Chesterton, *Twelve Types*, 25.
33. It did that for me.
34. Chesterton, *Twelve Types*, 7–8.
35. Though historians are often more circumspect about what they are able to achieve.

If I read a biography of Abraham Lincoln, I can ask questions about things that are left out. If his paternal grandmother's name is not mentioned, I am within my rights to ask what it was. Even if the answer had to be "no one knows," I could still assume that the question has an answer in the sense that Lincoln's father had a mother and she had a name. Even if her name is judged by the biographer to be unimportant to the task of telling of Lincoln's life, still she existed and had a name (she was Bathsheba Herring Lincoln). I can also increase my knowledge of Lincoln by visiting places he lived and reading biographies of other people of the time. Kentucky and Illinois are still there, and there are biographies of General Lee, General Grant, and a host of other people of that time.

Furthermore, the connections between Lincoln's life and our own are quite concrete. A consideration of the Emancipator might well include an account of the fortunes and misfortunes of the emancipated slaves and their descendants down to and including our own time. All the complex bits of the emancipation experience have a part in the world of Americans today.

The biblical story about Adam and Eve has a more specific didactic purpose than any account of Abraham Lincoln. I would be off the mark in interpreting it if I asked questions that are not considered in the story, not because no one knows the answers but because there are in a deeper sense *no answers*. What color was Adam and Eve's skin? In America race can be an important question, but to give Adam and Eve a particular skin tone would not suit why their story has been told to us. We could imagine innumerable other questions about Adam and Eve, say, for instance, whether they cooked their vegetables or ate them raw, but their story is a closed set in the sense that nothing matters that is not there, and interpretation does not serve us well by asking about what is not there.

Moreover, to seek connections of the story of Adam and Eve to contemporaneous history cannot lead to anything near as concrete and public as, for instance, an understanding of the experiences of post-slavery African-Americans. There were, according to the story, no other people at the time of Adam and Eve, which itself points to the story's most important assumption: those two were all of humanity. Knowing about what else was going on will not help us, because the story loses its point if anything else *was* going on with any other humans. Adam and Eve's story is universal, and it is closed. Everything there serves the story's purpose, and anything more would not.

The connections of their story to us are on a much broader level than anything that happened in the time of Lincoln. Those two people are all humanity at the beginning of the story of humanity, so their story brings all of us together in one category and accounts for our existence and our problems. So we read their story for what it says about us. The same might be the case, though not necessarily, for an account of Abraham Lincoln, but in a different and much more focused way (indeed, how could one explain American society of today without recounting the experience of slavery and its end?).

All this does not mean that we can denarrativize ("demythologize") the story of Adam and Eve and still fully get the lesson. It is as a story that it carries out its purposes.[36] But neither do we gain anything by trying to think of it as history. History has connections. When Lincoln was president, other things were happening in China. The story of Adam and Eve works by being the story of all humanity, by being in that way the *only* story. We can apply the resulting hermeneutic to all the Genesis 1–11 stories. There are reminders that what is said is about *all* humankind—in the creation accounts (Gen 1:26–28; "the man" in 2:5, 7, 15–17), in later echoes of the creation accounts (8:17; 9:1–2, 7), and in other places (5:1–2; 6:3, 5–7, 13; 7:23; 9:19). "All humanity" is still together as people begin to build the tower of Babel (11:1), but they are worried about losing their unity and being scattered (v. 4). They are right in anticipating that that will happen, but their solution does not work: when they are scattered (v. 9), that becomes, in fact, the end of "all humanity" as the focus of the Genesis narrative and as something that can act as a unit—the disappearance of humanity as a character in the story, so to speak. Thereafter Abram emerges as the focus (12:1).

So until Abram/Abraham, everything is about all humanity and describes and accounts for what all of us are like. Beginning with Abram, the concern is with Israel, and how *that* affects the rest of us (as promised in 12:3) has to emerge slowly, which is why the Bible is such a big book.

But there are still reasons for us to say that what is told of in Genesis really happened. The meaning of the stories does not emerge if we psychologize them, saying, for instance, "every person goes through what Adam and Eve experienced." That would, in fact, contradict the sense of the Genesis 1–11 stories, which is that humanity as a singular whole, not just as a bunch of similar neuroses, lives *together* in one big bucket of

---

36. See chapter 1 above, under "What We Have against Stories and What to Do about It."

trouble. Those stories are our collective history. They tell of "all humanity," something that finally emerged for residents of "Christendom," that is, Europe, only as recently as the Age of Discovery. Until we could know quite literally about all humanity, that is, about multiple cultures, we needed, perhaps, a myth of human origins to think about "all humanity."

HOW DID SIN BEGIN?

Universality

What is the origin of evil in the world that God pronounced "good" (Gen 1:10, 12, 18, 25, 31)? The Genesis 1–11 stories do not give us a complete answer. What they do say is that people do evil and that God is not to blame. That is, they tell us that evil does have an origin, but not in creation.

The Bible affirms the understanding that shows up in every human culture,[37] namely

- that some things that humans do are evil,
- that some things humans do are good: otherwise we could not know what we are talking about when we say that some actions are evil, and
- that we can, whether by instinct or with much thought, tell the difference.

The Bible adds to this something that most of us might agree to on at least a theoretical level, namely

- that the line between good and evil does not divide humanity—that is, that *all of us*, not just some of us, *do evil*.

Our tendency is to forget or deny that last item, at least in the heat of conflict, and some of us convince ourselves that there are, indeed, permanently bad people and permanently good people. Even the Bible is not entirely of one voice from verse to verse on the matter, but taken as a whole it seems clear: "Nobody is righteous. No, not anyone. Nobody gets it. Nobody seeks God. Everybody has gone off the tracks. Everybody is useless. Nobody does any good. *No, not anyone*" (Rom 3:10–12).

---

37. As far as I know. I do not count as counter-evidence cultures in which good and evil are disputed to such a degree that some people despair of knowing which is which.

That collection of statements seems to exclude any good from human actions, but really what it excludes with its "nobody" and "everybody" is any humans who have never done anything bad. We all get our chances to do wrong, and we all make use of those opportunities on at least some occasions. The question is not about quantity (am I more or less evil than my sister?) but about the mere fact: we all cross that line sometimes. Or perhaps we have been camped on the line long enough to forget its significance. At any rate, we are brought back to the "all humanity" in Genesis 3, 6, and 11. There is no distinction among persons; there is, rather, that simple "all." Every last one of us, just like the first of us.

It is good to dwell on that a bit more given our lazy and self-congratulating tendency to place the line between good and evil between people. If some people are really, really evil (Hitler was a favorite for a couple generations, or choose your favorite torture-and-murder perpetrator or drug-dealer or sex criminal), then we can divide them from ourselves. Some of us are aided in that when we see mugshots of rumpled and unhappy individuals, usually with darker skin than mine, on the evening news: they are criminals and we are not. Another bit of help might come from how descriptions of things like "antisocial personality disorder" are received in popular culture.[38] But the Bible as a whole places that line between God and us. He is good; we are not, and that "we" includes you, me, and all the other criminals. Rough news, and only hearable because the message of redemption is the next word.

It Is Not God's Fault

Let us dwell a bit on that line between good God and evil us. One of the things stories can do is to define right and wrong inside their own mini-worlds. The first *Star Wars* movie began by telling the back story with that long white-on-black prologue scrolling out of a distant heaven,[39] and there, right from the start, we learned to call one side "the *evil* empire." A storyteller can do that: set the parameters for the story by saying who is

---

38. The fact that "antisocial personality disorder" and "sociopath" have become so widely enrolled into our language is in itself indicative. It would be absurd for me to doubt the usefulness of the category or the diagnostic procedures (giving due respect to the *DSM*). But it would be good, broadly speaking, for us laypeople to think also about Michel Foucault's perception of the concept of mental health as a means of social control.

39. Or was it ascending into heaven? I have forgotten.

right and who is wrong. Usually it is less explicit than in *Star Wars*. There are less obvious or imperious ways to do it. But we still learn quickly that Heidi or the Lone Ranger is whom the reader is supposed to want to win.

As we read the Bible, it assumes that we will agree with it that God is correct in what he says. For instance, he said that the world he created is, or at least was at the time, "good," and the reader is expected to take that as a correct assessment. In the Bible, God is the one who is always right, though from page to page we often have to wait and see before he is proven right, or we have to work through arguments that he is right. And this extends beyond truth-telling to everything that God does. If I assume that at the end of the day (or the aeon) it will be shown that God committed some errors of judgment or ethics, then the Bible will either try to argue me out of that understanding or simply become incomprehensible or unbelievable for me.

The stories of the beginning of human evil argue for that assumption of God's rightness. The first story, the one about Adam and Eve, is assisted in affirming that God is not the originator of human evil by the pause it places between the completion of creation and the coming of evil (the aside in Gen 2:24 and the stative in v. 25), by its ascription of the suggestion of evil to a crafty animal, the snake (3:1, 4), and by the development of that suggestion by a human (3:6). Human existence and human evil are given separate origin stories, different beginnings, which is important because otherwise we might assume that sin and alienation from God define the way we have always been.[40] That the universe has a beginning means that God is its creator. That sin has a *separate* beginning means that it is not part of creation, that is, that God is not its originator.[41] Among the numerous possible philosophical objections to absolving God of any part in the origination of evil, most can be boiled down to an amalgamating of those two origins that the Bible keeps separate, or, that is, to the tension between these two statements, about both of which the

---

40. Cf. Bakunin, *God and the State*, 9: "The essential factor" in the "development of [distinctly] human animality," that which therefore makes possible "all that constitutes humanity in man," is "*the power to think and the desire to rebel*"; "Man has emancipated himself; he has separated himself from animality and constituted himself a man; he has begun his distinctively human history and development by an act of disobedience and science—that is, by *rebellion* and by *thought*" (12).

41. Attempting to protect God from blame by blaming, instead, "nature" or human nature actually ends up blaming God, the creator of that nature. Calvin, *Institutes* 1.15.1; 2.1.10–11.

Bible is clear: (1) everything in the world is either the direct or indirect result of God's creation, and (2) God is not the originator of human evil.

Saying God is not to blame depends, therefore, on the separation of these two origins. We cannot say that God is not to blame, or at least we cannot say it in quite the same way, if we presuppose that nothing like what these stories tell about happened in the human past.[42] We are thrown back on the stories in Genesis 2 and 3 if we are to have faith in what else the Bible says, namely, that God is good. The departure from an early human innocence did happen in some way. Creation itself was not faulty.

The Fall

The stories in Genesis 2 and 3, and indeed the rest of the Bible, do not try to solve the problem of the origin of human evil. For the most part, the Bible simply reasserts two basic premises. First,

> God Most High, the creator of heaven and earth. (Gen 14:19)
>
> You created my inmost being; you knit me together in my mother's womb. (Ps 139:13, NIV)
>
> Yahweh is the everlasting God, the creator of the ends of the earth. (Isa 40:28)

And then,

> God cannot be tempted by evil, and he does not tempt anyone. (Jas 1:13)
>
> God is light. In him there is no darkness at all. (1 John 1:5)

When the first temptation occurs in Genesis 3, the only ones present are Eve, the snake, and Adam. God seems to be out of sight elsewhere in the garden (v. 8), but the tension of this temptation taking place within his creation is present and is underlined by explicit identification of the snake as one of God's creatures (v. 1), which is part of the effort in Genesis to reduce the population of divine beings, in contrast to Mesopotamian myths. Furthermore, nothing is said about where the snake got (or how he formulated) the ideas he presents to Eve (ideas about "fallen angels" or Satan do not make an appearance in the story). Might God have been to

---

42. Attempts have been made to imagine how it might have happened early in human experience as reconstructed by paleontology.

blame for letting such a smart animal loose in the garden? Such speculation would take us out of the story, but we might be allowed to think that the situation in Eden was like that in the book of Job, where Satan acts as God's emissary when he brings every kind of trouble and hence temptation on Job. That this kind of tension could be felt is shown by the story of King David's census: he got the bad idea of counting up his military manpower from God (2 Sam 24:1–2), or was it from Satan, as in a later, more theologically cautious account (1 Chron 21:1–2)? Or was there a problem in how God created such that there was from the beginning that attractiveness to self-aggrandizement that the snake could appeal to in Eve? Again, the question takes us out of the story.

And the intent of Genesis 3 is clear enough: though God is the creator of our world, and there is evil in our world, God is not the source of evil. Creation did not include evil, and God is not to blame for evil. We cannot say that how we are now is how we were made, that God got it wrong. We cannot repeat what Emma Goldman said, "I do not believe in God, because I believe in man. Whatever his mistakes, man has for thousands of years past been working to undo the botched job your God has made,"[43] unless we remember that her words were directed not against God, whom she did not believe in, but against some sorts of belief in God. But for those who believe the Bible, creation and evil are separate. Take a breath between Genesis 2 and Genesis 3. To deny the separation between creation and evil would be to deny the beginning of the creation-redemption story, and thus at least alter the whole story.

Evil, however it originated, came into human experience through a human violation of the relationship between humans and God, portrayed in the Adam and Eve story as eating fruit from a forbidden tree. Though that event was followed by a progressive development that confirmed its significance and deepened its impact (the further stories in Genesis 4–11), something changed already with that single event to make all that followed possible (or, in general terms, even inevitable). It makes sense, therefore, to speak, as Christian theology has, of a "fall." How we are now is not how we were made, but here we are.

We also cannot say that the story of Eve, Adam, and the fruit just represents "what happens to each of us every morning" or that "we

---

43. Responding to audience questions during a speech in Detroit (1898), as recounted in Goldman, *Living My Life*, 207, and quoted in Gaylor, *Women without Superstition*, 382.

constantly face such choices." To thus psychologize the story,[44] would also not be true to experience: we simply do not face temptation as something new, but Eve and Adam did experience it that way. And now temptation followed by sin is always present as the continuous human condition and never begins afresh. For this reason, the biblical story tells us of *the* fall.

The Fall Is Part of the Creation-Redemption Story

Can we conceive of human freedom existing and not leading to at least one decision not to love God? That is, was the fall inevitable? Creation was not faulty, but how strong was the likelihood that it would become so? This question can be asking for speculation about no longer existing past possibilities, but if it is a question about what sort of story God initiated with creation, then the answer must be that the fall was completely foreseeable. Creation was not an experiment, and it has not gone awry from what God intended. God knew that he would redeem creation. Jesus did not come on a salvage mission. Rather, he spoke "things hidden since the world's creation" (Matt 13:35, quoting Ps 78:2). God knew that sin would come into creation and thus that creation would need redemption. God knew where the risky act of creating other wills would lead, and he took account of that knowledge before he created.[45] Milton expressed this by describing Adam as glad that he had sinned because his sin was a necessary step toward redemption.[46]

Whether sin was inevitable because humanity was created free has been a disputed point in Christian theology, and the weight of numbers has certainly been on the "no" side, which seeks to guard against any understanding of God as "the author of sin": "God has not compelled people to sin just because he created them and gave them the power to choose between sinning and not sinning,"[47] and one need not account

---

44. See the last paragraph under "Truthfulness" above in this chapter.

45. That the discovery of human freedom was prompted by someone who was neither God nor human but still "one of God's creatures" (Gen 3:1) may reinforce an understanding of human sin as existing as a potential before the fall. And so, perhaps, there is no need to call the origin of sin "inexplicable" or to derive it "from something external to the creation," as does Gunton, *Triune Creator*, 171.

46. *Paradise Lost* 12.469. The idea of the *felix culpa* had a longer history, e.g., Aquinas, *Summa Theologiae* 3.1.3, reply to objection 3, quoting "the blessing of the Paschal candle."

47. Augustine, *De Libero Arbitrio* 2.14–15.

for the existence of evil because it is simply "the absence of good,"[48] a vacuum so to speak.[49] On the other hand, it has been argued that where human freedom exists the possibility, even probability, of sin must also exist, even if God is omnipotent and entirely good. That is, God "could have forestalled the occurrence of moral evil only by removing the possibility of moral good."[50] Love for God is one possible outcome of human freedom, which would not be truly possible as the result of a genuine human choice if another outcome, namely sin, that is, the decision not to love God, were not also possible.

Furthermore, avoiding making God "the author of sin" becomes less important if we allow *time* to play a role, that is, if we think of creation as the initiation of the whole creation-redemption story. The fall has a place in the movement of the divine project of creation toward its goal. God's way of carrying out his creation intention assumed that the fall would occur and that redemption would follow. Creation is part of an ongoing project that includes upholding, provision, redemption, and eschaton. It is only the whole story that gives meaning to its beginning.[51] Redemption

---

48. Augustine, *Enchiridion* 11–14. "Absence of good" is not quite a fair representation of Augustine's term (*privatio boni*) or of his view, which is, rather, that evil can exist only in a good thing (such as creation or a human) by that thing being less good than it could be. Here again a distinction between the perfection of creation and the perfection of completion, or we might say "of potential," enters in (see chapter 4 above, under "For Space and Time").

49. In the same way, the idea of a single pre-fall purpose of God consistently sought by creation and redemption has been challenged on the basis that it takes Augustine's description of post-fall humankind as "unable not to sin" and applies it to pre-fall humanity. So Jewett, *God, Creation, and Revelation*, 495, against, among others, Barth. Jewett cites Amyraut as the opposite extreme—God's purposes were *changed* by the fall—and rejects it as well.

50. Plantinga, "Free Will Defense," 30. See Plantinga's article in full for a defense of this position. It would be most effectively challenged if an affirmative answer were given to, "Must I genuinely be ready to take either one of two possible courses of action—to perform or not to perform a given act—in order for my taking either one of these courses of action to be free?" (Nash-Marshall, "Free Will, Evil, and Anselm," 24), though the question is discussed widely. According to Nash-Marshall, Harry Frankfurt argued in "Alternate Possibilities and Moral Responsibility" that "alternate possibilities are not a necessary requisite of moral responsibility." The issue is whether freedom, by definition, requires indeterminacy, that is, what *we* mean by "freedom" (Nash-Marshall, 26, 26n6). For an entrée to further discussion, see Thiselton, *Systematic Theology*, 56–58. On the various answers to whether the creation-fall account makes God responsible for the origin of sin, see Williams, "Genesis 3."

51. So Barth, *Church Dogmatics* 3/1:229.

"is the completion of the whole project of creation, not the saving of a few souls from hell."[52] Genesis 1–2 tells of a beginning that points forward:

creation →

And the story proceeds to its eschatological end and goal by way of fall and redemption:

creation → fall → redemption → eschaton

The fall has been considered a reversal of creation,[53] but such an understanding is possible only if both creation and fall are considered apart from redemption. Redemption, for its part, can be considered a reversal of the fall, but it would not be needed (or possible) if the fall had not occurred. And the eschaton is not a reversal of anything that went before. It is part of the story. There is no regrettably lost alternative story.[54] No part of the story is fully understandable apart from the full story. It is in the new heaven and earth, not in Eden, that we see what God intended when he created.

---

52. Gunton, *Triune Creator*, 171.
53. So Moses Amyraut, mentioned in note 49 above.
54. For a survey of views of the relation between creation and redemption, see Gunton, *Triune Creator*, 11–12. The view represented here falls between the second and third in his discussion.

6

The One Problem

ODDLY DIVIDED

Ghosts and Dirty Jokes

ONCE THE TENSION THAT makes a story possible (and necessary) has been introduced, the storyteller might slow down to suggest that nothing is happening, indeed, that nothing can happen, to resolve the tension. It might simply be a device to keep the hearers listening. But in the story of humanity it seems very real: it can seem that we are left hanging, that we are stuck here, however that came about, in our current unsatisfactory, essentially unchanging state.[1] The halted middle—that is, the present—can seem to be the shape of our lives.[2] The deeper we think about our humanness, the more it can seem that nothing fundamental can change, except that death comes for each. And death separates us and so is evidence against any unity of humanity in one story. Till then, we go to the movies to see portrayals of a unity that we do not experience outside the theater emerging from challenges that are unlike the fragmenting challenges of real life (such as Arab and Israeli soldiers working together in *Independence Day*, 1996). There is no story about all of us together, no movement except that individualizing end, and till then the tension brought by the fall appears quite settled among us.

    1. Rom 7:24 can be taken as an expression of such stuck-in-the-middle despair, and its context shows the importance of the sense of moral failure involved.

    2. Creation and fall are left out as well because of an existentialism of our age that admits neither beginning nor end, confirming backhandedly a logic that says believing in creation implies believing in consummation (2 Pet 3:3–7).

The tension is not only among us but also in each of us, so that I am at odds not only with people unlike me but also with myself. Even with our ignorance of our origin, some hazy knowledge seems to hang around. We know enough to experience contradictions between this and that part of the human person, even if we are not sure what those parts are, whether those contradictions are "eternity in the heart" over against ignorance of God's work (Eccl 3:11), receiving God's commandment as both life-giving word and death-dealing deception (Rom 7:10–11), or stepping forward boldly while looking back nervously (Luke 9:62).

One thing is needed, and that is to locate ourselves in the story of creation and redemption. Until we find ourselves there, expanding knowledge of ourselves only expands the mystery. For instance, "we are scared of ghosts and laugh at dirty jokes."[3] That is, there is something odd about our relation to a world of spirits, even if we deny its existence, and about our relation to ourselves, experienced most in regard to our sexuality, even if we have it all analyzed and rationalized. "I do not think there is anything stupid or ignorant about howling at the moon or being afraid of devils in the dark. It seems to me perfectly philosophical. Why should a man be thought a sort of idiot because he feels the mystery and peril of existence itself? Suppose . . . it is we who are the idiots because we are *not* afraid of devils in the dark?"[4]

Terror and delight are oddly close to each other even if—and this is the normal state of affairs—we do not know why. Not just in enjoyment of horror stories[5] and fireworks at close proximity, but in life itself:

> I feel as if I were living in that roofless world of yours where men walk undefended beneath naked heaven. It is a delight with terror in it! . . . The world is so much larger than I thought. I thought we were going along paths—but it seems there are no paths. The going itself is the path.[6]

"Ah! The terror and the delight of that moment when first we fear ourselves! Until then we have not lived."[7] Rationalism has sometimes

---

3. In quote marks because I did not formulate the statement, though I do not know who did.

4. Chesterton, *Club of Queer Trades*, 186, on the lips of the character Basil Grant. I added the italicization.

5. As in, for example, the subtitles of *Hitchcock and Poe: The Legacy of Delight and Terror* (Perry) and *A Collection of Souls: Tales of Terror, Delight, and Magic* (Miller).

6. Lewis, *Perelandra*, 60.

7. Cather, *Collection of Stories*, 46.

mistaken its mission as being to rid us of such feelings, such mystery in human identity. We who have been affected by that mistake might forget the odd closeness of fear and alert enjoyment, but the point here is not that we fail to know that about ourselves but that we know it all too well. To whatever degree one of us tries to keep it all rational, that person receives odd reminders of our self-contradiction and fragmentation. We get, that is, reminders not of what we are in occasional weak moments but of the weakness that underlies whatever strength we lacquer it over with. Take nakedness, for example.

Nakedness

Nakedness became a problem for Adam and Eve (Gen 3:7–11), and it still is for their children. Their realization that they were naked did not come from an awakening of sexuality, as if by eating fruit from the forbidden tree they reached puberty. Their sexuality was already well in place (2:23–24). The issue of nakedness came up not after sex but after sin.

And it has become a multifarious thing. We are hung up about nakedness in all sorts of crazy, contradictory ways, some of us more, some less, though we can deceive ourselves about our supposed unhunguppedness as much as we can about anything. We have elaborate rules about what attire is acceptable where. Most of us do not want to be seen in public without our clothes, we have bad dreams about that, and we often do not like it when others impose their naked bodies on our vision.

In those dreams about being unclothed, nakedness is symbolic. Uncovered body parts is not the only issue involved in shame. This is shown by the ineffectiveness of the fig-leaf aprons Adam and Eve fashioned: before God, they still felt naked even with their brand-new clothes (Gen 3:7–8, 10). Awareness of God's close presence had changed: just being there with him felt like how most of us, in America at least, imagine being naked in public would feel. Even when God gave them their second set of clothes (v. 21), that was only enough to make it possible to go on living the scary sort of life we know outside Eden. And there is no better solution because the issue is not bodies. Even if we get over nakedness, we cannot get back to some kind of original, deculturized humanness. Any "normal" we possess or advocate is post-fall, and so is confused, fragmented, and unsure.

> You claim: "I am rich, I have acquired wealth, and I do not need a thing." But you do not realize that you are wretched, pitiful, poor, blind, and naked. I advise you to buy from me gold refined in the fire so that you can become rich, white clothes so that you can cover your shameful nakedness, and ointment for your eyes so that you can see. (Rev 3:17–18; cf. Matt 22:11–13)

It is all metaphorical: the Laodicean church members addressed here had no sense of themselves as "wretched, pitiful, poor, blind, and naked." Quite the opposite. But they were all those things, if only metaphorically, and their nakedness would be dealt with neither by some missionary's imposition of a culture-bound code (the baggy dresses that Pacific island women started wearing) nor by a reversal to a supposed pristine unclothed state, but by God's completion of redemption. Along the same line, everyone will be clothed in heaven, though in the biblical passages that refer to that (mainly Rev 3:4–5), the garments are metaphors for the healthy and unashamed state of those who wear them and for the redemption that has made those people so.

Along with whatever other reasons, we wear clothes to disguise ourselves, not just from others but each of us from himself or herself as well. Or we might call it giving ourselves an identity that goes beyond simple naked humanness, perhaps even one that distinguishes me from all the rest of you humans. Mark Twain imagined the Russian czar looking at himself naked in the mirror and seeing there that without his clothes he would be the same as other men, that the myths that allowed his family's thieving and brutal rule would be gone. At the end, feeling a bit discouraged about humanity because of the incongruity between the brutality of his reign and the adulation of the Russian people for him, the czar extends what he has said about his royal attire to the clothes of all people:

> Is the human race a joke? Was it devised and patched together in a dull time when there was nothing important to do?[8] Has it no respect for itself? . . . I think my respect for it is drooping, sinking—and my respect for myself along with it. . . . There is but one restorative—*Clothes!* respect-reviving, spirit-uplifting clothes! heaven's kindliest gift to man, his only protection against finding himself out: they deceive him, they confer dignity upon him; without them he has none. How charitable are clothes, how beneficent, how puissant, how inestimably precious! Mine are

---

8. This calls to mind the casual creation and destruction of a little world by "Satan" (the nephew of the biblical Satan) in chapters 2 and 3 of Twain's *Mysterious Stranger*.

able to expand a human cipher into a globe-shadowing portent; they can command the respect of the whole world—including my own,[9] which is fading. I will put them on.[10]

As such, clothing can represent whole environments. Václav Havel told of when, during a television weather report, "the sound cut out, though the picture continued as usual":

> The employee of the Meteorological Institute who was explaining the forecast quickly grasped what had happened, but because she was not a professional announcer, she didn't know what to do. At this point a strange thing happened: the mantle of routine fell away and before us there suddenly stood a confused, unhappy and terribly embarrassed woman; she stopped talking, looked in desperation at us, then somewhere off to the side, but there was no help from that direction. She could scarcely hold back her tears. Exposed to the view of millions, yet desperately alone, thrown into an unfamiliar, unexpected and unresolvable situation, incapable of conveying through mime that she was above it all (by shrugging her shoulders and smiling, for instance), drowning in embarrassment, she stood there in all the primordial nakedness of human helplessness, face-to-face with the big bad world and herself, with the absurdity of her position, and the desperate question of what to do with herself, how to rescue her dignity, how to acquit herself, how to be. Exaggerated as it may seem, I suddenly saw in that event an image of the primal situation of humanity: a situation of separation, of being cast into an alien world and standing there before the question of self.[11]

That wonderful habit of millennia, self-reliance, does not like to be interrupted. That moment of truth about humanness, of terrified embarrassment, sends us scurrying for cover so that we can again be the czar, the good citizen or good parent, the self-assured professional, the bad girl or bad boy, or whatever self-image we try so hard to live up to so as to protect ourselves from that truth about humanness. The Wizard of Oz commands himself as much as he does Dorothy and her friends: "Pay no attention to the man behind the curtain!" That is what the nakedness of Adam and Eve is about. To the degree that the coverings of routine,

---

9. I.e., his own self-respect.

10. Twain, "Czar's Soliloquy," 272. There is another clothes make the czar story in chapter 9 of Leo Tolstoy's *Ivan the Fool*.

11. Havel, *Letters to Olga*, 321–22.

rules, and roles are taken away, then we experience that confused, fragmented, and unsure post-fall "normal" and become aware of our naked humanness.

This difficulty with *this* nakedness is evident in one of the saddest and funniest things about humans. When one of us seeks a spouse, someone he or she will spend the rest of life with in a loving, mutually nurturing, and fruitful relationship, he or she begins by lying. Makeup and clothing are more carefully attended to, the caffeinated or alcoholic personality props are utilized, and the fake hipness (or holiness, if that is appropriate to the context) and fake intellectualism are put on display. A similar procedure is followed if one of us wants (to appear to want) to join a team of people committed to shared goals—what we sometimes call getting a job. In all such settings the layers of metaphorical clothing become endless, to where one might wonder if, as with an onion, there is no core, no *ding an sich* to the human except, perhaps, endless embarrassment and perpetual hiding.

Things might be different if Adam and Eve had gone to God and asked him to make clothes for them "so that we can stand to be around each other and, even more, so that we can stand to be around you." Instead, they sought their own solution and found it inadequate. The difference between their fig-leaf aprons and the animal-skin garments tailored by God (Gen 3:7, 21) was not the material but the maker.[12] What God gave them could represent grace, provision, and redemption given by him. Fig leaves could only call attention to human embarrassment by an attempt to hide it. So we have the choice between failing self-reliance and grace-filled sacrament. The fig-leaf shortcut looks attractive only because with it Adam and Eve do not have to ask God for his help. It is not a solution.

There is, in fact, no resolution without redemption. It seems absurd that life should be not only imperfect but unperfectable, but so it is—without redemption. I have a sense that my perpetual embarrassment is something I should be able to find a solution for, perhaps even a quick solution. *It is, after all, so irrational.* The cognitive therapy that begins with that statement might help, but it does not solve. It does not take me

12. The idea that an implied blood-sacrifice is what made the second set of clothes better is one of the ways in which Heb 9:22b, "without the shedding of blood there is no forgiveness," is overapplied. For the meaning in context of that verse, see Snyder Belousek, *Atonement, Justice, and Peace*, 192–208. A requirement of sacrifice is not accessible in the text of Gen 3, but the difference in who the tailor was is right there in the story: humans or God.

to some imagined "real self" that sheds that irrational feeling as unnecessary. The czar still looks in the mirror only after dressing.

Death

Numerous cultures have myths about the origin of death and about where dead people "go," so apparently death is something that needs to be explained. It is, of course, what always, without fail, happens eventually, but apparently humans consider it abnormal in some way. All those myths, those explanations, show that we have an instinctive belief in our natural immortality.[13] There is an odd incongruence: the inevitable has to be explained because it is opposed by what we more surely believe in, our own individual importance in the grand scheme of things.

Death is one of the things Christians have claimed far too much certainty about. Whatever we might claim to know, and on whatever grounds, we who are available to discuss it just do not know what it is like to die because we have not done it yet. Enough about that, though I do have an aside for readers who would point to experiences interpreted as returns from death, so-called "near-death experiences," and knowledge supposedly gained from such experiences: I am assuming that death comes once and is permanent[14] and that anything that does not have those characteristics is something other than death. Perhaps I am wrong about that, but there is nothing in such experiences to provide real evidence against my assumption. That strange things happen does not bind us to any preexisting mythological interpretation.

Death happened before there were humans (all those pre-hominid fossils), so we cannot say in any simple, literal sense that there was no death till after humans sinned. Whatever we might try to say on the basis of Genesis 3 and Romans 5 about the relation between the first sin and the fact that people die,[15] one thing is certain: that first sin quickly made killers out of humans (Gen 4:8).

Another biblical certainty is that death is not as overwhelmingly significant as it seems. It can be a metaphor for the now-normal human state of estrangement from God (e.g., Rom 8:6; Eph 2:1) and for

---

13. Primeval immortality, if the myth is of the origin of death; immortality of the soul, if the myth is of where we go after death. See Frazer, *Belief in Immortality*.

14. On the basis of human experience far more than of Heb 9:2.

15. I argued in chapter 5 that losing access to the tree of life was not a matter of punishment for sin.

the eternal state of those who remain in that alienation (Rom 1:32; 9:22; 2 Thess 1:9; Rev 21:8), and *what is represented by the metaphor surpasses the literal.* That is, physical death is of less significance, we are promised and warned, than continuing in that metaphorical "death," in, that is, alienation from God (Rom 8:10; Matt 10:28). And, by extension, life's reminders of death, that is, experiences of suffering, are likewise relativized (Rom 8:18).[16] Trying to figure out what Genesis 3 says about death may be a way of giving death more credit than it has coming to it. The relativization of death in the face of eternity is part of what we know ahead of time when we read Genesis 3 within the canon.

One place where that "death" metaphor becomes most powerful is in the face of *life*—life, that is, at its liveliest, this side of that first sin. Truth, here, is in the hands of the despairing. The liveliness of life so often comes down to the despairing attempt to escape the pulling asunder of the divided self or the perpetual embarrassment of those who are like the emperor in the tale, but in reverse: clothed but feeling naked.[17] Havel's story about the weather reporter could have gone on to what happened next and thereafter. If she is like some of us, she laughs about it now. But she may also be like those who can feel stuck there, inflating how foolish others think she is and how inept the incident proves her to be.

The Argument from Our Dividedness

So we can have a stack of metaphors, all for where we are now, after the fall, outside Eden, felt especially when the busyness slows down. How about this: "Since I walked through that puddle, my shoes (or my feet, if that helps the metaphor) don't fit. They feel like they're somebody else's." Or this, recalling Ecclesiastes 3:11 again: "I keep running into something in my heart (or head) that feels like eternity, and I can't figure out how it

---

16. Alongside this relationship of literal and metaphoric, there is the connection in terms of cause. "The death of the body follows spiritual death, or the death of the soul, including all the diseases and miseries by which man is surrounded from without" (Schmid, *Doctrinal Theology*, 238).

17. *The Emperor's New Clothes*, a story by Hans Christian Andersen, tells of an emperor promised a beautiful new set of clothes that will be invisible to anyone who is stupid or incompetent. The tailors are corrupt, and no one is willing to admit not seeing the wonderful garments, taken out on parade by the emperor, until a small child in the crowd points out that the emperor is naked. By that time, the tailors have skipped out of town with the costly fabrics.

got there. It certainly doesn't fit with what else is there or with anything I do." I am oddly divided.

This is in keeping with the apologetics I hinted at earlier:[18] the sense of something missing, of a memory of something never seen before, shows how disconnected we are from ourselves, from the truly human, which we have never witnessed or experienced but do know about. Feuerbach saw religious belief as a false projection of our own ideal self. A Christian response might ask why we should work so hard on conceiving an image of ourselves improved. The need for that unexperienced self-image comes from somewhere and is so inescapable a part of being human that it seems sensible to tie it closely to our origin. Biblical religion does us the favor of allowing us—or leading us—to acknowledge that we do not have in ourselves the ability to fulfill that image, that a description of what we are must include that we are unlike our own image of a better us. Faith leads us to acknowledge, that is, what we all know about ourselves. It is similar to a maturing child coming to accept that a heroic inner or hidden self, created in the face of fearful experiences and maintained through years of the same, is not the actual self. That image of a better me does correspond to something real, but that something is not me. It is God. Or perhaps it is fully redeemed humanity, prefigured in our creation and in the ideal human, Jesus.[19]

This argument is a variation on the updated Cartesian *ergo* represented by Chesterton's "I deny that biology can destroy the sense of truth, which alone can even desire biology. No truth which I find can deny that *I am* seeking the truth. My mind cannot find anything which denies [the existence of] my mind."[20] In the case of that image of a better me, if I reflect on my longing for what I cannot have, I thus identify something in myself whose origin I cannot account for. It is as if I remember a place where I have never been and do not know the location of. In fact, I *began*

---

18. See note 9 in chapter 1 above. Again I acknowledge contact with the form of *apologia* associated with C. S. Lewis (e.g., Lewis, *Mere Christianity*, 31–34; Maritain, *Approaches to God*, 109–14). Here a key issue is the degree to which perception corresponds to a real world. So Lewis, *Christian Reflections*, 57–71 (70–88 in the 2014 reprint). Perception exists in our minds, or, to press it to a Cartesian extreme (see note 20 below), in *my* mind. Here, the "perception" is an understanding in our minds about the world that includes spiritual reality, and ultimately God.

19. More about the latter in chapter 8, esp. under "Staying on the Human Course."

20. Chesterton, *Alarms and Discursions*, 260 (emphasis added). René Descartes reasoned that, if he inquired about his own existence, someone (he himself) was there to ask the question. Hence his conclusion, "I think, therefore I am," *cogito ergo sum*.

(whether "began" means "was born," "was created," or "evolved") with that dim perception of an ideal self. So I posit someone[21] outside myself from whom that thought or longing has come.

Similarly, the woman looking for the lost coin (Luke 15:8) is for Augustine a picture of himself looking for the image of God within himself, looking, that is, for himself, for the truly human. "If she had not remembered it, she would not have found it" because she would not have known to look for it. And she recognized it, having a memory of it, a mental image of it, with which to compare what she found. "When it is found, it is recognized by the inner image."[22]

But the memory offers little. Our existence as the image of God was changed by the fall to such a degree that we can hardly be blamed for not recognizing it for what it is. Our representation of God on earth was warped, perhaps gradually, as in Paul's description of the fall as a process over time in Romans 1. Rather than exercising dominion over other animals and worshiping God, humankind degraded itself with worship of itself and of the animals it was supposed to have dominion over (v. 23). The results included the further degradations of stupidity and sexual immorality (vv. 21–25). Or, as we see it in Genesis 3, the losses Adam and Eve experienced from the fall adversely affected their (and our) functioning as God's image/representative, including the loss of

- their simple understanding of God's words (Gen. 3:1–3),
- their ability to discern contradiction of God's words (vv. 4–6, 13),
- their freedom from shame (v. 7),
- their acceptance of God's presence (vv. 8–10), and
- their fairness in dealings with each other (vv. 12, 16).

They traded off the requisites of free relationality to gain something else, thus losing their own selves.[23]

---

21. A "someone" rather than a "something" because the personal is not generated spontaneously from the impersonal, though that is neither axiomatic nor unanswerable.

22. Augustine, *Confessions* 10.18 (27).

23. See Bonhoeffer, *Creation and Fall*, 62–66, on the image as freedom, relationality, and dominion, and Barth, *Church Dogmatics* 3/2:175, on responsibility and decision as the heart of humanness. See chapter 3 above, under "The Image of God" at note 32, for what Bonhoeffer said about human dominion over creation.

THE FIGHT

Envy and the Ritual of Accusation

Repeating a bit of what I said in chapter 2 (under "The Oddness of the Story"), "Exercise of power is what we understand. It is what makes sense to us, so it is what determines the resolution of human stories." Therefore, what we see in God's incarnation as Jesus is odd to us, "a reversal, an upside-down way of doing things." "Kenosis is a departure from *our* normal" because "exercise of power is how our thinking is structured this side of the fall." We can perhaps understand that odd thing, kenosis, better by examining its opposite, the human "normal," that is, the assumptions by which we live until we adopt God's odd ways for ourselves.

René Girard gives us much help in understanding desire and power.[24] His explanation starts from a basic part of being human, namely, the desire to be like others. This desire is not evil, but it leads to many evils. It does so because one aspect of desire to be like an admirable role model is competition: if you are more like my model than I am, then I must one-up you in some way or eliminate you. And the model is, of course, more like the model than I can ever be and therefore is my archrival. Desire to be like a model can therefore become desire to replace the model. The sum of many such relationships is social chaos.[25]

For instance, I can only be the best juggler of oranges if I out-do those whom I or others think are better at it than I am. If such an archrival also has a beautiful wife, whom I lust after, and plays guitar better than I do, all the worse. Envy can destroy me, but I can avoid that, or at least I think I can, if I can supplant that much-blessed juggler, that is, if I let my envy destroy him. But I may miss the fact that *he* envies *me* for something else, that all these considerations exist for him as well. And so we are caught up in "reciprocal escalation and one-upmanship."[26] If we live in a place without laws, we will fight.

That sort of chaos is not the end of the story, and here we come to the heart of Girard's thought. We humans do achieve order. We do get ourselves organized. The social contract is real, and its root is the desire

---

24. Among Girard's books, *I Saw Satan Fall like Lightning* is perhaps the most accessible. For an introduction to his thinking, see also Colloquium on Violence and Religion, "What Is Mimetic Theory?"

25. This works even if the model is not a real person but an ideal that I strive toward, because I will meet people who come closer to that ideal than I do.

26. Girard, *I Saw Satan*, 9.

to reduce the chaos so that we can survive. Because there are laws, jugglers and guitarists do not often kill each other. (In a certain country, during a recent period of relative lawlessness, nationally popular guitarists did kill each other for reasons only musicians can fully understand.)

But laws discriminate and do not involve us in admitting the real causes of chaos. The easiest way to get on death row in America is to have one's ticket stamped by inability to afford top-notch lawyers. The rest of us, who are not on trial, need not discover the real murderer as long as we think (or claim) that we have found that person, as long, that is, as society can act out the ritual of accusation, conviction, and ostracism or execution, even if we blame the wrong person. As long as we can blame, we can restore order, or so we think. Even if we know all too well that one execution, while it may satisfy the ritual of criminal justice, does not make a dent in whatever real chaos exists around us, we carry out the ritual. It is inconvenient to accept that we are all to blame (that all humans are sinners), so we achieve order by focusing the blame on some individual or some relatively small group. The basis of social order is the identification of that common enemy. To admit the real causes of the chaos would be to say that there is something fundamentally wrong with *all* of us, making us face that *one* problem, which has no such simple solution—or at least not one that we can accept.[27]

A classic example—or better, analogy—is the post-World-War-I German stab-in-the-back myth, particularly as expounded within Nazism. Nazis blamed Jews for Germany's defeat and humiliation, which was, viewed rationally, laughable. But the desire not to blame oneself (or one's people or one's heroes) is so strong that the irrational was believed. And still is, if we find analogies closer to home in, for instance, American anti-welfarism (blaming the poor), racism (blaming the descendants of slaves), anti-immigrationism, anti-whoever-the-president-is-or-recently-was-ism, or anti-what-have-you-ism. The desire not to blame oneself or one's people or all people, not to admit the real causes of chaos, is so strong that we find someone else, some small minority of the human number, to blame.

Satan is "the accuser." That is what his name means.[28] As such, he personifies both what we avoid—self-accusation—and how we avoid

---

27. "What is wrong with the world is most fundamentally that people respond to evil with evil" (Yoder, *War of the Lamb*, 54).

28. Or, more simply, "opponent"; Hebrew *śāṭān*. "Accuser" is certainly the role Satan has in relation to Job.

it—accusation of someone else. Because the ritual of accusation is an essential part of the foundation of social order, so Satan is "the ruler of this world" (John 12:31; 14:30; 1 John 5:19). Most of us, most of the time, want to be on the side of the accusers, not among the accused. Our role models, our heroes, then, are those who are shown to be right, who are righteous, or at least successful, at the end of the story.

Sin as Power Struggle

The model, then, the always successful juggler of oranges, becomes the rival. The one whom I admire becomes also the one whom I hate and the one whom I attempt to replace, by murder if necessary. For Adam and Eve, this was God. The desire for power, the desire to be "like God," lies at the root of the existence and nature of sin. As humans first contemplated the decision to violate their relationship with God, the snake presented the issues involved as a power struggle. The wisdom the fruit could give was needed for independence, for the ability to make one's own decisions, which, in their original relationship with God, Adam and Eve had had no need for. To live apart from God's will, apart from close relationship with God, requires that one have one's own "knowledge of good and evil." So eating fruit from "the tree of the knowledge of good and evil" is the route to independence.

Thus we have the desire to supplant or eliminate God, that is, the drive for self-divinization. That seems to be an obvious, non-theological understanding that no atheist should object to. The reason an atheist should be *militant* is because God (that we must say the *idea* of God here makes little or no difference) is in our way. Our carrying out some part of being ideally human is thwarted by the traditional transference of that ideal to an imaginary being who is—and this is precisely the problem—*not us*. To move toward that ideal, to give it human flesh, we must get rid of God, that unfleshly embodiment of our ideal. That is the simple reason for militancy in atheism. But there are people, Christians among them, who regard that very human need to shake off God as sinful, as, indeed, the very definition of sin.

Because we neglect that definition of sin, we can get hung up on behavioral details when we are thinking about sin and sanctification. We have a long history of using Christianity as an aid to telling children to be good and therefore of ourselves understanding it as such, since, after all, we were once children. Because we have that history, our understanding of sin often begins and ends with "is _____ action or behavior or habit sinful?" Thankfully, that tendency seems to be waning, and Sunday School is becoming a place for teaching more about Jesus and less about playground morality, at least from what I have seen of it. It has become harder to understand how easily some people said, for example, that C. S. Lewis was no ("real" or "born-again") Christian because he smoked. Not that smoking is good, but its goodness or badness is best dealt with outside the category of sinfulness, and, more germane here, sin is better understood without being weighted with answering questions about the goodness and badness of smoking and a host of other actions and behaviors. Along with that, heaven is better understood if we free it, too, from questions about whether Lewis's pipe will keep him out.

As with Lewis's pipe, so also the way of life of Richard, who lives on the street and is quite broken down by alcohol. He is, by his own profession, a Christian. The point is that we miss out on understanding both sin and salvation if we involve them too much with bringing Richard out from his situation. Changing Richard's life is possible—God has done harder things than that—but *how* it is changed is less a theological issue than something for a social service agency or the like. At any rate, I do not try to make Richard decide if he is a Christian on the basis of his way of life. That he is a Christian and an unreformed alcoholic are both true and are facts to be understood separately, just like C. S. Lewis's soul and his pipe.

Because we focus on behavior when we use language like "sin" and "sanctification," we miss both the unity of sin and the unity of sanctification. We might agree that the issue in sin and salvation is relationship with God, but we still often believe our faulty conscience when it says that what we need to do is to *be better people* in several detailed ways, focusing on behavior. Sin expresses a power struggle. Sanctification is a renunciation of the fight against God.

A human's striving for power is therefore an expression not of strength but of anxiety. "Our hearts are restless until they find their rest in you [God]" (Augustine, *Confessions* 1.1) because it is only by quitting the struggle for self-sustenance and by trusting God, who provides all we need, that we find rest from our anxiety. That Adam and Eve did not do so and that we do not do so is the cause of all human distress, competition, greed, fear, and violence.

Power Games

Remember Joe and Bob two chapters back?[29] They illustrated what happens when there is more than one will in the universe. Now think again about Joe's situation once Bob has entered the room and sat down. Joe is for the moment not God but one of us. He has two ways of getting Bob out of the favored chair.

One is persuasion. Joe can use any of a number of arguments relating to rules ("I got here first"), Bob's self-interest ("With your short legs, that chair over there would be more comfortable, and it's closer to the TV"), or prior treaties ("Remember, I reserved chair-choice to myself when I let you in"). His arguments can be truthful or not, relevant or not, honest or dishonest, and delivered with respect or not (though he might do well at least to fake respect, as a rhetorical strategy). The objective is the same. He wants to sit in the comfier chair (or he enjoys bossing Bob around chair-wise).

Or Joe can resort to violence. His violence can be of the sort used in the children's game of musical chairs or of a greater degree with more permanent and messy results. Again, the objective is all the same, and it is the same objective as he would have if he attempted persuasion. And if we thought of other means that stand on the line between persuasion and violence (say, threats of violence), gaining the objective would be the criterion for success, and the objective would still be the same.[30]

Or Joe might throw a noisy tantrum, hoping that someone will hear from the next room and intervene on his behalf. Regardless of the sincerity or falsehood of the tantrum (another possible rhetorical strategy), the objective remains the same.

And he might back up his argument or fisticuffs with prejudice, particularly if he wants other people in other rooms to think he might be righteous, or at least right, in his conflict with Bob—or if he wants to convince himself of that, since it is more enjoyable to be righteously selfish than just plain selfish. That desire to justify oneself is just as human as all this conflict over chairs.[31] At any rate, Joe might disqualify Bob by

---

29. See chapter 4, under "For Other Wills."

30. On persuasion, see further chapter 10 below, under "Persuasion." Regarding power exercised by both violence and persuasion, see, e.g., Caputo and Yount, "Institutions," 5–6. I am using "power" in a more restricted, hence less Foucauldian, sense here. But even with Foucault, room is left for a critique of exercise of power in human interactions (e.g., Caputo and Yount, "Institutions," 7–8).

31. See below, under "Legality and Other Means of Justification."

pseudo-scientifically proving that people whose names begin with B are incapable of understanding correctly what is involved in sitting in chairs. That would be every bit as sensible as arguments American racists have made.[32] And because Bob is, as a "B" person, so stupid, Joe is not addressing this argument to Bob himself. Perhaps Joe believes what he says. That would make it easier, but it is not necessary (claiming to believe his own arguments might be yet another rhetorical strategy). His objective remains the same.

If Bob is just as determined to maintain possession of the chair as Joe is to regain control of it, then Bob will respond similarly. He would not need to do so if Joe did not oppose him, but now his doing so demonstrates something that is a constant in human wars: we become like our enemies.[33] Bob may not use the same tactic: he may resort to violence in response to Joe's attempt at persuasion. But then Joe, given that excuse, is likely to become a partner in demonstrating that principle that we become like our enemies, meeting Bob's violence with violence.[34]

But, backing up to the beginning of the story, if Joe, who may now be God, wants Bob's *agreement*, then the situation changes. God may use violence,[35] but at every point in the Old Testament, what he wants is Israel's agreement. He wants Israel's will to match his, which is another way of saying that he wants effective covenant with Israel. Covenant is made effective through faithfulness, through love. God wants to *persuade* Israel, to *woo* Israel. God is not like Joe because for God the goal dictates the means of getting to the goal.

God thus messes up the rules of conflict. The distinction between goal (the chair) and means (persuasion or coercion) that a human Joe enjoys falls apart when he or Bob or Susie or Albert is dealing with God because God knows when we are lying and when we are speaking truth but without truth as our goal. No fooling God.

But with each other, that is a different story. Among humans there is hardly ever a reason to slow down the power games. We find it easier to overlook them, which is like overlooking the rhinoceros standing on my left eyebrow. The games are so pervasive, constant, and subtle that we

---

32. One major theme of Chesterton's *The Ball and the Cross* is how we humans dehumanize each other so that we can treat each other badly.

33. See, e.g., Seuss, *Butter Battle Book*. See further chapter 10 below, under "He Has Interrupted the Cycle."

34. The power games make us like our enemies. See Girard, *I Saw Satan*, 12–13, 15.

35. See chapter 2 above, under "Kenosis Is Not an Attribute."

forget that they are happening, that they, in fact, nearly define what we are. The hidden games of one-upmanship in friendly social conversation are as fierce in their way as any murderous inter-family feud, any saber-rattling among nations, or any playground bragging. The more a person is aware of his or her own thinking and of the distance between psyche and presentation, then the more he or she is aware, therefore, of all this gaming and how it rules each of us. If I thus say that an *it* (the game) rules *me*, I confess that the image of God, the one given dominion over other animate creatures, has become the slave to something not even worthy of a personal pronoun—and I am also thereby well on the way to acknowledging the apparent difference and even warfare between two things that share the name "myself." I begin to speak, then, as the confused "I" in Romans 7:7–25.

Legality and Other Means of Justification

Most of us, most of the time, as I said above, want to be on the side of the accusers, not among the accused. We want to be justified. Justification is a human need as fundamental to being human as our need to eat and breathe. It is part of who we are. Being able to say "I am right" in some particular circumstance is a great motivator. Pursuing justification takes up much of our time and energy. It comes from more than fear of consequences, be they judicial or relational. It is a matter of self-worth; we might even say it is a matter of giving self the right to exist. It is the only effective substitute we have for being good—if we restrict ourselves to our own resources and do not accept the different justification that comes instead by faith in Jesus (Rom 9:30–31).

Laws are useful to this hard work of justification because they give us standards for who is good and who is bad, and we like that. And the judicial system is useful because it carries out for us some responses to that goodness and badness so that we do not have to risk the chaos of doing that for ourselves. The responsibility for punishing is taken off my shoulders and given to "society."[36] We have, therefore, a tool by which to give accounts of praise and blame and to carry out some consequences of (responses to) praise and blame. "Law" in this sense includes social mores as much as it does written legislation, though the latter is, granted, more

---

36. Whether we think of Judg 21:25 (and 17:6) as describing a bad situation or a good situation, we should not miss that people were, as it says, doing what they thought was right, not whatever evil they thought they could get away with.

effective because it is less changeable, more official (or "legitimate"), and more definite. If I obey all the laws (and/or rules), then I am okay, and anyone in conflict with me must, ipso facto, be not okay. In other words, legitimacy, including what is customary and accepted along with written law, not only guards against chaos but also enables self-righteousness.[37]

Both law and custom are relational shortcuts. Any alternative would require more relational hard work and more accommodation to each other than we normally expend. Law and custom are, that is, tools by which we insulate ourselves from dealing directly with people. They stunt our relational growth, which is just what we want to do.

But self-justification need not end just because I lose in court. I can win at the level of my own understanding—my *self*-justification—even if at every other level I have lost. Even in prison, I can be certain in myself that I am right, and that counts for a lot this side of the fall.

This need for justification, to consider oneself right, avoids God's view, or it posits that God, being well-informed and intelligent, must agree with my self-assessment. Thus we reject both God's judgment and God's grace and substitute moral or social acceptability for acceptance by God, our righteousness for God's (Rom 10:3).

William Stringfellow, a lawyer by the way, spoke of the many different ways in which we seek to fulfill this drive to be justified: bearing pain, good works, good words, "relevance," or churchly pageantry.

> The pursuit of justification by any means—moralistic conduct, dogmatic conformity, charitable enterprise, daily work, or burnt offerings—is, in the biblical perspective, the essence of human vanity in its denial of God's freedom to affirm life without contingency, dependency, or equivocation. Such notions of justification refute God's capability of love.[38]

Stringfellow also saw the idea that God blesses the righteous (which has a tenuous place in the Bible) as making wealth itself a measure of this false

---

37. On the false distinction between violence and force exercised by a "legitimate" government, see Ellul, *Violence*, 84–88.

38. Stringfellow, *Keeper of the Word*, 65 (see also 133, 138, 140, 164); cf. Dostoevsky's "Grand Inquisitor," who is offended at Jesus's return because the church has the work of human happiness well in hand (Dostoevsky, *Brothers Karamazov* 5.5). Stringfellow wrote mainly against the implied atheism of some liberal Protestantism (see particularly Stringfellow, *Keeper of the Word*, 138), but what he says could be directed as easily against evangelicals, whether we think of conscious theological statements or the social mores of theologically informed or uninformed evangelicals.

justification.[39] And America's self-image as a nation shown by its success to be justified shapes much of our political rhetoric and government policies.[40] All this just illustrates the far reach of that drive for justification.

39. Stringfellow, *Keeper of the Word*, 245–50.
40. Stringfellow, *Keeper of the Word*, 227–32.

7

Myths, Heroes, and Monsters

ENDS AND MEANS

The Problem with the Problem

THIS COULD BE THE point at which I make the theologically or homiletically trite observation that the newspapers are full of bad news. (As we live through the death of print we will have to find another way of saying that.) And that should back up some part of whatever I have said about the pervasiveness of sin. My generation, those born within a few years after World War II, have learned well the preacherly and political uses of that cliché, and, sure enough, we really have been caught off guard by the big, scary, and unexpected several times. Exit Godzilla and enter Mothra.[1] Exit Soviet Union, but don't dare call that the end of our fears![2] But still, I am doubtful enough about letting interpretation of our times, untempered by the passage of time, serve as evidence for anything as important as sin. We need a longer, perhaps even theological, perspective in order to say anything like this:

> A knowledge of the sin and guilt of man in the light of the Word of the grace of God implies a knowledge that . . . history is, in fact, grounded and determined . . . by the pride of man; a knowledge that its course and aims and movements and beginnings and ends and new beginnings have one thing in common in

1. Or was it the other way around?
2. As Francis Fukuyama, "End of History?"; *End of History and the Last Man* were commonly misunderstood.

spite of all the differing and indeed opposing trends: that they all come under the judgment of God. History is concluded in disobedience.[3]

But however we react to the latest new and scary thing, God is still bringing about his purposes of redemption. Nothing we see or fret over means that the creation-redemption story has been abandoned. What shows up in the news is, rather, a series of reminders that the solution (to the *one* problem) does not come from our intelligence, righteousness, or organizational skills. History goes on, and the news will be as it has been. But Jesus remains "God's power and God's wisdom" (1 Cor 1:24).

Redemption comes not from our efforts but from outside us, which would not be a problem if it came from Superman. He upholds "truth, justice, and the American way" and thus represents what we would like to be or at least what we want our heroes and saviors to be.[4] Redemption by God is harder to accept because it comes from our enemy and because it questions and rejects the ways of negotiating life and the highest aspirations we have built up since the original rebellion against that enemy.[5] God gets things done not by the power plays that characterize human methods but kenotically, by what looks to us like an upside-down, backside-forward way of doing things but is really the way in which he has created the universe and the shape he has given it. We reject all that—indeed, it seems so obviously wrong that we do not have to think about it—because exercise of power is how our thinking is structured this side of the fall.[6]

Our inclination to reject that one true solution and the diagnosis that lies behind it has become a habit so deeply ingrained in us that it seems to be a sine qua non of humanness. Just as a successful revolution becomes institutionalized, so we live with amnesia about the initial rebellion, not to mention the trust in God that preceded the rebellion. We can solve human problems and sometimes do, but focusing on lesser

---

3. Barth, *Church Dogmatics* 4/1:505–6.

4. If you are not American, substitute any nationally and culturally appropriate superhero.

5. See chapter 5 above, under "Cain's Misinterpretation." "Being made sensible of his sin, and his danger, a Sinner will look for help and deliverance: but he will look every where else, before he look unto Christ" (Wesley, *Directions for Renewing Our Covenant*, 7).

6. See chapter 2 above, under "The Oddness of the Story."

problems outside the context of redemption by God can be like drying off our feet while drowning far from land.

False Endings

We have protected and justified our position away from God and our rejection of his methods—again, for so long that we have forgotten that that is what we have done and are doing. The shamed faces of Adam and Eve leaving the garden in medieval and Renaissance paintings are not our faces. We protect our position with what we can call "myths"—in the sense of commonly-held beliefs that do not line up with reality, though they may seem so obviously true that they are to some degree protected from questioning. They are also "myths" in the sense of ways of accounting, usually narratively, for what exists (or what seems to exist). Reasons for the way things are can be comforting even if they are not true.

They can also be called "false endings" or "dead ends" like the false endings in *Oliver Twist* that I mentioned back near the beginning of chapter 1. Many good things happen for Oliver, but his life cannot be secure until the fundamental problems, which began before he met the Dodger and multiplied thereafter, are solved. That is, the story cannot end until Oliver has a home and Fagin and Bill Sykes are dead, because even London is too small to hide in.[7] So also, in the life of humanity, our solutions along the way do not address the fundamental and original problem, so our history is very much one of misidentifying issues and solutions and therefore of incomplete problem-solving, because we are dominated by a belief about how things get done that disagrees with God's way of getting things done and therefore with the shape of the universe.

The disillusionment of the post-liberal age[8] has made it easier to see some of these dead ends, the diagnosis and solution myths active in our post-fall situation. The assumptions of classical liberalism can now sound foreign to our ears. For instance, it was said of William Godwin, certainly one of the founders of liberalism in the English-speaking world, that he

---

7. Unless it were to end tragically, with Oliver's death.

8. I am thinking here not so much of theology that has been characterized as "post-liberal" (among others, Hans Frei, George Lindbeck, and, in a different way, Thomas Oden) as of the disillusionment following on nineteenth- and twentieth-century political and social liberalism, that which made prophets of some nineteenth-century radicals, such as Michael Bakunin, in their disdain for idealistic liberalism.

was not singular, but was kept in countenance by many authorities, both ancient and modern, in supposing a state of society possible in which the passions and wills of individuals would be conformed to the general good, in which the knowledge of the best means of promoting human welfare and the desire of contributing to it would banish vice and misery from the world, and in which, the stumbling-blocks of ignorance, of selfishness, and the indulgence of gross habit being removed, all things would move on by the mere impulse of wisdom and virtue, to still higher and higher degrees of perfection and happiness.[9]

There might be some who still believe that great humanitarian possibilities are possible through the (US) Democratic Party, which can still, on festive occasions, invoke full-fledged liberal utopianism. But that is often displaced by a libertarian agenda and the entitlement language that is the less noble offspring of the Civil Rights Movement. If, putting a brighter face on it, we deal with individual problems without the aid of the old hubristic eschatological rhetoric (having to do with the lofty goals of liberalism, not the biblical eschaton), then we are also freer to examine our myths. In chapter 6 I mentioned myths concerning law and other means of self-justification. Here I will speak particularly about our exaltation and misunderstanding of knowledge, our myths of human goodness and maturity, and our myths of our freedom over against our subjection to transhuman powers.[10]

MYTHS OF KNOWLEDGE AND GOODNESS

The Knowledge Adam and Eve Wanted

As I described it in chapter 5, Eve and Adam wanted a life different from what God had given them.[11] They wanted to rise above simple conformity to God's will and gain their own "knowledge of good and evil," that is, discernment and decision making independent from God. The whole business was based on distrust of God, and with independent knowledge

---

9. Hazlitt, *Spirit of the Age*, 151.

10. I use "transhuman" not in its now normal sense, for technologically enhanced humans/humanity, but (as the best term I can think of) for powers that are far more than the sum of their human parts. See below in this chapter, under "Freedom and Captivity."

11. Again, "Adam, by longing for more than was allotted him, manifested contempt for the great liberality with which God had enriched him" (Calvin, *Institutes* 2.1.4).

Eve and Adam could become "like gods," supplanting the role in their lives previously played by God, the one who was, they thought, cheating them by withholding that higher existence. No doubt the immediate context suggests that we read the ambiguous phrase in Genesis 3:5 as "like gods," but the broader context of biblical monotheism makes it bolder: "like God." Grasping the one forbidden thing, the fruit of one tree, was the human declaration of independence from the old condition of submission to God's word. This disobedience was necessary for that sort of growing up, for becoming in that way "like God."

Not that the name of the forbidden tree can justify this interpretation in terms of ethical independence. "Knowledge of good and evil" in Genesis 2 itself (2:9, 17) is something simpler, namely "knowledge of good-and-evil," that is, knowledge of any and every sort, under the figure of two polar opposites, much as we might refer, conversely, to "nothing in heaven or hell."[12]

But the question does arise why the one prohibition should be tied to "knowledge," not only in the name of the tree[13] but also in how the snake, Eve, and God all describe what is sought and gained in eating the tree's fruit (3:5–7, 22). Furthermore, we find the same link in Romans 7:7–11, especially if that text is read as an account of Adam's experience.[14] "Sin took advantage" of the prohibition (Rom 7:8, 11), setting before Adam and Eve a decision between taking God's word as final and figuring things out for themselves (with a little prompting from the snake). Without the prohibition, the "do not" of Genesis 2:17, they would not have had any conception of doing a thing that went against God. The prohibition made possible the question of whether to do what God had said, and that question, helped by the snake's analysis of God's motives, opened a realm of new possibilities, which was entered by the decision against doing what God had said. Thus "sin took advantage" (Rom 7:7–11): the prohibition

---

12. So Rad, *Genesis*, 81–82.

13. Here a source-critical reading of the text provides a partial answer. The naming of the forbidden tree in 2:9, 17, came late in the development of the text. Its earlier namelessness is reflected in 3:3, 11, but after the addition of the "tree of life," the forbidden tree needed a distinguishing name. Therefore, that the tree is forbidden in 2:17 cannot be connected with "knowledge." The "knowledge" element drops out of the prohibition altogether. So, e.g., Westermann, *Genesis 1–11*, 223, 242.

14. So, e.g., Dunn, *Theology of Paul*, 98. The "I" as Adam is one of the ways in which we can read Rom 7:7–25. In Genesis it is, of course, the experience—or experiences, since they played different roles—of Adam *and* Eve that is involved. But, as was often done by Jewish writers of the time, Paul names only Adam.

in itself put Adam (and Eve) in a position of having to make a choice, in a position, that is, of ethical responsibility.

To continue letting God's word be decisive would have been simpler. Submission is simpler than choice. The possibility and responsibility of figuring things out would develop into a complicated ethical maturity.[15] "For Christian ethics, the mere possibility of knowing about good and evil is already a falling away from the origin. Living in the origin human beings know nothing but God alone," that *one thing*.[16] Obedience, "direct acceptance of God's lordship," lies "*outside* the opposition between good and evil, outside their tragic collision and antagonism," and therefore outside the whole enterprise of ethics.[17]

This is the case even if we understand the initial sin not as a decision against God but as a misdirected attempt to serve God creatively since, so Adam and Eve might have reasoned, God's instructions are an incomplete guide for human action. Humankind goes "back behind the given word of God to procure its own knowledge. . . . They renounce the life that comes from this word and grab it for themselves. . . . This is disobedience in the semblance of obedience, the desire to rule in the semblance of service."[18] The sin of our first parents was "pride," that is, "coveting God's likeness."[19] Their "desire for knowledge" arose from "their inordinate desire for excellence."[20] Their sin was hubris, a rising to responsibility and self-reliance, not a fall into degradation. It was not what we might associate with a sociopathic disregard of all society but more akin to the righteousness, even social righteousness, of the religious

---

15. Though see below for more about our supposed "Maturity."

16. Bonhoeffer, *Ethics*, 299–300; cf. *Discipleship*, 107: "Purity of heart here [in Matt 5:8] stands in contrast to all external purity, which includes even purity of a well-meaning state of mind. A pure heart is pure of good and evil; it belongs entirely and undivided to Christ; it looks only to him, who goes on ahead." Similarly, Barth, *Romans*, 428, with regard to the "attack on the presuppositions of all other ethics"; Kierkegaard, *Purity of Heart*, particularly chapter 3: knowledge of the *one thing* is blocked by knowledge of much.

17. Bulgakov, *Bride of the Lamb*, 151; cf. Hauerwas, "Explaining Christian Nonviolence," 172n9: John Howard Yoder "was not a pacifist" (though obviously he was) partly because he knew that answering Jesus's question, "Who do you say that I am?" must precede a commitment to any form of pacifism. "Christian nonviolence can, therefore, not be a position about violence abstracted from discipleship to this One as God's anointed."

18. Bonhoeffer, *Creation and Fall*, 116–17. Here already in lectures given in 1932–1933 we encounter Bonhoeffer's *homo religiosus*.

19. Aquinas, *Summa Theologiae* II-II.163.1–2.

20. *Summa Theologiae* II-II.163.1, reply to objection 3.

person. Degradation follows along later (Rom 1:21–28). Adam and Eve would thus be, dare I say, like the nineteenth-century reformist liberals who left it to later generations to figure out that Christian ethics cannot survive unaltered without Christian faith and discipleship to Jesus.

Does It Do Any Good?

Human knowing is often adequate, but always limited. In fact, "I know" carves out an exception to the norm, which is a much larger "I don't know." It is like me saying quite honestly that I know very little about auto mechanics (the norm) but have learned through repeated practice how to replace the alternator in a 1969 Opel Kadett 1500 (the exception). We are faced with a whole universe, but we have only such little bits of practical knowledge. We take this for granted because it is the human normal.[21]

Not so God. Discussion of the "attributes" of God[22] has sometimes distinguished between "negative" attributes, matters in which God is unlike us, and "positive" attributes, characteristics we have that God also has, but to a complete degree. For instance, a child might call out "present" after hearing her name at school, but God is present in the classroom and is also *omni*present, present everywhere. Knowing is a positive attribute: saying "God knows" does not say the same thing about God as "I know" says about me. If, for instance, knowing the future is impossible because the future actions of beings with free will cannot be known,[23] then the term "know" is therefore not quite sufficient or not quite appropriate when God is the subject. Or better, "God knows" implies no such limits. Furthermore, it does not matter whether God knows how to replace an alternator because he would just heal it or take a bus to work (and besides, he is already present there without having to leave home). The point here is that any idea of humans becoming "like God" must either assume countless qualifications or lead into impossibilities.[24] For Adam and Eve it was the latter.

---

21. On human "practical knowledge" over against God's knowing, see further Sparks, *Sacred Word*, 72–88.

22. See chapter 2 above, under "The Kenosis of Christ" and "Kenosis Is Not an Attribute," and chapter 3, under "God."

23. See the last paragraph of chapter 4 above, with note 53.

24. Aquinas says, for such reasons, "Our first parents did not covet . . . a likeness of absolute equality," "since such a likeness to God is not conceivable to the mind, especially of a wise man." The likeness to God they sought was "a likeness of imitation"

Submission to what God has said can sound oppressive to us, or it can sound like suppression of supposed natural human abilities to judge what is good and to take the initiative. It sounds like that at least partly because that effort to become "like God" happened so long ago: apart from the grace of God revealing it to us, we have no knowledge of anything outside the form of existence brought about by the ambitions of Adam and Eve, or whatever name we give to some distant ancestors.[25]

At our stage in human development, perhaps we can recognize more clearly that ethics—consciousness of our behavior toward each other—is knowledge essential for survival. We are far beyond Cain, whom God sought to bring from a religion of competition for blessing to a religion that takes into account how we treat our brothers. Or at least we know that we should be self-critical on that score. But reflection on "knowledge of good and evil" and its accomplishments can throw a salutary wrench into the works by discovering that it is not our ethical knowledge or enlightenment, even if we dress it in finer clothes than just those of knowledge useful to the survival instinct, that counts. What counts, instead, is hearing and heeding God's word, that *one thing*.[26] Or, with a hint toward chapter 10 below (under "Ethics"), what Christians have instead of ethics is discipleship to Jesus.

All this is true no matter how religious our "knowledge of good and evil" sounds, which brings us close to a Kierkegaardian critique: "An objective knowledge about the truth or the truths of Christianity is precisely untruth. To know a creed by rote is, quite simply, paganism. This is because Christianity is inwardness. Christianity is paradox, and paradox requires but one thing: the passion of faith."[27] If we elevate living by good ethics to the highest thing, then "The whole of human existence is entirely self-enclosed, and the ethical is at once the limit and completion

---

(*Summa Theologiae* II-II.163.2). But I am doubtful that we should think of such realism, wisdom, or humility on the part of Adam and Eve (or us), especially if it ends up making what they aimed for the same as the imitation of God Jesus told us to seek (Matt 5:48). Why should the snake encourage that? The snake's friend, the devil, seems to show just as little respect for Jesus's humility in Matt 4:8–9.

25. Bonhoeffer's critique does not mean that we should not "do ethics" in the sense of having criteria and applying our minds. It means, rather, that Christians' ethical work, however involved and busy it becomes, should have a single focus, on that "one thing," on letting God be God. On the historicity of the fall see chapter 5 above, under "Truthfulness."

26. So Jas 1:22–25, calling us not to ethics but to hearing and doing the word of God.

27. Kierkegaard, *Concluding Unscientific Postscript*, 1:230.

of our lives. Doing one's duty becomes sufficient, with the result that God becomes an invisible, vanishing point, an impotent thought unrelated to my life. His being is no more than the ethical itself, which fills all existence." "If the ethical is final, if it is the ultimate determination of life's meaning, then Abraham [having threatened to kill Isaac] should really be remitted to some lower court for trial and exposed as the murderer he is" rather than being honored as "the father of faith." But faith stands higher than ethics, and God is its center.[28]

The Joy of Knowing

The complexity of humanness, the sort of thing we saw instanced in the dating scene in the preceding chapter (under "Nakedness"), is not just a burden but also our delight. I have known people who spiced up their boring lives by imagining sudden illnesses so that they could ride in ambulances and others who knew they were the next target of hit men sent by the Mafia, the government, or extraterrestrials. But this love for complexifying life is not just the province of lonely neurotics who watch too much TV. It is also the pastime of educated, employed people who have families, hobbies, and friends and go to church. Knowledge is at the center of this complexifying and so is a commodity, just like marijuana, alcohol, and video games. I have heard that "no one learns to ride a bicycle by reading a book," but I am sure it has been tried.[29] In any craft, there are those who *know* more than they *do*. It is not just a matter of curiosity: it is cautious over-preparation. It is knowing *over* doing, knowing *rather than* doing, taking the safe road out of fear of the real road, the one that might arrive at a destination or teach a skill.

In accord with the three human drives named as "from the world and not from God" in 1 John 2:16 and the three temptations of Christ in the wilderness (Matthew 4 and Luke 4), Augustine identified three kinds of people.[30] One variety is "the curious," identified with "the lust of

---

28. Kierkegaard, *Fear and Trembling*, 83–84. Here, as always when reading Kierkegaard, I am dismayed by his individualism—as if faith were incompatible with community. Perhaps such was needed in his time and place.

29. I recently ran across an old book that presented itself as "a thorough course in how to swim."

30. More will be said about these groups of three in chapter 8, under "Staying on the Human Course."

the eyes" and Jesus's temptation to jump off the temple.[31] Their curiosity is "the joy of knowing things," not just what *we* might call curiosity or a quest for knowledge. It also includes the thirst for entertainment.[32] It is "a certain vain and curious desire, veiled under the title of knowledge and learning, not of delighting in the flesh, but of making experiments through the flesh. The seat whereof being in the appetite of knowledge, and sight being the sense chiefly used for attaining knowledge, it is in Divine language called 'the lust of the eyes.'" "Lust of the eyes" pertains not just to seeing, since we can say "see how it sounds, see how it smells, see how it tastes, see how hard it is. And so the general experience of the senses is called the lust of the eyes, because the office of seeing, wherein the eyes hold the prerogative, the other senses by way of similitude take to themselves, when they make search after any knowledge." It's not just a matter of pleasure. We will even stare at a corpse for the experience of seeing it.

> From this disease of curiosity, are all those strange sights exhibited in the theatre. Hence, men go on to search out the hidden powers of nature, which to know profits not, and wherein men desire nothing but to know. Hence, also, with that same end of perverted knowledge in view, magical arts are employed. Hence, also, in religion itself, is God tempted, when signs and wonders are demanded of Him; not desired for any good end, but merely to make trial of.[33]

Curiosity is the drug of choice or real religion of vast numbers of people. Indulgence of this habit has become illimitable with the advent of the Web, that supermarket of instant answers and random knowledge. Wikipedia is the high temple, a vast opium den for the addict-adherents of curiosity, and there is a "Random Article" button on every page. All of us can now know much more about things that we as individuals do not need to know anything about.

---

31. Augustine, *De Vera Religione* 38.70–71. What I say in this section about curiosity in *De Vera Religione* mostly summarizes Greer, "Sighing for the Love of Truth," 22–23. Greer contrasts this use of 1 John 2:16 with Augustine's later use of the verse in *Confessions* 10. For Kierkegaard's criticism of knowledge for its own sake, of knowledge or even "truth" for any other purpose than subjectively living in it, see, e.g., Kierkegaard, *Practice in Christianity*, 201–11; *Concluding Unscientific Postscript*, 1:192–230.

32. Augustine, *De Vera Religione* 49.94–95.

33. Augustine, *Confessions* 10.35 (54–55). For William G. T. Shedd's translation, see Augustine, *Confessions*, 286–87.

It did not have to wait on the Web. There were already history buffs, subscribers to magazines (*National Geographic* the best example), nosey neighbors, and celebrity followers. Many hobbies amount to tidbit-of-information collecting. There have long been people who could recite baseball statistics, capabilities of fighter jets, titles and dates of paintings, names and finely-differentiated products of fruit jar manufacturers, dates and results of gran prix circuit races, sources of different tobacco varieties, and so forth. Some people need to know those things professionally, but that often amounts to saying that they *need* to know in order to serve those who only *want* to know. Such professional knowers occupy much of academia, miles of bookstore shelving, and countless websites.[34]

Our dealing with this curiosity is, according to Augustine, part and parcel of our confrontation of the self-deception, complexity, and noise we hide behind. Curiosity is part of that seeking of distractive noise. It can be a way of avoiding self-knowledge and confession of sin. Augustine speaks in his *Confessions* of his readers as "a people curious to know the lives of others, but slow to correct their own. Why do they want to hear from me what I am while they are unwilling to hear from you [God] what they are?"[35]

We certainly can understand in our celebrity-eating time how the sins of others are more interesting than one's own. Because we do not remember the fundamental facts of our existence, our knowledge becomes shattered. "Thus, we do have some knowledge of individual verities, but we do not know *the* truth, the system, the unity of all truth in God. We do not know God, who is the ground of all things, and thus we truly know neither ourselves nor the world."[36]

The curiosity instinct is so great that some of us could not keep up with its feeding if we were to restrict its diet to what is really new and really true: "Give the people a new word and they think they have a new fact,"[37] and let curiosity be as gullible as it needs to be. The limitation of knowledge can be just as maddening for one person as for humanity:

---

34. This is not an argument against non-practical knowledge, mostly because I would not trust anyone, including myself, to determine for the rest of us what is practical and what is not—and because I have my own memorized and non-useful lists. I am pointing out that this curiosity is a characteristic of post-fall humanity. And I am not arguing against any particular quest for knowledge or against the general human quest for knowledge. I am describing who we are.

35. Augustine, *Confessions* 10.3.3.

36. Bavinck, *Created, Fallen, and Converted*, 78–99.

37. Cather, "Four Letters," 372.

"Death for us is all we have missed, all the periods and planets we have not lived in, all the countries we have not visited, all the books we have not read." "Death for the individual is the whole universe outside his consciousness."[38]

Curiosity is part of our fig-leaf clothing. It is as we realize our nakedness that a move against curiosity can be part of our redemption. Perhaps the staleness or death of curiosity experienced in depression can be such a realization of the nakedness of oneself or of all humanity. But a person seeking to know God thus both counteracts and makes use of curiosity.[39]

Maturity

Sometimes we greatly overestimate our accomplishments as humans. The people of Babel thought the universe should take notice of their mastery of brick-making and brick-stacking. To the universe, however, their accomplishment, tall as it was, was nothing, though God was concerned about humans getting bigheaded about it and what that would mean for their future. We have taken the technology of stacking bricks much farther, as we have the technologies of throwing rocks at each other, warding off rocks thrown at us, jumping up in the air (even to the moon, which still leaves the universe unimpressed), getting from place to place, sharing cute puppy videos globally in an instant, etc. Most importantly, the ancient technologies of hunting and gathering food, such that we now put the raw materials (seeds and cattle) in fields and feedlots where we will be able to gather the end products more easily and effectively. But we are still those excitable rock-piling, rock-throwing creatures.[40]

Our technological growth has not, in fact, been accompanied by ethical growth. Decisions that affect large numbers of us still get made by those whose only distinction is the possession of larger rock piles. And, partly as a result of that, resources that could go into problem-solving go instead into more rock-piling and rock-throwing. Those problems we are so slow in solving are generally of our own making, the results of our rock-piling, our rock-throwing, and our efforts to solve earlier problems similarly caused.

38. Zangwill, *Italian Fantasies*, 13–14.

39. E.g., Augustine, *De Vera Religione* 53.103.

40. In an old single-frame cartoon a crowd of early hominids is screaming and throwing rocks at each other, and one says to another something like, "I'm leaving. This meeting isn't going to settle anything."

There has never been a time when people are free enough from food-gathering, rock-manipulation, and problem-solving to take a view of the whole and figure out how humans should live. Or, should I say, never a time when those who *have* thought about it have been heeded. Or again, perhaps I should say, when an effort to heed such people has not resulted in fascism of some sort or other.[41]

My point is not that we could do that process of thinking and changing any better. Quite the opposite: we are beings that *do not* do it better. To say that we will just muddle along as humans always have might seem too pessimistic to some people, but it is true. We will, and the universe may never take notice,[42] no matter how great any of us thinks we are. We await the new heaven, the new earth, the new creation, by grace, whether we like it or not.

Idealism

There is an inevitable failure at the heart of what I have called both the normal pattern of human stories (in chapter 2) and the lie of the powers about power (see below) because meeting power with power only perpetuates and increases conflict, thereby increasing yet more the need to meet power with power. Whether in playground envy, professional rivalry, intra-family conflict, or conflict among nations, we go into battle with the assumption that we need to meet the enemy with weapons and methods similar to the enemy's or, we hope, better than the enemy's, whether those weapons are pistols or sarcasm, bombs or clever wit, fists or seduction. But they will not be better for long because the enemy studies us as well as we study the enemy. We thus become like the enemy, and the enemy returns the compliment. We carry on this cycle of "returning evil for evil" despite all the Bible has said about that (Lev 19:18; Prov 17:13; 20:22; 24:29; Matt 5:39; Rom 12:17; 1 Thess 5:15; 1 Pet 2:23; 3:9).

---

41. Cf. Carlo Cafiero and Elisée Reclus, preface to Bakunin, *God and the State*, 7: "Since the doctrinaires made their appearance, the true or pretended 'genius' has been trying his hand at wielding the sceptre of the world, and we know what it has cost us." Bakunin himself writes, "A scientific body to which had been confided the government of society would soon end by devoting itself no longer to science at all, but to quite another affair; and that affair, as in the case of all established powers, would be its own eternal perpetuation by rendering the society confided to its care ever more stupid and consequently more in need of its government and direction" (31–32).

42. Granted that it is hard to say what the latter would mean to people of our age.

It goes along with this and is particularly significant for the American self-understanding that, while we are outmatching the enemy and being outmatched by the enemy, we maintain the illusion that we are, at some sort of core level, unchanged by the experience. We are, we think, and this applies at the playground and in those other arenas, the same idealistic or blessed or righteous people we always were. We still identify with the experiences and desires (however legendary) of our ancestors or with the good kids we were before we got to the playground. After all, what we do once we get to the playground or the battlefield is, so we think, intended merely to defend those blessings and ideals. Nonetheless, we become like the enemy in how we treat ourselves as well as in our weaponry, trading our small freedoms, for instance, for the "vigilance" necessary, we think, to fight, for instance, Communism in the 1950s or Islamic terrorism more recently. We become like our enemy. It is fundamental to who we are as humans, not just Americans, after the fall.

Perhaps we can recognize this more clearly if we look at the experience of some people on the other side of the world. After the end of the Soviet Union, some Russians found that, while life might be better on average, they missed the idealism of Communism.[43] If that idealism, so foreign to us, could be important to some people, then can we see more clearly how our ideals are important to us, even while we do not seem to be coming closer to living up to them?

FREEDOM AND CAPTIVITY

HAL and Other Homicidal Deities

We have a habit, but less so as the years go on, of talking on the telephone with people we do not know, generally after an interval of being on hold. In the early days of this habit the unknown person would be sitting at a computer terminal, and we would often hear that person say *"The computer* won't let us do that," the prohibited "that" being something we thought needed doing in order to progress to some next step. If you think back far enough, then some of us had only a vague idea of what *the computer* was, but, whatever it was, it had the authority to say "No." Perhaps, then, given that ability to speak, *the computer* was not a what

---

43. I encountered Russian people saying that about themselves, fortunately for me while practicing their English, on two Russian websites that have long since disappeared. They seemed to think this a rare sentiment among Russians.

but a who. That is, it was an invisible entity that spoke and demanded obedience, much like a god.

The ritual saying "the computer won't let us" was an acceptance of submission and a counsel to others that they also submit. It was sometimes "the computer *can't* do that," but that amounted to the same thing, like the polite HALspeak circumlocution "I'm sorry, Dave. I'm afraid I can't do that" (*2001: A Space Oddyssey*). Saying it either way was a surrender of our place in creation, our dominion, to someone we barely knew how to name and certainly never saw, if indeed there was a visible aspect to the thing.[44] We accepted our demotion into a dehumanized position, lower than that given to us in creation and imposed by this invisible ruler.

Now, living in a better informed era, we know that that prohibition—"the computer won't let us"—was really just about limitations of software, and that, with more thought and communication up front in the design and code-writing, fewer such impossibilities emerge. So *the computer* can be demoted from deity to its proper role of impersonal tool, though we might think computers now exercise a collective godlikeness as *the internet*, though I will not go into that here.

All this is an example and analogy for much of what we experience of life. Just as we submit to the rules of the game of one-upmanship, as I described in chapter 6, so we submit to countless other cultural norms, ideological requirements, and faceless institutions. And, faceless or not, they act in ways that only things with personhood (a three-word oxymoron) can do, such as make decisions, issue orders, set standards, and approve or disapprove. When we speak of what they *decide* or *do*, we are conceding that they are worthy of such personhood. The basic premise of corporate law—that corporations can be treated as persons—is just an extension of our normal way of speaking. We give away some of our humanness to these non-human entities.

My favorite example of such rulers is called "the economy." For example, "I can't get a job because the economy is unhealthy." It is often true, but how many people saying such things could say what "the economy" represents? Or "It's the economy, stupid." As a mantra for a political campaign (Bill Clinton's in 1992) it was perhaps useful, but did it not assume and build on our inability to point to "the economy"? Where

---

44. I saw a computer for the first time in the early 1960s. It filled the basement of a large building and kept track of electric bills for a couple million people. It could also play a few monophonic tunes. That is not counting an earlier encounter with a garage-sized thing that could play tic-tac-toe as well as any kid I knew.

is "the economy" located? Which way should I point? Is our ignorance on such details simply part of acknowledging that we humans, along with any policies and plans we might come up with, must submit to this unseen but pervasive entity?

Such things have their own lives apart from my life or yours. We do not necessarily know when or how we submit to them, or even that we do so. But submit we do, and thereby we admit to our rulers that we, the humans, are of less importance than they are. Did we ever respond to "The computer won't let us" with "But we're the humans! God gave us dominion over the earth! Why do we let the works of our hands tell us what we can't do?" The same was observed about a similarly faceless institution before computers and even telephones: "You remember Thurlow's answer to some one complaining of the injustice of a company. 'Why, you never expected justice from a company, did you? they have neither a soul to lose, nor a body to kick.'"[45]

Who Are They?

Giving up our freedom has been a human thing to do since we started living together, which may mean before we started being recognizably human. Two people who are married to each other make compromises in order to preserve their togetherness, not so much between him and her as between the solo self and the dual us. And that difficult process is like nothing next to what each of us does for the sake of larger collectivities such as cultures and nations. It is necessary to submit in such ways for our collective safety, though I will want to think later about the meaning and appropriateness of that word "necessary."[46] At any rate, it is what we do to control the chaos that has resulted from our competition.

It began with Cain. His story and that of his descendants in Genesis 4 give us the best clues of how we got into this situation of subservience. His parents had believed the snake's lie that we live in a competitive universe, that God was their rival. Cain carried that understanding into his worship of God, thinking he was in competition with his brother for God's blessing. He thus failed to understand what God wanted and that how he dealt with his brother mattered in how God dealt with him. Then

---

45. Sydney Smith quoted in Holland and Austin, *Memoir of the Reverend Sydney Smith*, 1:376.

46. See below under "Fear Not" and chapter 11, under "Why We Obey Laws."

he failed also to believe God and so retreated into providing for his own defense by flight and by city-building. Later, Cain's descendant Lamech, also believing that we live in a competitive universe, ramped up the self-reliant aggression and violence.[47] The myth of competition became self-fulfilling in that believing it was true made it true, and competition and self-protection have snowballed as we become like our enemies, like each other, that is.[48]

By establishing walled cities and laws, humans join together for collective defense, thus increasing their chances for individual and collective survival but surrendering their freedom, including their freedom to decide whether to survive or to sacrifice oneself for the collective good (or for a principle of, say, nonviolence). Nowadays it might be not a walled city but a well-armed nation, but each represents a truce among a lot of people for the sake of carrying on warfare against others—outsiders—more effectively, and against enemies within the camp, that is, those nonconformists and disrupters we call "criminals."

And so we have not only governments but also a broader array of what we can call "institutions," unlocatable but powerful, faceless but very active *things*, the structures humans place over themselves in an effort to contain their chaos. These entities take on a life of their own beyond their existence as human collective action, so that, again, we give them personhood and, indeed, let them rule over us. With these non-human powers come their myths, mainly that of their inevitability—that is, the myth that we have no alternative to submission to them.[49]

With this submission, there remains for humanity no story, because a story requires freedom, exercise of will, and movement toward resolution. God's provision has been rejected in favor of human self-determination, but that has paradoxically led those whom God created free into a situation in which they give up self-determination. Our unfreedom means that we limit the use of our imagination in thinking about ethical possibilities: out of fear of each other and subservience to the institutions,

---

47. See chapter 5 above, under "Cain's Misinterpretation," on all that.

48. Quoting Pogo's "We have met the enemy and he is us" became a cliché, but perhaps you have forgotten it, and there is no better way to describe the human situation. On René Girard, see chapter 6 above, under "Envy and the Ritual of Accusation."

49. "Slaves lose everything in their chains, even the desire of escaping from them: they love their servitude" (Rousseau, *Social Contract* 1.2).

the highest we ever rise is the best of the same old evil alternatives,[50] so that our best ethics is merely disguised "returning evil for evil."[51]

What Are We Afraid Of?

Those partly personalized but hard-to-locate entities such as computers and their rules for us, cultural norms that discourage any attempts to question them, and faceless but powerful institutions have been identified with what is referred to by the New Testament (mainly Pauline) language of the "powers and principalities" (e.g., Eph 1:21; 3:10; 6:12; Col 1:16; 2:10, 15) in discussion of the latter for a few decades now.[52] There are a number of such Pauline terms for the "powers and principalities."[53] Sometimes an apparently impatient Paul says in effect, "*Whatever* is out there!" in an attempt to get past any attempt at analysis.[54]

There is one point at which, it seems to me, this identification of the institutions and ideologies of our age with the powers spoken of by

---

50. Language often used in reference to democratic elections, especially those limited by a two-party system—and that usage captures well what I mean here.

51. See Yoder, *War of the Lamb*, 39.

52. Most prominently, Wink, *Naming the Powers*; *Unmasking the Powers*; *Engaging the Powers*. Earlier, Berkhof, *Christ and the Powers*; Stringfellow, *Ethic*, 75–111; *Free in Obedience*, 49–73; *Keeper of the Word*, 187–292; Wink, "Stringfellow on the Powers"; Ellul, *Ethics of Freedom*, 144–60; *On Freedom, Love, and Power*, 96–97; Yoder, *Politics of Jesus*, 134–61, 140n5, 159. See also Dawn, *Powers, Weakness, and Tabernacling*, 1–34. A root of this understanding of the "powers" was nineteenth-century radicals' emphasis on "critique," specifically "critique of institutions," which they regarded as a fundamental part of "thought leading to revolution" (e.g., Marx and Bakunin). In other words, rhetorical analysis to discover the fundamental message underlying much of our talk, which is about persuasion, coercion, and power. Such analysis is, if anything, the dominant pattern of thought of our Nietzschean age.

53. Plural or singular *archē* and *exousia* in 1 Cor 15:24; Eph 1:21; 3:10; 6:12; Col 1:16; 2:10, 15; Titus 3:1; *archē* in Rom 8:38; *archōn* in 1 Cor 2:8; *exousia* in Rom 13:1–3; 1 Pet 3:22; also other terms in most of those same passages.

54. Thus he piles up terms in Rom 8:38–39 (and in v. 35 in another way); Eph 1:21; Col 1:16. In 1 Cor 8:4–6, he pushes past both those who believe there are many "gods" and "lords" out there and those who are quick to deny that there are any, moving toward what is important "for us," affirmation of "one God the Father and one Lord Jesus Christ." Along the same lines is his use of "all" and "every": what he says about these forces is applied to "all," that is, *whatever* might be out there, with no exceptions; they are all defeated, but they all still oppose us (1 Cor 15:24; Eph 1:21; Col 1:16; 2:10; "or any others" in Rom 8:39; "none" in 1 Cor 2:8). Whatever we say about the "powers" will affect how we understand the demons Jesus exorcised (e.g., Luke 11:14) and the New Testament's portrayal of an overall realm of evil (e.g., Luke 11:15; John 12:31; Eph 2:2; Col. 1:13; Rev 9:1–11; 12:7–10).

Paul goes astray or misleads. The "powers" are said to have been created by God (Col 1:16), and some interpreters have taken this to mean that government, for instance, was created by God.[55] And, because they now oppose God's purposes and people (e.g., Rom 8:38), the powers must also be fallen from their creation goodness.[56] But it seems better to speak of our governments and other institutions and our ideologies, totalitarian and otherwise, as not created and therefore not completely identifiable with the Pauline powers—not created or fallen but existing only as human collective action necessitated by the fall. They are not created and fallen alongside humanity, but are fallen *as* human.[57]

Those who fell could only be created personal beings, whether just humans or also angels/demons,[58] so whomever we say is fallen we thereby ascribe personality to. That, I think, would be giving too much credit to the government or the church or marriage or Nazism or whatever. A healthier theological assessment of government can come from such a post-fall view of its origin.[59]

A way around my objection might be to emphasize that what God created was not any specific government or any specific ideology of collective action but the *possibility* of human collective action, of compromise, and of broad sets of ideas to undergird such action. But the more we make such a distinction, then the more we thus affirm that the institutions and ideologies are not what God created. The language of the "powers and principalities" is useful in our understanding of the transhuman institutions and ideologies of our day,[60] and I will follow it to some extent, but not in all that has been said about it.

Why not take all that New Testament language about "powers and principalities" "literally," that is, as referring just to supernatural beings

---

55. E.g., Stringfellow, *Ethic*, 78–80; Yoder, *Politics of Jesus*, 142. The willingness to regard the powers/government as part of creation is perhaps partly due to discomfort with an ongoing direct providence/upholding (see chapter 2 above, under "The Kenosis of the Trinity," and chapter 5, under "Life Goes On"). So Yoder, *Politics of Jesus*, 141. Government as created has also been aided, though not correctly, by Rom 13:1–2, 6.

56. So again Stringfellow, *Ethic*, 80–82; Yoder, *Politics of Jesus*, 141.

57. Again (note 48 above), "We have met the enemy and he is us."

58. Surprisingly, perhaps, to some, there is little to nothing in the Bible about a fall of anyone other than us humans. The notion of an angelic fall is locatable in the Bible only because we bring it to the text as an interpretive lens.

59. I will say more about this in chapter 11.

60. See Stringfellow's narration of his experience in two classrooms, *Free in Obedience*, 50–51. On "transhuman," see note 10 above.

rather than to the big institutional monsters of our own age? The reason is found in the focus of human fear. If we ask what in any given age people are afraid of without themselves quite being able to identify it, then in Jesus's and Paul's age that would be some sort of amalgam of government, disease, famine, insanity, and gods and other spooks. In our age, after the Industrial Revolution, it would be big social forces, ideologies, institutions, and apparently constant technological change.

That does not exclude the more "literal" demonic from our interpretation because calling those things we most fear and least understand "demons" is a quite sensible thing to do. With this interpretation of the New Testament texts we are admitting that some things are beyond our rationality and (though a scientific age might call it heresy) will always be. Let us hear Chesterton say it again: "I do not think there is anything stupid or ignorant about howling at the moon or being afraid of devils in the dark. It seems to me perfectly philosophical."[61] The problem is not in being afraid but in not acknowledging that we are afraid and that our fear is at least human and perhaps even rational.

There is no absolute distinction in the Pauline language between human powers and demonic powers. With the terms used[62] it is clear that Paul (or perhaps a Paulinist author in some of the texts) is sometimes referring to human governments (Rom 13:1–7; 1 Cor 2:8; Tit 3:1) and sometimes to non-human forces (e.g., Eph 6:12; another author in 1 Pet 3:22). But it can occasionally be hard to decide which, or perhaps both human and non-human are intended (Eph 1:21: "not only in this age but also in the age to come"; 3:10; Col 1:16; 2:15; Rom 8:38; 1 Cor 2:6; 15:24).[63] This is striking to us in our age, but it makes perfect sense given that government could be just as dangerous and even more mysterious in ancient times than in ours.[64] So a term like "transhuman" becomes useful. Rather than speaking of some sort of transference of language in one direction or the other ("the biblical writers used terms originally applied to government also for the demonic" or vice versa), it would be more in

---

61. Chesterton, *Club of Queer Trades*, 186.

62. See note 53 above.

63. So Yoder, *Politics of Jesus*, 139–40n4. On the complexity of the issue in discussion, see Yoder, *Politics of Jesus*, 160.

64. Government is mysterious now because it is so complex and hides so much of its activity, but it was less visible then because, without television, there was no need for it to hide. It might become visible only when tax collectors or soldiers came through one's village.

line with the Bible's manner of expression to see some area of overlap and ambiguity, making use of the same terms quite natural.

So, for example, the portrayal of imperial governments as monsters in Daniel 7–8 and the transfer of earthly battles to heaven in, for example, Daniel 10:13 and perhaps the reverse in the book of Revelation. When armies met, their gods fought also. Similarly, some of the witnesses of Jesus's exorcisms, which raised so many questions (e.g., Matt 12:23; Mark 1:27), might well have said "if Jesus can exorcise demons, then he might be the one to get rid of the Romans and the unfaithful Jews" (and some did "come to grab him to make him king," John 6:15). So we are not out of line to see the exorcisms as part of an announcement of a new age definable in political terms.

The relationship between spiritual and political that we see in the Bible is different from our time's thinking, making the identity of "the powers" ambiguous in some contexts. The politics of the spiritual realm (Mark 3:24–26) and the politics of Rome and Judea are not easily distinguishable. The meaning of Jesus's "house" (Matt 10:25) and Satan's "house" (Mark 3:27) is, in our terms, both spiritual and political. There is no dividing one sort of realm from the other.[65]

Fear Not

Even as we muddle along, God might be having a good laugh at things we are terrified of. For instance, horses, which as weapons of warfare assumed such an importance in the time of the Old Testament that people could say things like this and be easily understood: "They have horses and they're headed this way! We are doomed!" (e.g., Jer 4:13; 6:23; 8:16; 50:42), "He has horses, so he is a powerful and wealthy king" (2 Chron 9:25–26), or "*They* have horses, so they are a wealthy people" (Isa 2:7). But alternatives to those kinds of statements come into view when attention is given to the actions of the God of Israel: "Sing to the Lord because he has triumphed gloriously: he has tossed horse and rider into the sea" (Exod 15:1, 21).[66] "Some people trust in chariots and horses, but we trust

---

65. For this reason our avoiding politics in our preaching and teaching is misled. We do it only for convenience' sake, because of our worldliness and dividedness. More about that as well will come in chapter 11.

66. Pharaoh's horses were both mounts and chariot horses (Exod 14:9, 23; 15:19). Note the contrast between "the horses of Pharaoh with his chariots and his horsemen" who "went into the sea" and "the people of Israel" who "walked on dry ground in the

in the name of the Lord our God" (Ps 20:7; similarly Pss 33:17; 147:10; Prov 21:31; Isa 31:1).

Horses, especially with chariots, carried the same sort of emotional force then as nuclear weapons, terrorists, and rogue governments exercise now. They were barely believable weapons, known mainly through rumors, pointed at the biblical "us." So it stands to reason that we also have similar choices between trust in our age's equivalent to armed charioteers and trust "in the name of the Lord our God." God's inevitable victory reduces whatever we fear to simple mortal human (or equine) status: "The Egyptians are human, not gods, and their horses are flesh, not spirits. When the Lord stretches out his hand . . . they will all die" (Isa 31:3).

The same is also true of those other powers, those that exist only as our collective action, the transhuman institutions and ideologies. Taking the eschatological long view, participating, that is, in the movement toward that final end, robs them, too, of their importance and makes possible our thinking now outside captivity to the myth of their inevitable power.[67] They are robbed of their power not only as we say that they, like Pharaoh's horses, are mortal, but also as we say what they really are: they are only human, though they (that is, *we*, since that is who they are) impose beliefs about their inevitability that cannot ultimately be enforced. They exist only as our belief about the efficacy of power, though they disguise themselves as much more than that, as that which exists apart from us and without which we cannot do. It is no surprise that we think in these ways, given our assumptions about the necessity of power,[68] but even now they are falling before Jesus and those whom he is liberating.[69]

Those powers are nothing without our belief in them, without our attributing personality to what does not possess it apart from our acting as if it did. We become healthier as we see them shown for what they are, when we describe them exactly, refuse to give them personality, and

---

midst of the sea" (Exod 15:19). For other statements like those in the Exod 15 victory songs, see Deut 11:4; Judg 5:22; Ps 76:6; Isa 43:17; Jer 51:21. The victory is always God's (cf. the promise in Deut 20:1).

67. See Yoder, *War of the Lamb*, 39.

68. See chapter 2 above, under "The Oddness of the Story," and chapter 6, under "The Fight."

69. Jesus already before the cross saw the collapse of Satan's rule (Luke 10:18; John 12:31; 16:11; cf. Luke 11:20–22), part of which comes as the freeing of people from the myth of inevitability of institutions.

assert our place in creation against our inventions, which would otherwise steal that place from us.[70]

Are government and other institutions "powers of evil"? Yes, but not because of any connection with Satan and demons. They are evil, rather, because they are us. Not (or not mainly) us as created but us as fallen. They can become demonic as Satan attacks us through our collectivities. One of the ways this is done is in the inflation of their importance, the myth of their necessity and inevitability. But the collectivities are necessary in the sense that they exist where fallen humanity exists. They have become part of our nature, our definition, but as fallen, not as created or as sanctified. We begin to see their passing from existence as we look forward to that final defeat of evil.

70. As done by, e.g., Stringfellow, *Ethic*, 76; *Free in Obedience*, 52; Yoder, *Politics of Jesus*, 142.

8

Redemption

GRACE

Divine Illogic

WE NEED TO BE reminded constantly of grace because it lies so far outside our expectations, even while it is the ground of our continued existence and our place in the story of creation and redemption. We believe that we inhabit a universe in which coercion solves problems and in which righteousness is getting our fair deserts, but we are actually in a universe in which kenosis and grace are fundamental. Our creation, then the provision for our needs, which continues even after sin, and then our redemption from sin and its deadly effects are all one package. It will be completed, tied up, and delivered in the eschaton, which completes the story. All of it is founded on grace.

Grace is, by definition, non-routine, unexpected, gratuitous. "Where is the grace,"[1] Jesus asks, if you do what is expected from mere self-interest, "if you love, do good, and are generous with a reasonable expectation of return" (Luke 6:32–34)? Even banks do as much. But to love and care for those you are least expected to love and care for and to give to a thief or to one who can be trusted *not* to pay back (vv. 27–30, 35): it makes no sense to do so. That is grace.

In the same way, God. Creation, provision, redemption, and completion are all because of grace, all beyond what can be expected and

---

1. "What sort of grace is that for you?" (Luke 6:32, 33, 34), usually translated, "What credit is that to you?" or the like.

therefore beyond what makes sense. It was while we were still God's enemies, those who try to supplant him, that Jesus went so far as death on the cross—while such generosity was undeserved and therefore unexpected by those who live by the usual assumptions (Rom 5:6–8).

Because creation, provision, and redemption are all included in the same package (the one story), provision is a sign of redemption. Because God provides, he is known as "Father": fathers give fish and eggs, not snakes or scorpions (Luke 11:11–12; cf. 6:36). If I expect to receive snakes and scorpions, or, more likely, if I look at my over-easy with toast and think it is a scorpion, it is because I do not see God as Father. But if I expect the egg because I think I deserve it, then, still, I do not know God as the Father he is. My expectation is based on who I think I am rather than on who he is. But even as God's enemies we are told that God is indeed "Our Father." He becomes that when we learn to trust his care for us, even though it is undeserved.[2]

For instance, the prodigal son, the child who did his utmost to make himself an enemy to his father.[3] My visual idea of that father as he runs out to welcome his son home (Luke 15:20) is captured by "The Little King," a short and rotund comic strip character of the past, particularly in a strip in which he is inspired by passing footracers and takes off running in his polka-dot underwear.[4] Without his royal robes, his body is drawn as a circle. The Little King and the prodigal's father both look comically out of place as runners.

The comedy works not just visually but in the whole character of the father. This would have been more obvious to those who heard Jesus tell the parable, though some were probably not so much amused as shocked. Instead of acting like a commendable head of his family, the father first gives in to his son's outrageous request for an early pay-out of his inheritance (v. 12) and then seems to reward his son for recklessly blowing the whole bundle.

The prodigal's brother is more sensible, as is the prodigal himself once he has sobered up. As the prodigal rehearses the speech he intends to recite to his father (vv. 18–19), he has already come to expect the same

---

2. See further Segundo, *Grace and the Human Condition*, 4–9.

3. Picking up that story from where we left it in chapter 2, under "Kenosis and the Creation-Redemption Story."

4. It can be seen at https://en.wikipedia.org/wiki/File:LittleKing1.jpg. Unlike the unclothed royals of chapter 6 above (under "Nakedness" and "Death"), this one is quite unselfconscious.

thing that his brother has always preferred, namely that their father's giving respond to each son's past responsibility or lack thereof. But that sensible expectation is not met.

In fact, nothing happens in the parable to make the father's actions, either before his younger son's departure or after his return, sensible. The father is, in fact, a bit of a buffoon. "Mercy is comic, and it's the only thing worth taking seriously."[5] Just like that father, grace is comical, shockingly so. We would rather, like the prodigal's older brother, have everything follow the rules and everyone get what they deserve. We apply such rules to ourselves and to each other all the time. No wonder, then, that when grace breaks out the older brother is mad as hell (vv. 28–30), much like some vineyard workers who wanted recognition for having worked longer than some others (Matt 20:11–12). But if logic and sense prevailed even over God, we might as well eat pigfeed and not go home.

Gospel Stupidity

When God speaks, he speaks of grace. And so his words are necessarily illogical and nonsensical. It is not by a simple application of exegetical logic that we understand them in the manner in which they were spoken. "No one will enter the kingdom of heaven without becoming a child" (Matt 18:3, heavily paraphrased), that is (this is at least part of the meaning), without becoming more open to God's nonsense.

The meaning of grace is that the more we structure happiness or justice, the less we can receive happiness or justice from God. This is so because our best, most rational knowledge has no place for grace. Like the prodigal's brother and the early-bird vineyard workers, we want things to make sense. However things might look to God (and our mental periscopes cannot rise to that level), grace is counter to order and structure as we conceive them.[6] It does not complete some structure that we already know. It is not carried out according to a list of standard procedures that we already have in hand. God breaks the rules—any rules that we could know or formulate—to love us.

Listen to Paul: "When you look around the church, do you see any so-called smart people? Do you see people who know all the rules? God

---

5. T Bone Burnett, from the song "The Wild Truth" on the CD *Talking Animals*.

6. Which is why the tit-for-tat logic of Proverbs can seem out of place in the Bible, read as the revelation of grace.

knows that that sort of knowledge doesn't get anybody closer to him. God wants to save people who believe our stupid sermons" (1 Cor 1:20-21). "Divine power" sounds like it should be the name for something spectacular, obvious, and triumphant, but Paul identifies it (v. 18) with his own stupid preaching about the gory and deliberately humiliating execution of a man regarded as a possible revolutionary leader (Luke 24:21). Or maybe "divine power" should be the name for an argument that wins by being devastatingly logical, but certainly not for the words of an admitted (and somewhat hysterical) non-eloquent like Paul (2 Cor 10:1, 10; 11:6; 13:3). So much for how it ought to be. Those expectations have been discarded.

We do not normally like being recipients of this grace. Grace is an odd story, and we hear it at the expense of our self-reliance:

> The worst possible injury is done to us.... We cannot appropriate either the virtue of righteousness or the glory of justifying ourselves (a glory that is so important that many tales and legends finally come to a climax in it, as the hero triumphs through a thousand tests and then at the last receives the supreme reward that he has won, [which] always corresponds to either absolute love or absolute purity, that is, the righteousness obtained at the cost of so many trials in a conquest that is strictly anti-Christian, the quest for the Grail and the Lancelot cycle being a mere parody of revelation). The declaration that we are justified by grace, by the sovereign love of God manifested in the death of Jesus, dispossesses us of something that we regard as essential, namely, that we should fashion our own righteousness.
>
> To come to the point of putting ourselves in God's hands for justification goes against the grain and causes us to bristle.... The one condition for coming to the eucharist is the admission that we are not worthy.[7]

Because the radical change that occurred in the fall collides with the creator's love, redemption occurs. Left to ourselves, we can imagine redemption being abandoned because sin is stronger than our worthiness. Or, instead of despairing in that manner, we can imagine redemption being glossed over as unnecessary because sin is not all that big a deal or because of some "redeeming quality" in us. But sin *is* that big a deal because it violates our humanness, and the consequent state of human worthiness

---

7. Ellul, *Subversion of Christianity*, 160. One could object to the last sentence in this quotation on the basis of 1 Cor 11:27-28.

is ignored because it cannot rise to any significance. Instead, the creator's love is stronger than all other considerations, and he does redeem us.

HOW DOES GRACE HAPPEN?

Theories

How does it work? Here we are thinking about both what God does to save (in this chapter) and what we do to receive salvation (in the next chapter). From God's side we talk in terms of "theories of the atonement,"[8] and of what *must happen* in order for salvation to occur,[9] but immediately the question arises why anything "must happen" if God's grace is as decisive as it is. Could God not just say "let the sinners in!" much as he said "let there be!" at creation?[10] But perhaps the better question is not what *must* happen for atonement to occur but what has, in fact, happened apart from any question of necessity. At any rate, asking "how" in regard to grace can be a way of affirming the binding of Christian theology to narrative forms: something *happens*—in time, so that there is a before and an after—for grace to be effective as grace. Grace does not simply exist: it happens. It is not just God's mindset or mood, but God *doing* something. And, incidentally, our salvation is not dependent on our understanding of the mechanics of salvation, which is a good thing.

Theories of the atonement can be sorted into three or four basic groups:[11]

---

8. "Atonement" means simply "reconciliation," but it carries with it thoughts of the hard work involved in bringing together and making peace between parties who have been at odds with each other.

9. What "has to happen" starting earlier (particularly Irenaeus, *Against Heresies*, e.g., 3.17; 3.18.4), but certainly from Anselm on, is mainly that the mediator be both God and human. Hence the title of Anselm's *Cur Deus Homo*, "Why the God-Man." The same thought is found in, e.g., Calvin, *Institutes* 2.12.1–3; *Theologia Germanica* 3. And, along with that, the necessity that the divine-human mediator die.

10. Anselm, *Cur Deus Homo* 1.1: "And this question, both infidels are accustomed to bring up against us, ridiculing Christian simplicity as absurd; and many believers ponder it in their hearts; for what cause or necessity, in sooth, God became man, and by his own death, as we believe and affirm, restored life to the world; when he might have done this, by means of some other being, angelic or human, or merely by his will" (Sidney Norton Deane's translation in Anselm, *Proslogium; Monologium*, 178–79).

11. The third and fourth in my list are usually one, as in the classic work comparing theories of the atonement, Aulén's *Christus Victor*. Such comparisons of "theories" are found in many systematic theologies. Kärkkäinen, *Christ and Reconciliation*, 298–314, is particularly helpful and accessible. Schmiechen, *Saving Power*, is a book-length treatment with some innovative suggestions.

1. Jesus stood in our place, taking on himself a legal penalty or obligation that we owe, but he does not.

2. Jesus's death is the complete expression of divine love and human obedience and convinces us to change our ways and be reconciled to God.

3. Jesus handed himself over to death and the devil as a ransom for us, but thereby fooled the devil, who did not realize just who he was dealing with. A metaphor used for this view is that of the fishhook: the devil bit into the bait, which is Jesus's humanness, but was caught by the hidden hook, which is Jesus's divine nature.

4. In more general terms, Jesus went into battle against the hosts of death and the devil and defeated them on our behalf.

It is often forgotten that these "theories of the atonement" do not cancel each other out. We need not pick just one. In fact, writers who are most identified with a particular "theory" are often the very ones who can easily call on the broader range of language ("theories") about the atonement.[12] And each of the "theories" has a basis in Scripture; each vocabulary set began in the Bible.

In what I like to call *governmental* understandings of atonement (number 1 in the list above) what *must happen* is dominant. The basic idea is that we have obligations to God that we have not fulfilled and cannot. Or we deserve a punishment that must be inflicted in order for God to accept us but that would also annihilate us. It would not be right or would perhaps even be impossible for God to accept us on any other basis. For him to do so would be to violate his own nature. So Jesus has fulfilled that obligation (though he alone among humanity did not owe it) or taken that punishment on himself (though he did not deserve it) in order to win our salvation. The nature of God—God's justice or honor, what it is possible for God to put up with and still be God—is fundamental.[13] But Jesus has dealt with that. He offered himself in sacrifice to "appease the just anger of his Father."[14]

But again, is not speaking in that way of what *must happen* a constraint on grace? Is "justice" something that limits God and that therefore

---

12. This is one of Schmiechen's main points throughout *Saving Power*.

13. On Anselm speaking of God acting because of necessities imposed by his nature, see note 3 in chapter 3 above.

14. Calvin, *Institutes* 2.12.3.

is like a god above God?[15] Furthermore, any demand for "the righteous distribution of rewards and punishments"[16] or the like is not answered or satisfied but canceled or contradicted or rejected by grace, as in the family of the prodigal.

Talk of Jesus accomplishing something that allows a change in the Father's attitude toward us seems plainly contradicted by New Testament statements regarding God's love for humanity as the basis for atonement (e.g., John 3:16; Rom 5:8). We might say that any such obligation or demand for punishment is "thrown out of court," but really we must depart completely from the courtroom as a metaphorical environment for understanding God. Grace, therefore God's disposition toward us, is a *departure* from rules, from justice, evidenced in events like God's change of plans because of his favor toward Noah.[17] This does not mean that substitutionary ideas of the atonement have to be abandoned altogether, but it does mean that we have to be careful about what they involve us in saying or assuming about God.

Jesus Does It Right

Jesus was like us in being tempted, but unlike us in not sinning (Heb 4:15; cf. 2 Cor 5:21; 1 John 3:5). However we understand the mechanics of grace—on any theory of the atonement—the sinlessness of Jesus, his complete obedience of God, has to be fundamental (as suggested in Heb 7:26–28; 9:14; 1 Pet 2:22–24). Following the same list of four theories as above:

1. If Jesus took a penalty on himself, he could only do so as one who did not have that same penalty due to himself already, and so he had to be sinless.

2. If Jesus's death is the complete expression of divine love and human obedience, then it could be that only because he was completely sinless.

---

15. See again chapter 3 above, under "God" and in note 3, on God and necessity.

16. "That form of moral excellence which demands the righteous distribution of rewards and punishments which renders it certain, under the government of God, that obedience will be rewarded and sin punished" (Hodge, *Systematic Theology*, 2:489).

17. See chapter 5 above, under "Life Goes On."

3. If Jesus fooled the devil by handing himself over to death, then that could only work because he was what the devil did not expect, namely, sinless.

4. Or if Jesus took the field against the hosts of death and the devil, then he fought them by withstanding temptation and remaining sinless, even while those held captive by the devil were in that state of captivity because of their sins.

But could Jesus have done otherwise? Could he have sinned? It is hardly a simple question since either answer, yes or no, leads into difficulties.[18]

Sinlessness here can be thought of as an aspect or manifestation of divinity. The traditional answer to *"Could* Jesus have sinned?" is "no" and is coupled with his being God: he was able to resist temptation because he was already perfect, because he was God.[19] "God who incarnate in the virgin's womb came into the world without sin, carried within him nothing of a contrary nature. He could then be tempted by suggestion; but the delight of sin never gnawed his soul, and therefore all that temptation of the devil was without [i.e., outside] not within him."[20] Temptation remained external to him because there was nothing in him to answer to it.[21] Or, putting it into more human terms,

> the admission into his mind, even for a moment, of such evil thoughts, and especially their assuming for him the guise of a temptation, are suppositions wholly incongruous with his character. According to the explanation itself [of Jesus's temptations in the wilderness], he repelled them at once with strong abhorrence. There was, then, no trial, no temptation. Our Lord could not be tempted to do what was abhorrent to his nature,

---

18. The discussion can seem somewhat pointless: Could we recognize as human Jesus's thought processes, if we knew what they were, which we do not? How could we understand what it is like never to deviate from obedience to God, to be in that way "the complete human"? Indeed, we need to bear in mind the complexity of the question of *any* person's freedom in situations where character and temptation meet.

19. This has historically been referred to as the "impeccability" of Christ. That is, Jesus did not sin because, as God, he could not sin. See chapter 2 above, under "Jesus the Impossible," on the two natures, human and divine, of Christ.

20. Gregory (I do not know which Gregory) according to *Catena Aurea*: Aquinas, *Commentary on the Four Gospels*, 1:118, on Matt 4:1–2. That is, temptations could come to Jesus from outside him, but there was nothing in him, no desire, to respond to the temptation. So also *Glossa ordinaria* according to *Catena Aurea*: "He saw not, as we see, with the eye of lust, but as a physician looks on disease without receiving any hurt" (Aquinas, *Commentary*, 127).

21. This is generally based on an overanalysis of Jas 1:14–15.

and what he recognized as so sinful that (to use the conceptions and language of his countrymen) the mere imagination of it was to be ascribed to Satan.[22]

But if "in all things like us, yet without sin" in the Chalcedonian Creed[23] means that Jesus, being God, could *not* have sinned and therefore faced no genuine temptation,[24] then, it seems, Jesus was other than human,[25] the temptation accounts in Matthew 4 and Luke 4 are false, or they present Jesus as trifling with the devil, and Hebrews 4:15 is faint comfort.[26] The "no" answer thus seems in danger of reducing Jesus's humanness.

One alternative would be to say that Jesus, being human, simply was not sinless and that to say otherwise is to deny to him what seems essentially human.[27] More about that after a few paragraphs, but here I will just note that if we take what we learn about humanness from ourselves and apply it to Jesus,[28] then the idea of his sinlessness is a problem, because sin seems to be fundamental to who we are. Then either Jesus is not quite human or the claim that he is sinless is wrong. But sin is not part of

---

22. Norton, *Translation of the Gospels*, 2:32, 34 (quoted), 43.

23. Similarly, the Anglican *Articles of Religion* 15: "Christ in the truth of our nature was made like unto us in all things, sin only except, from which he was clearly void, both in his flesh, and in his spirit. He came to be the Lamb without spot, who, by sacrifice of himself once made, should take away the sins of the world; and sin (as Saint John saith) was not in him."

24. See note 20 above.

25. If temptation is "an objective occurrence without any fundamental subjective component," can it be called "temptation" such as we experience? That is asked by Shuster, "Temptation, Sinlessness, and Sympathy," 199; also, e.g., Thielicke, *Evangelical Faith*, 2:378. A "docetic" christology is one that denies that Jesus was human. The sort of semi-docetic results one can get by following through on a doctrine of the impeccability of Christ is seen clearly in Augustine. See Dorner, *History of the Development of the Doctrine of the Person of Christ*, 1:77; Augustine, *Literal Commentary on Genesis* 10.20; Aquinas, *Summa Theologiae* III.15.1; cf. Williamson, "Hebrew 4:15," 7: Jesus's sinlessness, at least as it is spoken of in Hebrews, is not what he "possessed when he began his struggle with temptations, a kind of built-in pre-disposition against sin which would have infringed the reality of his humanity." See note 54 below on the timing of Jesus's perfection.

26. Here we are faced with a version of the divine-human incompatibility spoken of above in chapter 2, under "Jesus the Impossible," which has always carried the temptation to deny either divinity or humanity to Jesus.

27. E.g., Williamson, "Hebrews 4:15"; Knox, *Humanity and Divinity*, 106.

28. As one must do to write a biography of Jesus. See Carl Braaten in Braaten and Jenson, *Christian Dogmatics*, 1:520, on the effects of this normal biographical assumption on life of Jesus studies and theology.

the basic definition of humanness.[29] As created, we are "very good" (Gen 1:31), and sin comes later to already-existing humanity.

And there is a less drastic version of a "yes" answer to "Could Jesus have sinned?": Jesus *became* perfect by resisting temptation (as suggested by Heb 2:10; 5:9–10; and the "therefore" in Phil 2:9). This does not mean that he sinned and then learned how not to sin[30] but that his *completion* (his becoming "perfect" in that sense)[31] came as a result of his having faced and defeated temptation. But here we are in danger of ending up with an adoptionist christology, that is, of regarding Jesus's position as Son of God as a reward for his obedience. And it is as the one who was *already* God's Son that he faced temptation (Heb 5:8; the heavenly voice in Matt 3:17; 17:5, etc.).

The term "sinless" itself captures nicely the character of most discussion of Jesus's sinlessness, which takes place in negative terms, that is, in terms of what Jesus was not or did not have prior to his having any chance to sin, that is, before he had been born, and in terms of what he did not do rather than what he did.[32] It would be better to think not in terms of an abstraction such as "sinlessness" but in positive narrative terms,[33] that is, in terms of what Jesus did as he faced specific temptations and did not sin in those concrete circumstances. This will bring us back to our focus on kenosis as having to do with will and obedience.[34] So the sinlessness of Jesus is, from this perspective of attention to the narrative, not so much a pristine purity as a habit of responding to decision points with submission to God and acceptance of a specific role as a victim of human violence. That is, indeed, what the Gospels tell us about from beginning to end. And the same is what Paul tells us about in Philippians 2:6–8 as he passes on to us what appears to be a deliberate reversal of

---

29. E.g., John of Damascus, *Exposition of the Orthodox Faith* 2.12 ("sin is the result of the free volition humankind enjoys rather than an integral part of its nature"); Gregory of Nyssa, *Great Catechism* 5; Aquinas, *Summa Theologiae* III.15.2. Shuster, "Temptation, Sinlessness, and Sympathy," 199n6: "Immaturity or lack of knowledge or experience is not the same thing as sin; growth and development can be pure"; similarly, Ullmann, *Sinlessness*, 146.

30. So Williamson and Knox; see note 27 above.

31. See similarly about humanity as a whole chapter 4 above, under "For Space and Time."

32. We will return briefly to this issue (below, under "Jesus, Warrior and Son").

33. This rather stretches the meaning of "narrative" but is a common enough usage nowadays. The sense is "in terms of events, not from a timeless, abstract perspective."

34. See chapter 2 above, under "The Kenosis of Christ."

a Prometheus or Adam myth, of, that is, a tale of one who *did* grasp at being equal to the gods.[35]

The idea of Jesus's sinlessness may have begun, or gained its greatest traction from, the fact of his trial. He was executed, and a natural response for his followers was to say "but he was innocent!" (e.g., Matt 26:45, 55, 59–60; 27:3–4, 18–19, 23–25).[36] Then this sort of concern is taken back into earlier parts of the Gospels' narratives to account for the plain fact of hostility toward Jesus on the part of many elite Jews (e.g., Matt 12:24–29; John 8:46). That may be how the Christian tradition of Jesus's sinlessness began, but it is not where that tradition stayed. It went, rather, into thinking about Jesus's humanness (Heb 4:15) and about atonement and sanctification through him (2 Cor 5:21; Heb 7:26–27; 9:14; 1 John 3:5), aided by the Torah requirements for sacrifices (1 Pet 1:19, tied to the defense of Jesus's innocence in vv. 22–23).

Staying on His Own Course

The temptations Jesus faced, according to the Gospels, were both particular to him and also like those facing all of us. That is, first, they were focused on derailing or reshaping his specific mission, but, second, they were also like the usual temptations faced by humanity and thus showed that he was made of the same stuff as we are.

First, then, the temptations of Jesus had to do with whether and how he would carry out his particular mission: he was tempted to use his position as God's Son for the popular or spectacular quick fix (Matt 4:3, 5–6; 27:40, 43; Luke 11:16; 23:39), he was tempted to self-aggrandizement at the cost of loyalty to his mission (Matt 4:8–9), and he was tempted to abandon the course that was leading to his crucifixion (Matt 16:21–23).

---

35. So, e.g., Yoder, *Pacifist Way of Knowing*, 29. Another way of thinking about the sinlessness of Jesus in narrative terms is seen in, e.g., Drown, "Growth of the Incarnation." It is as Jesus grows up and is "made perfect through suffering" that God is revealed; Jesus required "struggle and temptation in the attainment of his positive righteousness. To make that righteousness a necessary result of his sinless endowment would be to unmoralize his life" (Drown, "Growth of the Incarnation," 517). For Jesus to "help those who are tempted" (Heb 2:18)—for him to be our model in that regard—his temptations must have been real, must have presented real options to him. And without real temptation there cannot be real righteousness (Drown, "Growth of the Incarnation," 519–20).

36. We need to be careful not to read that defense with the assumptions of modern jurisprudence. Pilate could afford to do the prudent thing (like Caiaphas in John 11:49–50), so any critique we might make of his decisions in regard to Jesus are off the mark.

REDEMPTION 143

Jesus's disciples often aided the devil in this sort of temptation. Repeatedly, after Jesus told (or retold) them of his coming crucifixion, they showed that they either did not understand or did not accept his mission:[37]

predictions of the cross		temptations	
the first[38]	Matt 16:21	Peter, representing Satan, rebukes Jesus.	Matt 16:22-23
	Mark 8:31		Mark 8:32-33
an extra	Matt 17:12	The disciples are unable to carry out their mission of healing.	Matt 17:16-17, 20 (cf. 10:8)
the second	Matt 17:22-23	The disciples' competitiveness comes out.	Matt 18:1
	Mark 9:31		Mark 9:33-34
	Luke 9:44		Luke 9:46
the third	Matt 20:17-19	The disciples are again competitive.	Matt 20:20-22
	Mark 10:32-34		Mark 10:35-39
an extra	Matt 26:2	The disciples put almsgiving above recognizing Jesus's sacrifice.	Matt 26:8-9
an extra	Luke 22:22	The disciples are competitive.	Luke 22:24[39]

Then in Gethsemane Jesus prays three times (Matt 26:39, 42, 44; Mark 14:35, 36, 39; only twice in Luke 22:42, 44; also Heb 5:7) because he is tempted to abandon his mission, and his disciples are again of no help.[40] He is mostly silent at his trial (Matt 26:63; 27:12, 14; Mark 14:61; 15:5; Luke 23:9; John 19:9), and on the cross he rejects the sarcastic advice to draw on his privileges as God's Son to save himself (Matt 27:39-44; differently in Mark 15:29-32; Luke 23:35, 39).

37. John 13:8 picks up characteristics of two of the Synoptic passages: Peter rebukes Jesus, as in Matt 16 and Mark 8; Jesus insists on his role as servant, as in Matt 22 and Mark 12.

38. All three of the particular formal predictions of the cross appear in all three Synoptic Gospels, but Luke varies in whether what I call the "temptations" are joined to the predictions. On these three predictions and their settings see further chapter 10 below, under "Metaphors for Followers."

39. After all this, Luke 22:28 seems tongue-in-cheek.

40. Note these links in the Gethsemane accounts to other temptation passages: (1) "Pray that you do not enter into temptation" (positioned differently in regard to the three Gethsemane prayers, Matt 26:41; Mark 14:38; Luke 22:40, 46), recalling the Lord's Prayer, "Lead us not into temptation" (Matt 6:13; Luke 11:4). (2) "An angel appeared from heaven to him and strengthened him" (Luke 22:43), recalling the angel of Matt 4:11.

It can seem that these temptations had primarily to do with suffering, which Jesus could have avoided by the devil's suggested different way to fame. Suffering loomed before Jesus in Gethsemane and did certainly occur on the cross.[41] But such a view of his temptations may rely too much on the significance of suffering. One can sin and suffer (1 Pet 2:19-20). Jesus's suffering was significant as a result of his following through on the method of kenosis, of complete submission to the will of God and to absorbing what humans could do to him rather than fighting back. It was specifically in holding to that course to and through the cross that Jesus was sinless (John 10:18; 1 Pet 2:22-23). He was totally committed to obeying God and fulfilling his particular mission (John 4:34; 15:10). He followed the pattern of kenosis by his subjection to the will of his Father.[42]

Staying on the Human Course

But, second, Jesus was "tempted in all things, just like us" (paraphrasing Heb 2:10). He is of the same stuff as we are (vv. 11, 17). It was only as human that he might defeat the devil (v. 14). So Hebrews 2:18: "since he suffered by being tempted, he can help those who are being tempted," which refers not just to sympathy or spiritual aid (cf. 4:15) but also to the necessity that the redeemer be a tempted human. That is, "he can aid the tempted" by pioneering the new humanity through the thicket of his own temptations.[43]

---

41. So, e.g., Shuster, "Temptation, Sinlessness, and Sympathy," 205: "the possibility that his mission could be carried out without suffering, that all this pain was not only terrible but unnecessary."

42. Cf. Aquinas, *Summa Theologiae* III.20.1.

43. "By suffering for us He not only provided us with an example for our imitation, He blazed a trail" (*Gaudium et Spes* 22). In *Smyrneans* 4.2 Ignatius wants his own suffering to be "in the name of Jesus Christ, so that I suffer together with him. I endure all things because the one who makes me able is the complete human (*ho teleios anthrōpos*)" (my translation; see chapter 10 below, under "Perfection," on *teleios*). Similarly, Jesus "offered himself to be tempted in order that he might be also a mediator in overcoming temptations, not only by helping but also by example" (Augustine, *On the Trinity* 4.13[17]). The "blazing of the trail" includes Jesus's submission to the baptism of repentance (Matt 3:11-15) according to, e.g., Aquinas, *Summa Theologiae* III.15.1: "A penitent can give a praiseworthy example, not by having sinned, but by freely bearing the punishment of sin. And hence Christ set the highest example to penitents, since He willingly bore the punishment, not of His own sin, but of the sins of others."

Just as we go to Jesus for an understanding of God rather than beginning from a general understanding of God,[44] so also with the humanness of Jesus: rather than bringing an understanding of humanness to our task of understanding Jesus as a human,[45] we work toward an understanding of what it is to be human from our knowledge of Jesus. He is how we know about what is human.[46] From reflection on ourselves, we learn about humanness off-track. In Jesus we see what we cannot conceive of in ourselves: the continuation of God's human project.[47] I said earlier that sin is not part of the basic definition of humanness. In fact, the definition of humanness is Jesus, and as we learn about humanness from him, his sinlessness becomes part of a full understanding of humanness as part of God's "good" creation. He is the presentation of what we were created for and of what the future of the redeemed is, of, that is, our sanctification.

God's project in creating humans was not complete at the beginning. Jesus is "the final measure of the nature and destiny of humankind."[48] Apart from knowing him, we can hardly imagine "what we will be" when that destiny is fulfilled, but we know that we will be "like him" (1 John 3:2; cf. 1 Cor 13:12).

Humanity was protected from self-divinization and from self-destruction, and no doubt has been protected against those two ways of ending God's human project far beyond the stories in Genesis 1–11 that tell us about them.[49] But with Jesus there was something new: a human who cooperated with God's plan, who, that is, said no to the devil. So, in partial agreement with the ransom theory of the atonement, the devil *was* faced with what he did not expect, but with two differences: First, it was not so much Jesus's *divine* nature as his carrying through of *humanness* that hooked the devil. Second, it was not just Jesus alone. Jesus is the new

---

44. See chapter 2 above, under "Beginning with Jesus."

45. The method of biography. See Braaten and Jenson, *Christian Dogmatics*, 1:520.

46. On not bringing an anthropological a priori to christology, see Barth, *Church Dogmatics* 1/2:40, 44. *Gaudium et Spes* 22 again: "The truth is that only in the mystery of the incarnate Word does the mystery of man take on light. For Adam, the first man, was a figure of Him Who was to come [Rom 5:14], namely Christ the Lord. Christ, the final Adam, by the revelation of the mystery of the Father and His love, fully reveals man to man himself and makes his supreme calling clear."

47. "To find that true and essential nature of man, we have to look not to Adam the fallen man, but to Christ in whom what is fallen has been cancelled and what was original has been restored" (Barth, *Christ and Adam*, 75).

48. Braaten and Jenson, *Christian Dogmatics*, 1:525.

49. See chapter 5 above, under "Cain's Misinterpretation."

Adam, humanity beginning over again (1 Cor 15:45), and ultimately the devil is gagging not just on one person but on a vast crowd.

That Jesus succeeded where we fail is emphasized by the parallels between his temptations in Matthew 4 and Luke 4, the temptations Eve faced, and those that humanity in general faces according to 1 John 2:16:

Jesus's temptations (taking them in the order in Luke 4:3–12)	1. hunger	2. a vision of the authority and glory of kingdoms	3. testing God
Eve's temptations in Gen 3:6	1. The forbidden fruit is "good for food."	2. The fruit is "a delight for the eyes."	3. The fruit can "make one wise," that is, "like God, knowing good and evil" (v. 5).
"all that is in the world" (1 John 2:16)	1. "desires of the flesh"	2. "desires of the eyes"	3. "pride of life"[50]

So Jesus, facing similar challenges at the beginning of his mission to those faced by Adam and Eve (who were "all humanity": see chapter 5 above) as their mission began, succeeds where those first humans failed. He stayed on the course of being human and did not fall prey to what took them and all of us off that course. The snake/devil made his speech to Jesus as he had to Eve, but he gained no ground. Jesus is therefore the complete human, not only "the image of the invisible God, the firstborn of all creation" (Col 1:15) but also "the eschatological Adam," the human who made a fresh start for humanity (1 Cor 15:45).[51]

The temptations of Jesus also parallel those faced by Israel during the wilderness wanderings (Exodus–Deuteronomy):

Jesus's temptations	1. hunger	2. the glory of kingdoms	3. testing God
the Israelites in the wilderness	hunger (Deut 8:3; Exod 16:3–4; Ps 106:14)[52]	seeking a God who is shinier (Exod 32:1–6; Ps 106:21)	testing the LORD (Exod 17:7; Deut 6:16; Pss 95:8–9; 106:14)

---

50. Observation of the parallel sets of three dates back to Augustine and extends also into the three theological virtues (the Pauline trio of faith, hope, and love), Augustine's description of three kinds of people (e.g., *Confessions* 27.4; see chapter 7 above, under "The Joy of Knowing"), three of the four cardinal virtues (which are prudence, courage, temperance, and justice), and almsgiving, prayer, and fasting, the three life-disciplines that Jesus (in Matt 6) shows can be enrolled in the forces of human pride and one-upmanship. See Greer, "Sighing for the Love of Truth," 23.

51. See further Barth, *Church Dogmatics* 1/2:126, 129.

52. See chapter 5 above, under "What Sin Is," on the exodus generation's distrust

There are other parallels, which make it even clearer that we are to connect Jesus's temptations with Israel in the wilderness:

Deut 8:2	God led Israel		"in the wilderness	for forty years	that he might humble you, testing you to know what was in your heart, whether you would keep his commandments or not."
Luke 4:1–2	Jesus was led by the Spirit	and fasted	in the wilderness	for forty days	so that the devil could test him over against God's purposes for him.
Exod 34:28; Deut 9:9	Moses	fasted	while Israel was in the wilderness	forty days and nights	as he received the law.
Deut 9:18	Moses	fasted	while Israel was in the wilderness	forty days and nights	as he bore the sins of the people.

Furthermore, both Israel's and Jesus's identity as "S/son of God" are connected with their temptations (Deut 8:5; Luke 3:22, 38–4:3, 9). So, here again, as with "all humanity," Jesus, facing similar challenges at the beginning of his mission to those faced by the people of Israel as their mission began, succeeds where they failed. Jesus stayed on course.

The New Beginning

Jesus provides that new beginning and brings along with him the great crowd of his disciples. He carried out his mission and accepted the way of the cross. In doing so, he was fully human, more human than you and I are. It was as God was "leading [us] to glory" that Jesus was being "completed *through* sufferings" (Heb 2:10), brought not only *through* childhood *to* adulthood but also *through* his disciples' misunderstandings and the cross *to* completion of his mission.

---

of God's provision. Jesus's response to the first of his temptations, "Not on the basis of bread alone will humankind live, but on the basis of every word coming from God's mouth" (Matt 4:4; Luke 4:4, quoting Deut 8:3), picks up on the creation context of the manna incident: the Israelites did not trust provision through the creating word but wanted to be provided for as they had been as slaves in Egypt (Exod 16:3; Num 11:4–5, 21:5).

For Irenaeus, the mission of Jesus is what we might call a "redo" of Adam and Eve.[53] As the first couple initiated humanity, so Jesus was the new/last Adam, the initiator of the new humanity. But while they gave in to temptation and were derailed from their mission, Jesus fought the devil and stayed on course.[54] Adam and Eve took us along with them on the course of rebellion against God, but Jesus brings us along with him in a new obedience in the Spirit. "As by the disobedience of the one man, who was originally molded from virgin soil, the many were made sinners and forfeited life; so was it necessary that, by the obedience of one man, who was originally born from a virgin, many should be justified and receive salvation."[55] Jesus has, "in his work of recapitulation, summed up all things, both waging war against our enemy and crushing him who had at the beginning led us away captives in Adam."[56] "He commenced afresh the long line of human beings, and furnished us, in a brief, comprehensive manner, with salvation; so that what we had lost in Adam—namely, to be according to the image and likeness of God—that we might recover in Christ Jesus."[57]

Or, in the language of an understanding of the atonement as sacrifice, Jesus offered up the once-for-all sacrifice by offering up himself (Heb 7:27; 9:26). From what we have seen in the Gospels about Jesus's

---

53. Irenaeus's term is *anakephalaiōsis*, "recapitulation," based on *anakephalaiōsasthai*, "to unite," in Eph 1:10. This idea was not completely original to Irenaeus, who drew on Paul, Ignatius, and Justin in this regard.

54. Whence the importance of Jesus being completely human and having "passed through every stage of life" (Irenaeus, *Against Heresies* 3.18.7). *Gaudium et Spes* follows the course set by Irenaeus but places Jesus's perfection before his temptation rather than after: He "entered the world's history as a perfect man, taking that history up into Himself and summarizing it" (*Gaudium et Spes* 38).

55. *Against Heresies* 3.18.7; similarly 3.21.10, etc.

56. *Against Heresies* 5.21.1.

57. *Against Heresies* 3.18.1. Thus Irenaeus is again helpful in retaining the story structure of our understanding of creation and redemption. As we have seen, the unity of creation and redemption was an essential part of his response to the Christian Gnostics, for whom the fundamental human problem was creation, not sin. He responded that the creator of the physical world and the redeemer are one and the same God, that redemption does not save us from the creator's sin or mistake but completes the creator's purpose (see chapter 1 above, under "The Unity of the Story"). And Irenaeus's commitment (along with that of others) to Christian retention of the Hebrew Scriptures and to the unity of the creator and the redeemer served as a counterweight to the impassible God of the philosophers (see chapter 2, under "God the Impassible"). And the understanding of the fall as also part of the one story of creation and redemption (chapter 5, under "The Fall Is Part of the Creation-Redemption Story") also owes much to Irenaeus.

many temptations and his anticipation of the cross, we know that such use of sacrifice language speaks of more than his death. It is in the whole course of Jesus's cooperation with God, his acceptance and carrying out of his mission, that he offers up himself. The sacrifice metaphor includes the cross, but is not restricted to the cross (Heb 9:14; 1 Pet 1:18–19, etc.).

Jesus did not face down the devil so that we do not have to, any more than he went to a cross so that any of us can avoid the cross that he tells us to take up.[58] But "he learned obedience from what he suffered, and having (thus) been completed, he became the source of eternal salvation for all those who obey him" (Heb 5:9–10). And just as we carry the image of the first human, "the man of dust," so we are coming to bear "the image of the man of heaven" (1 Cor 15:49; cf. Rom 5:14–18; more about that in chapter 10 below).

THE POWERS ARE DEFEATED

Jesus, Warrior and Son

Jesus was not dragged kicking and screaming "into the wilderness to be tempted by the devil."[59] Rather, he went as a warrior eager for battle. "He was led [by the Spirit into the wilderness] not against his will or as a captive, but by a desire for the fight."[60]

But this warrior was not some sort of supercop or he-man. We should not overemphasize or get hung-up on any advantages he took into the battle. Indeed, as I have mentioned, he treated such advantages, which the devil associated with the title "Son of God" (Matt 4:3, 6; Luke 4:3; 9; cf. Matt 27:40, 43), as themselves temptations to deviate from his mission. It was as one who is tempted and therefore "weak"—that is, all too human—that Jesus was most in tune with his mission (Isa 53:4–5; Luke 22:38; Phil 2:7–8; Heb 2:18; 4:15; 5:2). Unlike the superhuman or mechanical-marvel heroes of popular culture, Jesus, after a forty-day fast,

---

58. Matt 16:24; Mark 8:34; Luke 9:23. See chapter 10 below, under "The Cross-Bearer." Why do we sing songs in church that say that Jesus "bore (or 'bears') my cross for me"? What is meant might be correct, but the expression certainly obscures Jesus's "take up your cross."

59. As Mark 1:12 is sometimes read (e.g., Hooker, *Mark*, 49) because it uses *ekballein*, a verb also used in exorcism accounts, e.g., Mark 1:34, 39. Other uses of the verb (e.g., Matt 9:38; Mark 1:43) make it clear that little more need be implied than what Matthew and Luke say with "led by the Spirit" (Matt 4:1; Luke 4:1).

60. Jerome according to Aquinas, *Catena Aurea*, on Matt 4.

was simply hungry (Luke 4:2) and did not either drop names to the maître d' or perform miracles to hurry along dinner.

Jesus is called "God's Son" also by the heavenly voice, though without the devil's "*if* you are . . ." He thus receives from heaven both encouragement before and congratulations after his triumph: "You are my beloved Son, in whom I am pleased" or words to that effect,

after he has been baptized and before he goes into the wilderness to be tempted:	Matt 3:17; Mark 1:11; Luke 3:22
after he has withstood temptation by Peter (Matt 16:22–23; Mark 8:32–33) and has affirmed Peter's place in the inner circle (Matt 17:1; Mark 9:2):	Matt 17:5; Mark 9:7; Luke 9:35; 2 Pet 1:17
as he faces death (John 12:23–25, 27–28, 31):	John 12:28[61]

The affirmation that Jesus is in fact God's Son comes from the Father as Jesus moves his mission forward by stepping away from what the devil wants him to think of as privileges of that sonship. This choice between two ways of being God's Son might be thought of as the decisive event of kenosis, even more than the cross is, and thus as the center, the hinge-point, of the story of our creation and redemption.

Tying Up the Strong Man

When Jesus is accused of being in league with the powers of darkness (Luke 11:15-23, paralleled in Matt 12:24-30; Mark 3:20-27), he explains his work of defeating the devil and freeing us from the devil. A man has come along who does not speak because of a demon inside him. The man is imprisoned and the demon is the jailer. So when the demon is sent packing by Jesus, the man is freed and speaks (Luke 11:14 and the parallels). Some of those who witness this seem confused (v. 15): "He expels demons by Beelzebul, the prince of demons." Their illogic, pointed out by Jesus, shows that they oppose Jesus but do not know how to make sense of what is happening.

His response begins with a proverbial description of the confused state that they apparently think the devil's realm is in (11:17-18). He also speaks of their own sons exorcising demons (v. 19). Better than trying

---

61. Cf. Matt 12:18; John 5:37; 6:27; and the same sort of heavenly affirmation, now because Jesus has "loved righteousness and hated wickedness," Heb 1:9. He is not named as "God's Son" in John 12:28, but he has named the Father twice in the context (vv. 27, 28).

to identify those "sons," we should hear Jesus throwing his questioners' confusion back at them and rubbing in the point of the non sequitur of Beelzebul casting out his own demons: "How would *your own* family survive such division?" To their criticism, Jesus suggests that the confusion or illogic is not in Beelzebul's house (i.e., the devil's family) but in their own houses.

Having drawn the parallel between Beelzebul's house and their own, Jesus exploits it further:

- If Jesus is not in league with the devil but with God, then God is coming as king *against* Jesus's critics (taking *epi* in 11:20 in the same sense as the two instances of the preposition in vv. 17–18; cf. 10:19).
- If Beelzebul's house (now his dwelling place) is being ransacked, as in the exorcism they have just witnessed, then apparently someone stronger than Beelzebul, Jesus himself, has come against Beelzebul (vv. 21–22).
- If the critics are not on Jesus's side, then they are opposed to him (v. 23), with the implication that, as he has done with Beelzebul, Jesus will defeat them and ransack their houses as well.

The Methods of His Warfare

Luke 11:21–22 mixes battle language into the parable of the householder being tied up and robbed (unlike the parallels, Matt 12:29 and Mark 3:27). Battle language is so commonly used in the New Testament for the conflict between Jesus and Satan's realm (e.g., in the book of Revelation) that we hardly think it metaphorical to speak of "spiritual warfare."[62] But it is metaphorical: Jesus does not meet the devil on the devil's terms, and they do not approach each other with similar weapons.

We see the disparity in an odd thing about the battle scenes in Revelation: the battle is always over before it begins. There is no description of the battle because there is no battle. The foes approach, and the side of evil falls before they make contact (Rev 12:7–8; 16:14–19; 19:11–21). The choice of weapons is also odd: the believers conquer their accuser "by the Lamb's blood and the word of their testimony" (12:10–11). As Jesus leads his army into battle his "sword" is what he says (it "comes from his

---

62. So also with courtroom language and "final judgment."

mouth," 19:15). So even where battle language is used, the metaphor has to be twisted around some to accommodate the truth of Jesus's so-called "victory."

God has defeated the powers of evil by means that appear paradoxical in our world because of the understanding of power that exists in this world, which is under the control of "the powers." God did not defeat the powers by exercising power, which would be to grant the truth of the lie told by the powers, which is that exercising power is all that can matter. That lie is what I have called (in chapter 2) "what makes sense to us, what determines the resolution of human stories." God defeated the powers, instead, by kenosis—by sticking to his decision not to use violence or coercion. He has kept his commitment to that decision as far as the cross.[63] And "the cross cannot be defeated, for it is Defeat."[64]

We might picture another kind of typical scene (you have seen this in movies) being twisted around. The big strong man wades into a fight and says "The violence stops here!" But this time he does not knock heads together to make his point or to hint at what he is capable of. Instead Jesus steps into the fight and says "The violence stops here! But not because I am stronger and therefore more effectually violent than everyone else but because I am weak and I absorb violence without returning it, without becoming violent in return, which is the normal human way of doing." "He was insulted, but he did not return it in kind. He suffered, but he made no threats and gave himself to the one who judges justly." That is how "he carried our sins in his body on the tree" (1 Pet 2:23-24).

As we saw in chapter 2, this follows the pattern of creation:

In creation	Similarly, in redemption
God placed limits on the exercise of his sovereignty	God in Christ "emptied himself"
(though he still had all his sovereignty),	(though he still possessed all that he had before),
to create those who could love him.	to restore our freedom to love him.
He thus exercised his sovereignty over the eschatological end of the story.	He will therefore be recognized eschatologically as Lord by all.

---

63. Where Christ is, God is, so it is God—all of God—who accomplishes atonement. The actions of God *ad extra* involve the whole Trinity.

64. The words of McIan, a central character in Chesterton, *Ball and the Cross*, 207.

God's paradoxical method is thus the accomplishment of his will by surrender. This is the one battle in which the victor has neither become like the enemy nor taken up the enemy's methods, unlike all our wars. God accomplishes his goals by means that allow the exercise of the human freedom to reject him and even to kill him. God has consistently acted paradoxically, when judged by the standards of the powers and by the human standards for story construction, which are one and the same, thus proving that both are wrong.

But What Is the Theory?

Therefore, "the cure for evil is suffering."[65] By "not returning evil for evil" (Rom 12:17) but meeting evil with suffering, Jesus deprived the universe of any symmetry in the meeting of good and evil.

> The gospel is not about delegitimizing violence so much as about overcoming it. We overcome it partly by demythologizing its moral pretensions,[66] partly by refusing to meet it on its own terms, partly by replacing it with other more humane strategies and tactics of moral struggle, partly by innocent suffering, and partly by virtue of the special restorative resources of forgiveness and community. Yet all of those coping resources are derivative. At bottom violence is judged—*critiqued* in the deep sense of the verb—because of the passion events.[67]

Along with any honor we give to the traditional theories of the atonement, we should also say that the cross works because it throws a wrench into the works of the human habit of meeting evil or violence with the same, thus bringing it to a halt.

But is it not odd that we say anything like "the cross works"? Does that mean that we have applied some sort of effectiveness criterion and found that Jesus dying accomplishes whatever our objective is? Then perhaps our theology is like Caiaphas's political pragmatics (John 11:49–50; 18:14). We should be careful of expressions like "the power of the cross" because they might be validating the cross by some sort of effectiveness test, and, more obviously, because we have received those very words, "the power of the cross," from the same context in which Paul tells us

---

65. Yoder, *War of the Lamb*, 54, summarizing Tolstoy's understanding of the gospel.
66. See chapter 7 above, under "Fear Not."
67. Yoder, *War of the Lamb*, 41; cf. 54–56, 207n16.

that God's power is nothing like what we think of as power. That "power," God's power, would be canceled out were Paul to try to advertise it with "words of eloquent wisdom." It is, rather broadcast by a "word" (Paul's actual preaching) that looks just plain stupid to those who do not receive it (1 Cor 1:17–18, 21, 23–24). When we speak of God's "power," we are likely to be misunderstood, as if we were referring to something more powerful than Anthony Joshua and the United States Navy rather than something that could also be called "the weakness of God" (v. 25).[68]

The cross is not a battle banner but a lousy way to die.[69] It is the cross most completely when it leads nowhere, where it makes no sense, where it is futile, apparent futility being one sure sign of the stupidity spoken of in 1 Corinthians 1. This applies to and perhaps even negates theories of the atonement as well, since they are about what the cross *accomplishes* and about *our understanding* of how it accomplishes that, our understanding being another form of that stupidity in the eyes of those who do not receive the word of the cross.

A similar way in which the criterion of effectiveness invades our thinking is how quickly we sometimes try to find meaning or consolation in misfortune or tragedy. "It was for the best that. . . ." "What God was doing in these awful circumstances. . . ." Part of suffering is lack of what we call "meaning." The futility of suffering helps us remove our faith from understanding, which is, again, possibly no more than a form of foolishness, and transfer it to God, and take our hopes away from "meaning" and transfer them to the one hope that God will be glorified, and let that be enough.[70] What is "of ultimate importance" is "that the reality of God show itself everywhere to be the ultimate reality."[71] "Suffering love is not right because it 'works' in any calculable short-run way (although it often does). It is right because it goes with the grain of the universe, and that is why *in the long run* nothing else will work."[72]

---

68. See above, under "Gospel Stupidity."

69. That it came to be used as a battle banner is just plain weird and a serious hindrance to any Christian testimony in succeeding centuries.

70. This is a good part of the burden of Hessert, *Christ and the End of Meaning*, as opposed to books that cater to our mania for "meaning," even while perhaps steering it in gospel directions, such as Chaddick and Borlase, *Better*.

71. Bonhoeffer, *Ethics*, 48.

72. Yoder, *War of the Lamb*, 62.

The Reversal That Is Not Really a Reversal

The key that unlocks the path from conflict to resolution in nearly all stories is the finding and using of some means of power by which the hero, heroine, or heroic people reaches the goal that is the story's resolution. Power in some form is the one thing that allows the story to be moved to its completion. It is the ability to control something, or quite often someone, outside oneself. If I determinatively influence, change, stop, or start the actions of someone else to conform to or carry out my will, then I am exercising power. Normal stories respond to and encourage an understanding of myself and others in which the getting and exercise of power is central.[73]

The dominant pattern of the biblical story, the story that Christians believe, goes in quite a different direction. It is by refusing to use power that God (and God's people, as we will see) move toward the end of the story. This is completely counter to what humans believe is natural and logical. It is this unnaturalness of the story of creation and redemption that is so hard to accept, grasp, and retain and that has so often gotten Christians searching for expressions of the gospel that are versions of a more normal story of finding and using power but that are not true to the gospel.[74]

God sent the one by whom he created everything,

> but perhaps he sent him, as one might suppose, to rule by tyranny, fear, and terror? Certainly not! On the contrary, he sent him in gentleness and meekness, as a king might send his son who is a king; he sent him as God; he sent him as a human to humans. When he sent him, he did so as one who saves by persuasion, not compulsion, for compulsion is no attribute of God. When he sent him, he did so as one calling, not pursuing; when he sent him, he did so as one loving, not judging.[75]

The defeat of the powers by means of the cross and resurrection of Jesus brings a reversal of what is expected or normal. The myth of power is rejected:

- "Many that are first will be last, and the last first" (Matt 19:30).
- "Those who humble themselves will be lifted up" (Luke 14:11).

73. See chapter 4 above, under "For the One Story."
74. See chapter 10 below, under "False Endings."
75. *To Diognetus* 7.3–5, as translated in Holmes, *Apostolic Fathers*, 707.

- "Whoever loses his life will keep it" (Matt 10:39).
- Those who mourn a loss that others only gloss over are those who receive God's comfort (Matt 5:4).
- They move from frustration to certitude (Romans 7–8).
- And they grasp salvation not by grasping resources they already have: in this way Paul in Philippians 3:7–11 is like Jesus in Philippians 2:6 (and cf. Luke 14:33).

We can speak of all this as a principle of reversal that is basic to the creation-redemption story. But in the meek inheriting the earth or the last becoming first we discover what has been true from the beginning. This apparent reversal or paradox is how we are brought out of the false myth of power and into the true physics of creation.

9

How the Odd Story Converts Us

FAITH

Divine Kenosis

THERE HAS BEEN A question hanging about the premises, somewhat like the pachyderm in the parlor, perhaps as early as chapter 2. When we speak of kenosis as submission to the will of another, can we name that "other"? Of whom does Jesus make himself the slave according to Philippians 2:7? Whose slaves do we become if we follow him in kenosis? Two easy, "when in doubt" Sunday-school answers, are confirmed by Paul as he calls himself "a slave *of Christ Jesus*" (Rom 1:1; Phil 1:1) and as he explains at some length how he has "enslaved [himself] to *all*" (1 Cor 9:19) for the sake of his preaching of the gospel.

Here the focus will be on two other answers, which are possibly even more vague but are clearly connected to the meaning of kenosis for all of us as those who are redeemed by Jesus. The first is simply "the other." If we take the advice in Philippians 2:3–4, which of course leads into the kenosis of Jesus in v. 7, spotting the "others" and their needs becomes first priority.

The second answer takes us back into the heart of how Jesus accomplished our redemption. He followed his own counsel in Matthew 5:39: "Don't fight back against the evil one." Let "the evil one" have his way. "The evil one" is whoever insists on his or her own way, including the devil but not only the devil. So Jesus lets the devil and other opponents have their own way rather than calling down fire or angels to defend himself or his honor (Matt 26:51–54; Luke 9:52–55). There is the fishhook of the resurrection, so the devil does not win in the end, but the way to that end is the way of submission to the cross. Or sometimes, as we adopt Jesus's methods, it is for us a way more annoying than deadly, such as letting ecclesiastical pains in the neck have their way.

In the same way, God holds out salvation to us, but continues to follow the kenotic model by not forcing the issue. He submits to the will of the other, of "the evil one," who is not only the devil but also you and me. Salvation is not forced. Salvation is for all, but all who hear the gospel are, by hearing it, given the freedom to accept or reject it.[1] It tells a story and asks "Now, is that your story, or are you going to stand outside it?"

Salvation is received, and while we sometimes speak of faith as a "requirement" for receiving it, how we hear that might mislead us. Faith does not open the door: it walks through a door that is already open. Salvation comes "by grace, through faith," but faith is a small thing next to grace in the redemption equation, as Ephesians 2:8 goes to some pains to remind us. Accepting one's place in the one story of creation and redemption is not a meritorious act. It is, rather, an acknowledgment of lack of merit, a giving up on oneself.

Redemption is universal, though the appropriation of it is not. God's goal of having his love returned still, as always, includes human freedom not to return God's love. So God's way of redeeming extends to how redemption is appropriated by individual humans: God does not override the human will. God continues to accomplish his goals by means that allow the exercise of the human freedom to reject him, even to kill him.[2]

Faith Comes by Hearing

It is, in fact, the story itself that makes the difference, which takes us back to what I said in chapter 1 about the "point" of the story. King David was changed when the prophet Nathan's story of the murderously greedy rich man became a story about himself, though not in the way he first imagined (2 Samuel 12). He had written the end of the story himself by following the normal pattern of justice and condemning the man, so he had

---

1. What of those who never hear? I, at least, have no ready answer, but the question is to some extent theoretical since it can be asked only by those to whom it does not pertain.

2. A universalist view of salvation eventually eliminates this freedom from the picture.

no argument when that man became himself. With this reversal of his role from judge to malefactor, the king might have learned about a new way of being king, not as an autocrat but as a lover of justice, even when it went against him. He perhaps began to learn about kenotic kingship, the ways of a ruler informed by the ways of God, a ruler who surrenders self-interest for love of "the least of my brothers" (Matt 25:40).

Repentance begins when the hearer enters the story of creation and redemption, when the hearer begins thus to exercise faith. The "point" of that odd story is the point at which it becomes a story about me. That is faith. "The kingdom of God"—more exactly, the manner in which God rules—is as odd as a mustard seed that grows into a tree (Matt 13:31–32): mustard seeds simply do not produce trees. It is as odd as neglecting ninety-nine sheep to find one (18:12).[3] Ditto the foolishness of preaching and faith (1 Corinthians 1 again): who could have imagined that this unworthy thing would lead to salvation?[4]

Jesus's parables work in the same way as Nathan's parable: it is as a parable takes on the specificity of a story about me, that is, when its "point" is discovered, when I discover my real role in it, that it can call for repentance. The intention of the parables is to "bless" the hearers by "turning them away from wickedness" (Acts 3:26). That is, the intention is to *convert* the hearers.

The hearers of a parable are judged by the manner of their hearing. Some gain by their hearing, and others lose (Matt 13:11–13, 19, 23). It is only with the passage of time that it becomes apparent which is which (v. 30). The "children of the kingdom" (the "righteous") and the "children of the evil one" (the "stumbling blocks and doers of lawlessness") are indistinguishable until the judgment (vv. 38–43, 49). But now Jesus seeks hearers who will drop everything for the *one* thing (vv. 44–46).

There is thus for each hearer a movement farther in the direction indicated by that person's hearing of the parable, be that toward conversion or toward stubborn refusal. This confirmation of a person's direction can look like a reversal: "I came into this world for judgment, so that those who don't see can see, and so that those who do see will become

---

3. Some older commentaries are quick to say that the other sheep are not neglected. E.g., Alford, *Greek Testament*, 1:584; more recently, Keener, *Matthew*, 452. But placing the parables in their cultural context need not mean adding to their content to make them other than laughable or shocking in that context. If the ninety-nine were looked after, why mention that the shepherd left them? So, e.g., Craddock, *Luke*, 185; Huffman, "Atypical Features," 211.

4. See chapter 8 above, under "Gospel Stupidity."

blind" (John 9:39). This is so because "seeing," that is, knowledge of how religious discourse is supposed to work, can get in the way of "seeing" in the sense of following the converting path of the parable. Knowledge is fine, but shrinks to nothing next to love (1 Cor 13:2, 8), and this is not the love that is easy but the hard love of fellow church members and other enemies. Not that positively responding disciples understand everything immediately. Far from it (Matt 15:17; 16:9, 11; Mark 4:13; Luke 18:34).

JUSTIFICATION

Who Is Justified?

Hearing a parable can thus raise the question "Which character in this story is like you?" and then turn the tables on the hearer, as in the parable of the Pharisee and the tax collector (Luke 18:10–14). Two men, who are different from each other, pray, and then one comes away from praying "justified" and the other does not. The difference between the two going into the story is that the Pharisee is likely to be respected by the audience, and for the same reasons that he respects himself (vv. 11–12), and the other is not respected. One is a good Jew, and the other is a bad Jew. But the difference is different coming out of the story because they have opened themselves to God's opinion by going to pray. Then the second man, who is a tax collector and therefore despised, is justified, and the Pharisee, whom the hopefully righteous in the audience have identified with from the beginning, is not justified (v. 14).

We use the word "justified" to judge a person's actions, often taking into account the prior actions of other people:

- "Am I *justified* in doing this?"
- "Do his past actions *justify* my avoiding any further dealings with him?"
- "Is it right for us to sue them for all they're worth? That is, are we *justified* in doing that?"

Here, "justified" means morally acceptable or permissible, and we apply it to people as well as actions: my actions are justified, or I am justified. It is what we respond with when we are accused, criticized, or ridiculed. If my justification of myself and my actions is accepted, then I need say nothing more, and my critics can say nothing more.

But it is different when we speak of being accepted by God. Paul used "justified" in that sense (e.g., Rom 3:20–4:8) and made it clear that a person being justified—accepted by God—is not dependent on his or her actions being justified. Instead, being justified before God is something received as a gift (3:23–24). Justification in that sense comes by God's grace, by way of the death of Jesus, to those who have faith in Jesus.

That in itself may not have been in question. Rather, for some of the people who received Paul's letters the issue was whether they should adopt some or all of the practices required in the Law of Moses—not to gain God's acceptance but to maintain their possession of it. But Paul sought to neutralize any such distinction between achieving and maintaining justification (Gal 4:9; 5:1–4).

We can say that Jesus's story about the Pharisee and the tax collector sets these two uses of "justified," that of justified actions and that of acceptance by God, over against each other.[5] The first man, as far as most Jews would have been concerned, is justified by his actions, by his way of living, and the second is not. The Pharisee is good, the tax collector is not. It would be easier to excuse any bad behavior on the part of the good man than to excuse the whole evil life of the tax collector. But the Pharisee, though he is justified as far as he himself and people like him are concerned, he is not justified before God. It is a very different thing to be judged by ourselves or our neighbors than to be judged by God.

What makes the difference is how the two men pray. The first prayer *claims* justification—acceptance by God, the second *leads to* justification. The man who claims everything receives nothing, and vice versa. God chooses the sinner's prayer, the prayer that claims nothing, to be that which he accepts. The terms God has set for his acceptance of people take into account something altogether other than morality and religious observance. God has chosen those who pray the tax collector's prayer.

Which is shocking, even to Christians, perhaps most to Christians. Perhaps the best way to understand how most Christians have thought about such things is to picture someone in Jesus's audience asking "Then what happened the next day, specifically with the tax collector? Did he give up tax collecting? If so, then did he pray in the temple a year later and say 'God, I thank you that you brought me out of that evil business, that I am no longer like my cousin Harry, who is still in the tax collecting business'? Did his prayers start to take into account his improved life?

---

5. Though the language is not as Pauline as it may first appear to be.

Did they change from being the sinner's prayer to something more like the Pharisee's prayer?" Or what if the question from the audience is "Was the tax collector able to *maintain* his justification once he got it? What did he have to do *next*?"[6]

But the story does really end with Jesus's pronouncement that the tax collector was justified. It is God who justified the tax collector, and if justification requires any maintenance, it will come in the same manner as justification came in the first place, by God's acceptance of the person who prays the sinner's prayer today, tomorrow, and every next day until the end of life. Everything the most sanctified Christian saint has comes from the sinner's prayer, not because that person has prayed it once but because it has become his or her continual prayer.[7] We never come to the point where the rules are returned to the human normal; God does not in the end start assessing people in the ways that we do.

Jesus is insistent on this. His story of the prodigal and his brother and father (Luke 15:11–32) is like the story of the Pharisee and the tax collector: the party is for the one who repents, not for the one who has no need to repent (cf. 15:7). The repeated "they have their reward" in Matthew 6 (vv. 2, 5, and 16) means that those who are justified according to their own standards, like the Pharisee in the parable, thereby set themselves outside the one story. They have reached their end already and therefore have no eschatology and no story.

Whose Justification?

As I mentioned in the last subsection of chapter 6, justification appears to be a fundamental human need. Pursuing it takes up much of our time and energy. It is a need to consider oneself right, and it has to be understood ultimately as a rejection of God's judgment and God's grace. It is a constant attempt to substitute "justification" in the sense of moral acceptability for "justification" in the sense of acceptance by God, reaching for our righteousness rather than God's (Rom 10:3).

The best understanding of sin says that if, for example, I come out of a dispute with someone and ask myself whether I did anything wrong, the answer is Yes, always Yes, and no amount of comparing my supposed

---

6. What did another tax collector do the day after he had been called by Jesus? He went to a party with his old and his new friends (Matt 9:9–13).

7. This is in essence what Gal 3 says. It is also the basis for the repeated use of the "Jesus prayer," the prayer for mercy, in Orthodox devotional practice.

righteousness to that of the other person will change that, no matter how much of a jerk he is. In complicated situations, I am never completely pure in motive or action. That that is also true of the other person is not my business. The universality of sin applies to each of us in each and every day. There is more to sanctification than I know, but it is certainly a good general rule that we do not reach some level where the occupying power of sin has been flushed from all sides of all our interactions. The tax collector's prayer does not become obsolete, which means that the rules I want to follow when I ask whether I did anything wrong in a situation do not count, so I may as well not ask. If I imagine that anything I do can be a substitute for the tax collector's prayer—his "God, have mercy on this sinner!"—I am wrong.[8]

Augustine spoke of "that affection of the mind that aims at the enjoyment of oneself and one's neighbor without reference to God," calling it "concupiscence." The opposite of concupiscence is love for God, living "with reference to God." Our love for God is weak or twisted because we do not have (nor do we want) a right understanding of God. We prefer what destroys us, which is lack of relationship with God. Beginning with Eve, we believe the lie that God is not committed to our welfare and sustenance. Instead of receiving from God, we worry over what God is requiring of us, over whether he really wants to receive any person who comes in faith. We teach fear of non-Christian ideologies, we feel we must go to war to protect—to protect what?—we require of people something that has sometimes been called the "Protestant work-ethic," we give people spiritual disciplines that imply that we should be uneasy around God or that we are alienated from God because of our lack of effort or self-integration or because of our possession of bodies. We misinterpret the parable of the widow and the judge (Luke 18:2–7) to say that God is hard to get things from.

It is not that spiritual disciplines—perhaps better "life disciplines"—are valueless. Quite the opposite. But we do better if we undertake them to open ourselves to God, not to convince God or even ourselves of anything. We do them best because God is full of grace toward us, not as if we have to get something by all our work. Benedictine monks, for instance, turn from three central expressions of power (which is anxiety

---

8. And because that prayer is always accepted, it can be a way of departure from fear: "Throw yourself upon him. Do not fear. He will not pull away and let you fall. Throw yourself without fear, and he will receive you and heal you" (Augustine, *Confessions* 8.1).

for self): sex, individual choice, and possession. So celibacy, obedience, and poverty are ways of teaching oneself about renunciation of power, about taking up the way of kenosis, and about giving care for oneself over to God. If I do not seek sex, rights, or possessions, I can be more open to receive sustenance from God.

Self-Justification

Whenever a person tells a lie, the truth is there standing alongside the alternative that the liar wants others to believe or, in the case of self-deception, that the liar wants to believe. In the grand human deception that stands behind all our little deceptions, the truth is the fact of sin, and the lie, the desired alternative to the truth, is that I (or my group) have done good and *am* (or are) good, that I have my own righteousness (Rom 10:3).

To claim one's own righteousness is to erect a barrier against God's righteousness (again Rom 10:3). This is the effect, but it is also the *purpose* for claiming one's own righteousness: to be independent of God and his righteousness. Claiming to be good is how we run from God. It is the leafy aprons made by Adam and Eve (Gen 3:7). Adam and Eve fell not out of a desire to be bad but out of a desire to be independent of God. And once this independence was achieved (as far as it could be), the constant human practice of self-justification kicked in. Celebrating one's own goodness like the Pharisee in the temple (Luke 18) is a way of escaping from the reality of our universal sin and from God's annoying questions (Gen 3:9–13).

It is for this reason that the desire for justification is like hungering and thirsting. It drives us and permeates everything we do till we receive from God.[9] Until we do that, we examine our consciences only to see whether to count a particular situation as gain or loss in the matter of self-justification. (As an example, the answers found by that praying Pharisee in the temple fell on the gain side.) This kind of accounting relies too much on that faulty knowledge of good and evil that we picked up at the fall. It is subject, that is, to human deceitfulness, to our common lack of self-knowledge.

---

9. See the last paragraph of chapter 6, above, including note 38, on William Stringfellow's identification of the many different ways in which we seek to fulfill this drive to be justified, which "refute God's capability of love."

The *correct* answer is always "yes, I did sin," in every situation and circumstance. Even where I can say that someone else did something really bad, there I was still what I am, still one who does at least some things badly. And why should I make sin or lack thereof a matter of comparison, as the Pharisee in the temple did? The only reason for doing so is to make the whole topic of sin, of my standing before God, serve the desire for self-justification.

All good things and all goodness come from God. To be in right relationship with our creator is to receive good, not to (claim to) do or be any good that is our own. The desire for independence that led to the fall is expressed in a desire to believe oneself good, which saves us from having to receive good from God. So we deceive ourselves, and often part of this self-deception is a belief that that goodness of our own gets us closer to God. It does not. It only helps us avoid our need for God's goodness.

When the self-deception fails, as it did for that other man in the temple, the tax collector (Luke 18:13), despair is the result.[10] Despair feels like considerable distance from God. But that long distance is measured not from God but from righteousness of our own, from ourselves as little gods, in effect. Despair is much closer to God and *his* righteousness, his justification of a person, than one's own goodness can ever be (Luke 18:14a). As another tax collector and a certain unrespectable woman experienced (Luke 19:8–10; 7:36–50), one does real good out of gratitude, as part of receiving, not out of the old desire to *be* good, that is, to have one's own goodness.

So we must follow a paradoxical route to God and to goodness. It is paradoxical for us, but in the universe as God created it, it makes complete sense. Receiving good rather than achieving it seems unworthy to us (cf. Rom 9:19). God giving good rather than requiring it of us might seem like a bad way to run a moral universe, but that is only because we are misled by our constant effort to establish our independence of God. Knowledge of God in Christ is more important than doing good (Hos 6:6; Phil 3:8–10) and precedes doing good (Phil 3:9; 1 John 4:10, 19; Prov 1:7a). "Knowledge of good and evil" leads to shame, division, and death (Gen 2:16–17; 3:6–12, 21–24) and to knowledge of sin (Rom 3:19–20).

Our natural inclination is to be like the Pharisee praying in the temple. How natural? About like head up, feet down instead of trying to walk

---

10. Why a tax collector? Not because they were particularly bad people, but because they were despised. If we despise the Pharisee for being a Pharisee, then we are likely to get the story the wrong way around.

about the other way around. We do really have to be turned completely upside-down. Giving up self-justification is that unnatural, but it is really being turned right side up, being brought into line with how the universe works. That Pharisee's problem was not with his acts of righteousness. There was nothing wrong with his religion, even if we have been taught to dislike it. The problem was with his self-deception, his lack of comprehension of his sin, that is, of himself. The key message here is about justification, that is, that other justification, justification before God. It is reached through the tax collector's despairing prayer.

CONFESSION AND TESTIMONY

Retelling the Story as My Story

Redemption is appropriated by those who accept the confession of the community of redemption as their own. The confession is a recitation, in fact, of the one story of creation and redemption, where God has consistently acted paradoxically when judged by human standards. Conversion comes when a person understands that story as his or her own and thus rejects the standards of the powers and the lie that subjection to the powers is inevitable and unavoidable. It is for this reason that baptism, creed, and testimony have always come together.

The all-important question in revivalistic Christianity is "Do you have a testimony?" That focus is one reason that denominational distinctions have gradually (over two hundred years or more) become less significant. The line that distinguishes the authentic Christian cuts through denominations, nations, ethnicities, and languages and rests squarely, so it is understood, on having a testimony. If I can give my testimony, I can thereby interpret my life-story in the language of grace. I can identify myself by means of a personal narrative that is part of the grand narrative of God's creation and redemption of humanity in Jesus. My testimony is my adoption and personalization of the creedal narrative (Jesus died and rose *for me*) and is thus my ticket of admission to the baptismal water and the believing community. Augustine in the *Confessions* is as good an example as any.

Of course, like any other Christian practice, having a testimony to give is no guarantee against hypocrisy or self-deception. But it does set *appropriation* of redemption at the center, which is good. It is tied to the individualism of modernism, America, and the frontier, but not insolubly because it attaches the individual to the community by bonds of tradition, sentiment, and confessional statement. Sometimes a believer will feel bad that his or her testimony has nothing new, that it is just like testimonies that have been given countless times before. But it is actually a good thing to use well-worn language to understand and to give testimony to one's own experience. Thereby the believer identifies with those who have walked that path before and discovers that his or her story is like the stories of others and the story of the community as a whole.

Going Public and Uniting with the Community

My existence as a Christian begins when I confess, that is, when I agree with the gospel. Other ways of saying that are that I *believe* the gospel (Mark 1:15) or believe in Jesus (Matt 10:32; Luke 12:8; Acts 16:31) or in his resurrection (Rom 4:24; 10:9; 1 Pet 1:21) or confess that he is Lord (Rom 10:9; Phil 2:11), Messiah (John 9:22), and Son of God (1 John 4:15). The gospel tells of the coming, life, death, and resurrection of Jesus and of the salvation that is won by Jesus for those who believe. When I agree with the truth of that story, I become one of those who believe. And this confession is made publicly (Matt 10:32; Luke 12:8).

Agreement with the gospel is not something given with being human or being of any particular nationality, or something that comes natural for anyone. It is, in fact, though it is "the one story," an odd story, a story that runs counter to what being human (post-fall) causes us to expect as a normal or possible story.

That one story is all-encompassing and includes within it one's understanding and interpretation of everything. So there is never a boundary in my life or my thinking around what agreement with the gospel affects. Because the gospel makes a claim to everything, then everything is changed for me by my agreement with it. Therefore, believing the gospel entails repentance. Everything I do is now to be examined, changed, and reshaped by the gospel. My understanding of everything I experience or encounter is characterized by my faith—if, indeed, I have the faith I claim to have—in the gospel. I now interpret myself, my experiences, and the world through the gospel story.

Having thus begun by confession, I continue by my continuing testimony to the gospel, that is, by indicating my continuing agreement with the gospel and by giving my agreement personal specificity by naming the events that make up the narrative or process of my coming to and continuing in agreement. Thereby, I and the gospel interact to shape what I am. As the language of the gospel comes to be the language I use to describe myself and my experiences, then I not only interpret my experiences through the gospel story but also interpret the gospel story through my experiences. So my testimony shapes my ways of acting and thinking.

The community of those who believe is present alongside me in every step along the way. I have heard the gospel through the testimony of those who believed already before me, I understand the total claim of the gospel because of that testimony, I shape my testimony according to the language of that community, and I allow myself to be shaped by socialization into that community. My confession/testimony is the means by which I claim membership in that community. And ideally that is all that is needed. I need nothing else, such as social class or geographic origin, to be recognized as a bona fide member, though the community does have to decide regarding the validity of my confession according to standards it has developed by its own encounter with the gospel. Like those who believed before I did and through whose testimony I came to believe, I become an advocate for the gospel by my testimony, whether by the affirmations made in shared worship, by individual worship, by speaking to others about the gospel, or by action shaped by the story.

All that is a bit too much on the sunny side and perhaps gives too much credit to the wisdom of the community. Agreeing with the gospel is not given with being human, but it can nearly seem so because the Christian community gives us the words, forms, and context for doing so. The community can certainly make being a Christian far easier than any recognition that the gospel makes a claim to everything. It can make being Christian seem normal and can blind us to the connection, as in the book of Revelation (6:9; 11:7; 12:11; 17:6), of "the testimony" to martyrdom. We adapt our retrospective testimonies to the community's language and thus further affirm our identity with the group and become spokespersons for the group,[11] but that makes it neither easy for the community's discernment, especially where being a Christian has become normal or desirable,[12] nor a sure and certain way to become disciples of Jesus. When the community marks the path too clearly, it affirms its identity as an institution, as a "power," and identifies faith with conformity. "The

---

11. See Segal, *Paul the Convert*, 29; Jacobs, *Looking Before and After*, 35-40.

12. See Jacobs, *Looking Before and After*, 35-37, on how Jonathan Edwards and other eighteenth-century pastors confronted such questions about "the testimonial ritual."

institutional power to teach is [the] counterfoil" of obedience to the gospel, and the gospel enables me to "trust myself to walk on the surface, without being engulfed by institutional power. You certainly remember how Peter just walked out on the waves of the Lake of Genesareth on the Word of his Lord. As soon as he doubted, he began to go under."[13] This freedom can be terrifying, but it is where faith is clearest. So faith might often involve not conforming to the community, but then that could draw us into another long paragraph of consideration of the dangers of individualism. Such alternation between community and individual might be necessary, but for now the Book of Life is closed (Rev 20:12), and faith made certifiable would not be faith.

FREEDOM

Restored

A result of that first decision not to love God is that people believe that their captivity to sin is final and unending (though this is usually experienced as toleration of limits rather than as captivity). It is thus that we have become subject to the powers of evil. But those powers can only pretend to exist independently outside human sin. The inevitability of their power is itself a pretense, a lie, the myth by which unredeemed humanity lives. Nonetheless there is, for humanity in that state of subjection, no story, because a story requires freedom, exercise of will, and movement toward a new state.

As God carries out redemption, he restores to humanity freedom to return his love. He thus makes it possible for people to escape deception by the powers of evil, which is humanity's self-deception, and thus to regain a story understanding of their existence: movement is now possible. The atonement, however we might understand its working, is thus God's defeat of the power of sin and restoration of freedom to human wills that have been enslaved to those powers.

Human freedom, even restored by the atonement, is not absolute. The decision whether to appropriate redemption is strongly influenced, even though not completely determined, by such factors as whether a person was raised in a Christian home and community or never heard the gospel or was incapable of understanding it in even the simplest way.

---

13. Illich, "Educational Enterprise."

Human community, that place where God's image is most clearly seen, has also become the setting that keeps humans from choosing redemption. Again, completely determinative or completely insignificant are not the only possibilities for such influential factors. I am inclined to give some weight to New Testament suggestions that judgment is in accord with knowledge (Luke 10:13; 12:48; John 9:41; 12:48; 15:22, 24; 1 Tim 1:13; Heb 10:26–27; 2 Pet 2:21). Fortunately none of us needs to know precisely how to distinguish sheep and goats (Matt 25:31–33). That is a matter for God to deal with. And if there is any caprice in the distinction, it is not God's[14] but that of the world affected by human sin: all the hindrances in the way of a person's choice for salvation (their lack of freedom in that sense) are ultimately part of living in a world affected by sin.

To redeem, God makes "a new creation" (2 Cor 5:17; Rev 21:1). But by his grace the new creation includes the old. Redemption is not the sort of deal that God offered Moses (Exod 32:10), something like "I'll get rid of rebellious humanity and start over." God does not discard or destroy the old creation. The original goal, the existence of creatures who can love (and are therefore other wills), is still sought. The possibility that the human creature will not love God obviously still exists and is carried out. God carries out redemption, in fact, by restoring to humanity the freedom to return his love. Freedom thus restored is real freedom.

For Us and for Creation

Redemption frees us from Cain's misinterpretation so that we need no longer believe that God is against us and therefore have to take care of ourselves.[15]

Redemption frees us from the neglect of worship of our creator that goes hand-in-hand with worship of the created. It frees us from our habit of remaking God as Superman and from the alienation from God that is called spiritual "death."[16] It frees us from our misunderstanding of God as the stony-faced enforcer of rules to see him as the gracious father who breaks expectations and rules.[17]

---

14. See chapter 4 above, under "For Other Wills," on predestination.
15. See chapter 5 above, under "Cain's Misinterpretation."
16. See chapter 6 above, under "Death."
17. See chapter 8 above, under "Divine Illogic."

Redemption frees us from self-reliance, the need to self-justify, from false endings that gloss over the human habits of sin, and from the hard work that comes with "knowledge of good and evil." We are freed for reliance on God's word.[18]

Redemption frees us from the spiral of mimetic violence and makes of us those who forsake violence, who give up the competitive and coercive game, who allow room for other wills, who do not live life like a game of musical chairs in which the point is to gain space by bumping others out of it.[19] The way by which our redemption was won and by which God is revealed to us (Rom 5:8) shows us also how life can be lived without competitive violence. Redemption demotes fear of death and so frees us to speak unashamedly (Matt 10:27–28).

Redemption frees us from the illusion that what the institutions say is irresistible, from the limitations they place on what we do or say, and from the need to serve their perpetuation. It frees us from the myth of the inevitability and permanence of sin, the myth that sin defines us. It opens a hole in the closed system of the lie, of resignation to sin. It lets in light and allows humanity to have a story, the story of creation and redemption.[20]

The creation-redemption story includes everything God has created. Creation, provision, and redemption are all one project. Therefore, it is only the whole story that gives meaning to creation,[21] and redemption "is the completion of the whole project of creation, not the saving of a few souls from hell."[22] Redemption does not just pull some selected sinners out of the conflagration the rest of creation is destroyed in. Instead, it includes all of creation and affirms the goodness of creation.

A theology that is only natural theology, such as deism, cannot perceive the creation-redemption story. It starts outside the confession and stays there, where creation stands alone doctrinally, and so can eliminate any God-given meaning from the continuation of time. But starting within the confession, considering creation as part of the larger creation-redemption story, binding it together with soteriology, christology, and eschatology, makes something quite different of creation. The actuality of

---

18. See chapter 7 above, under "Myths of Knowledge and Goodness."

19. See chapter 6 above, under "Envy and the Ritual of Accusation" and "Power Games"; Yoder, *War of the Lamb*, 177.

20. See chapter 7 above, under "Freedom and Captivity."

21. So Barth, *Church Dogmatics* 3/1:229.

22. Gunton, *Triune Creator*, 171.

human freedom does not entail that God has stepped back out of involvement with creation or that his involvement can be reduced to impersonal forces such as "natural law," "progress," or "evolution." Nature may work on its own, but creation does not. God moves creation toward its goal. However modern we are, we cannot start thinking we live in a world that continues apart from God sustaining it.

Because "creation is affirmed and not denied, elected and not rejected, it is the object of God's good pleasure."[23] But all creation is now in bondage to the power of sin and "eagerly awaits the revealing of God's children" (Rom 8:19). God saves those who believe the gospel because he loves the whole cosmos (John 3:16), that is, what is temporarily, at best, the devil's kingdom (John 12:31; 16:11; 2 Cor 4:4; 1 John 5:19; Rev 12:9). God's ultimate plan is to "unite in Christ all things in heaven and earth" (Eph 1:10). Creation is not complete: it waits for us; its redemption from death is contingent on the completion of our redemption (Rom 8:19–21). The fragmentation and conflict we see are not final.

"The crucified God is the visible certainty that creation is already an expression of love: we exist on the foundation of love."[24] The kenosis of the dying Christ is thus the confirmation of the kenotic love of the creator for what he has created, and the resurrection of Christ is the sign and beginning of the success of that love, of that creation, of that cross. What is in the package cannot be broken down or separated. "Only if the being of creation is good, only if trust in being is fundamentally justified, are humans at all redeemable. Only if the Redeemer is also Creator can he really be Redeemer."[25]

---

23. Barth, *Church Dogmatics* 3/1:366.
24. Ratzinger, *In the Beginning*, 99.
25. Ratzinger, *In the Beginning*, 100.

10

Following

WHOM WE FOLLOW

Jesus Is Our Teacher

IN THE SCHOOLS OF the Greek and Roman philosophers who were the founders of the Western philosophical tradition, the objective was usually not so much to teach particular ideas as to demonstrate ways of disciplined thinking and inculcate a way of life in which such thinking could be carried out. Otherwise, how could Aristotle have been a student of Plato?[1]

Many Jews of Jesus's day thought the coming age, in which they would be liberated by God from subjection to non-Jewish rulers, was waiting on the time when all Jews would be living by the Torah, the law of the Jewish people. In the age to come the Jewish people would live in their homeland, which would be purified of all non-Jewish religion, and they would worship their one God, subject only to God's law, not to any foreign rulers. But in the meantime it was necessary to understand the Torah and teach observance of it to all Jews. During the time of Jesus, individual teachers of the Torah were surrounded and followed by their disciples, who were thus learning life. So when Jesus called particular

---

1. Pierre Hadot's interpretation of the Greek and Roman philosophers included these key themes: (1) the students of the philosophers were not so much taught a system of philosophical doctrine as made apprentices to a manner of life characterized by wisdom, clear thinking, and virtue; (2) the "spiritual exercises" of Christian writers (e.g., Ignatius of Loyola) were in literary and intellectual continuity with writings of the philosophers. See, e.g., Hadot's *Philosophy as a Way of Life*, 81–144, esp. 82–83.

men to "follow" him, there could be no doubt of his meaning.[2] He was a Jewish teacher of Jews, and was, in fact, regarded as a teacher of the Torah.

In both settings, the teacher-disciple relationship was intended to make of the disciple a duplicate of the teacher both in manner of life and, eventually, as a teacher of others. So the disciples of Jesus are those who adopt the manner of life lived and taught by Jesus. Like teacher, so the student, such that they have a shared reputation (Luke 6:40; Matt 10:24–25; John 13:16; 15:20).

He Has Interrupted the Cycle

But there is more here than a way of life or even a way of dying. Jesus is like no other teacher because in him humanity's path has been redirected. In ourselves we are stuck in the pattern of inevitable and repeated failure resulting from the normal human practice of identifying enemies and then meeting them by becoming like them, and then believing the lie that we are unchanged by doing so. Jesus was different. He was accused and not vindicated, at least not publically.[3] He took up the cross and refused both our methods and the ends we seek.

> When they insulted him,
>   he didn't give it back in kind.
> When he suffered,
>   he didn't make threats. (1 Pet 2:23)[4]

The pattern has been broken by Jesus, not just by himself and for himself but also for us and then, as we come to be conformed to him, by us.

---

2. That they were men and not women was customary and, we can say, necessary because of the difficulties that would have come with having female disciples in that time, but would not in ours.

3. Christians have sometimes insisted on the illegality of Jesus's trial and condemnation: he was innocent, they say. This began at least as early as the second-century *Acts of Pilate* and continues now on many preachers' websites. Why? To make of Jesus a law-abiding citizen? But from the perspective of the forces set against him, Jesus was not innocent, and we would do well to allow that he might have been at least somewhat offensive. So also Stringfellow, *Free in Obedience*, 50.

4. To Jesus's weakness (see chapter 8 above, under "Jesus, Warrior and Son") compare Paul's use of "weak" in his descriptions of his own mission in 2 Cor 10–13 and of the church in 1 Cor 1:26–29: in Pauline terms "weakness" and "boasting" are opposites, and Paul must "boast of [his] weakness."

Jesus thus, returning to Philippians 2:6–8, became not just any human but the ideal human as defined not by a normal story but by the odd story, the story of creation and redemption. He became, that is, the one who stays the course of being human, who does not fall prey to what took away Eve and Adam and all of us, the one who humbles himself, makes himself a slave, is obedient, and takes that obedience even so far as an ignominious death. And we can add to this, on the basis of John 13:1; 1 John 3:16, and other Johannine passages, that Jesus became the one who loves completely, beginning to end, taking that love so far as that ignominious death (Rom 5:6–8). He is the one who "goes Adam's route, but in reverse,"[5] who does not grasp at being "like God" by a supposed route of independence like Adam, Eve, and all their Promethean offspring, by, that is, attempting to supplant God, but who completely submits to God (John 8:28). He is thus the "faithful witness" (Rev 1:5; 3:14), the new beginning of humanity, and the faithful image of God (Rom 8:29; 2 Cor 4:4; Col 1:15).

He Is Our Model

It is in doing similarly, by accepting suffering and staying the course of our mission, that we follow Jesus. But that is what we receive more than it is what we do. After Jesus's death on the cross and his vindication by resurrection, God sent the Holy Spirit, another expression of his presence, so that he can live within us. Because our becoming like Jesus happens by the Spirit and as the result of the Spirit's presence (Gal 5:22–23), we admonish each other not to live better but to allow the Spirit free rein. Our admonition also includes instruction in what the Spirit is trying to accomplish (hence, for instance, that list of fruits of the Spirit in Galatians 5), and always *as* what the Spirit is trying to accomplish.

It is thus that we become "like God," not in the way sought by Adam and Eve but by means of Jesus.

> For by no other means could we have attained to incorruptibility and immortality, unless we had been united to incorruptibility and immortality. But how could we be joined to incorruptibility and immortality, unless, first, incorruptibility and immortality had become that which we also are, so that the corruptible

---

5. Ratzinger, *In the Beginning*, 75.

might be swallowed up by incorruptibility, and the mortal by immortality, that we might receive the adoption of sons?[6]

Jesus is "the beginning" of all the good that can happen among us because he is "the firstborn from the dead" (Col 1:18; cf. Acts 26:23). The image of God is renewed in those who believe in Jesus (Col 3:10; cf. Eph 4:15).

Our sanctification is not like polishing a car (or a decorative cross) but like driving on a rough road. It is like being nailed to a cross while praying for the crucifiers (Luke 23:33–34). Where we become "complete/perfect/mature (*teleios*) as [our] heavenly Father is complete" (Matt 5:48) is not in some sort of rush-of-light glorification but in loving our enemies (vv. 43–47).[7] This presupposes not that we have risen above the possibility of having enemies but that we do, in fact, have enemies, and not that we are no longer tempted but that we are, like Jesus, in the thick of temptation.

What we see first and last when we look at Jesus as our model is his kenosis. We see him as the one who set aside glory (what we would call "reputation" in non-theological contexts) to become a human, even a slave, and even the one who is expendable for the sake of others (Phil 2:6–8). It is thus that we come to understand both God (see again chapter 2) and completed humanity (chapter 8), so our understanding of God and of our way of life as Christians meet in Jesus. He is the one who, in whatever he does, does it as God and as human. Therefore, with a full and orthodox christology, our following of Jesus becomes imitation both of God and of the one who is the complete human. And so, while we base our imitation/following of Jesus on the story about him and the account of his teachings in the Gospels, we also base it on christology, on an understanding of Jesus the slave as God and human. "In short, the most plausible explanation of the rightness of a kenotic ethic is a kenotic doctrine of God. The connection is that such a way of life is imitation, reflection of the character of God. Only if kenosis is somehow in harmony with the ultimate character of reality should it be regarded as expected to be anything but foolishness." And in fact kenosis *is* "the underlying law of the cosmos."[8] If God's perfection were best seen in acts of power, then the ideal expression of his image, both original and renewed, would also be acts of power. But with the kenotic God, we go in quite a different

---

6. Irenaeus, *Against Heresies* 3.19.1.
7. See the last subsection of this chapter on *teleios*.
8. Murphy and Ellis, *On the Moral Nature of the Universe*, 174, 251.

direction.⁹ "So that the cause of all diseases might be cured—that is, pride—the Son of God came down and was made low. Why are you proud? God became low for you. You might perhaps be ashamed to imitate a lowly human, so at least imitate the lowly God."¹⁰

This Christ, the new image of God, the one who has rejected the devil's way and broken the cycle of increasing weaponry, is being formed in believers as they are transformed into the image of God by the work of the Spirit (Gal 4:19; 2 Cor 3:18; 4:4, 6). They cooperate with this process, and, because of the kenotic grace of God, that cooperation or lack thereof can be decisive (Rom 12:1-2; Gal 5:16, 25; Phil 3:7-14).¹¹ But the transformation is, nonetheless, the work of God's Spirit. That difficult (see Romans 7!) last of the Ten Commandments, the one against coveting (Exod 20:17), is fulfilled in us as we step out of the power games in imitation of Jesus.¹²

METAPHORS FOR FOLLOWERS

The Cross-Bearer

The narrative of self-enslavement and obedience as far as crucifixion of the one who was "in the form of God" (Phil 2:6-8) is echoed by a substantial theme in the Gospels: there, too, Jesus is the servant who goes to the cross. Just as Paul uses the Christ hymn to reinforce a call to surrender to the interests of others (Phil 2:3-4), so Jesus repeatedly makes the course of his life, leading toward his death, the pattern for the lives of his disciples. Because he is our teacher, we follow him in self-abasement, self-enslavement, and going to the cross.

This pattern of the cross reflected in discipleship shapes much of the interaction of Jesus and his disciples in the Synoptic Gospels between Peter's confession at Caesarea Philippi (Matt 16:13-20; Mark 8:27-30; Luke 9:18-20) and Jesus's entry into Jerusalem (Matt 21; Mark 11; Luke 19). It is particularly in connection with the three Synoptic predictions of his crucifixion and resurrection that Jesus teaches about following him. Chapter 8 above (under "Staying on His Own Course") looked at these

---

9. This is stated less briefly and more forcefully by Placher in *Narratives of a Vulnerable God*, 3.
10. Augustine, *Tractates on the Gospel of John* 25.16.
11. See above, the first subsection of chapter 9.
12. See Girard, *I Saw Satan Fall*, 12-13.

passages from the perspective of the disciples' role in the temptations of Jesus. Here we focus on the three metaphors for discipleship that Jesus offers in the teaching segments: cross-bearer, child, and slave.[13] Each of these three figures exemplifies kenosis, submitting to the will of "the other"/"the evil one," and each is preceded by the disciples' reaction to Jesus's prediction of his death and resurrection. And each of these teaching segments includes one or more of Jesus's eschatological reversal sayings, either with the prediction, as part of the metaphor, or following after the metaphor.[14] These teaching segments are also linked strongly with the question, always present in the Gospels, of Jesus's identity and authority.

the question of Jesus's identity and authority	Matt 16:13–20	Mark 8:27–30	Luke 9:18–21
first prediction of crucifixion and resurrection	Matt 16:21	Mark 8:31	Luke 9:22
reaction: Peter is offended	Matt 16:22	Mark 8:32	
discipleship: death by crucifixion	Matt 16:24	Mark 8:34	Luke 9:23
eschatological reversal: death and life	Matt 16:25	Mark 8:35	Luke 9:24

Peter's answer to that question at Caesarea Philippi (Matt 16:16 par. Mark 8:29 and Luke 9:20) counters the popular identification of Jesus with the prophetic tradition by giving him a royal title.[15] Jesus confirms Peter's acclamation (Matt 16:17), and that the other disciples accept it is seen in Jesus's warning to all of them (16:20) not to shout it about. Later, Jesus assures the disciples that some of them will live to see "the Son of man coming *in his kingdom*" (16:28).[16] But the "prophet" identification of Jesus never goes away, and the transfiguration of Jesus (17:1–13) goes

---

13. In the Gospel of John the cross is a throne, which is saying something quite different but to a similar end: to see what kind of king Jesus is, we look at the cross.

14. The eschatological reversal sayings include life-death sayings such as Matt 16:25 par. (also in, e.g., Luke 14:26; 17:33) and sayings in which not death but social status and rank are at issue, as in the teachings that follow the second and third predictions of the cross and resurrection.

15. That the category "prophet" was considered a thing of the past is shown by the way it is invoked: Is Jesus one of the prophets of old returned? But John the Baptist was a recent person regarded by many as a prophet, and so saying Jesus was John returned was another way of placing him in that ancient category.

16. The parallel texts do not explicitly speak of Jesus as a king: "the kingdom of God come in power" (Mark 9:1), "the kingdom of God" (Luke 9:27).

back to that explanation of Jesus and links him specifically with John the Baptist (16:12–13), that is, with the tradition of Israel's prophets being killed by Israel (e.g., 1 Kgs 19:10, 14; Jer 3:20; Matt 5:12; 23:29–34; 1 Thess 2:15).

After the first cross prediction, between Caesarea Philippi and the transfiguration (Matt 16:21 par. Mark 8:31 and Luke 9:22), Jesus makes submission to the same form of death as his a prerequisite for discipleship (Matt 16:24–26 par. Mark 8:34–37 and Luke 9:23–25; also stated negatively in Matt 10:38–39 par. Luke 14:27).[17] In all these cross-discipleship passages (add Luke 17:33 and its reversal saying to those just named), the downward spiral is the way the teacher goes and the way the disciples follow. It determines both his nature—christology—and theirs—discipleship.

The Child and the Slave

second prediction of crucifixion and resurrection	Matt 17:22–23	Mark 9:31	Luke 9:44
reaction: the disciples are distressed or confused	Matt 17:23	Mark 9:32	Luke 9:45
discipleship: becoming like a child	Matt 18:1–5; 19:14	Mark 9:33–37; 10:14–15	Luke 9:46–48 (18:16–17)
eschatological reversal: social status	Matt 18:3–4	Mark 9:35	

After the second prediction come some of Jesus's "child" sayings (others of which are in Matt 19:14; Mark 10:14–15; Luke 18:16–17). In the narratives surrounding these sayings low social status is represented literally by the presence of children or a child. High social status is represented by the term "greatest," which is introduced in a question asked by the disciples (Matt 18:1) or in an argument among the disciples stemming from status rivalry among them (in Mark and Luke). The explicit lessons attached to the present child or children, except in Matthew 18:5, are

17. From our position (and the Gospel writers') after Jesus's crucifixion, his teaching here is heard as a metaphor derived from his own crucifixion. But not so for those who first heard this "take up your cross." Crucifixion could stand in for violent death of any kind, much as one might draw a thumb across his or her neck today without intending a reference to throat-slitting in particular. See references in Allen, *Matthew*, 111. Knowing how offensive Jesus might have been (see note 3 above) helps us understand better how he might well have anticipated how badly things would go for him and for his close followers.

variations of an injunction to assume the status level of children in order to enter God's kingdom (Matt 18:3–4; Matt 19:14 par. Mark 10:14 and Luke 18:16; Mark 10:15 par. Luke 18:17).

eschatological reversal: social status	Matt 19:28–30; 20:16	Mark 10:29–31	Luke 18:14, 29–30
third prediction of crucifixion and resurrection	Matt 20:18–19	Mark 10:33–34	Luke 18:31–33
reaction: the disciples jockey for position	Matt 20:20–21, 24	Mark 10:35–37, 41	(Luke 18:34 repeats 9:45)
discipleship: becoming a servant	Matt 20:20–28	Mark 10:35–45	(Luke 22:24–27)
the question of Jesus's identity and authority	Matt 21:23–27	Mark 11:27–33	Luke 20:1–8

After Jesus's third prediction of his suffering and crucifixion, Matthew and Mark tell of the incident initiated by two disciples, both sons of Zebedee, attempting to circumvent or solve this whole issue of who is or will be "greatest" among them by a formal petition to Jesus (cf. Esth 4:11; 5:1–8; 7:2–4). The disciples' competition with each other, as a reaction to Jesus's prediction, demonstrates their denial of the coming crucifixion or simple disinterest in it. They already regard Jesus as their king, most explicitly according to Matthew (Matt 16:16, 20, 28; 20:21), hence the appropriateness of the petition. The words of the brothers' request (through their mother in Matthew) and Jesus's words in reply make "greatest" more explicitly a matter of political position. This time, low social status is represented by the "servant" or "slave," and Jesus links the issue of the disciples' ambitions to his own path toward death by referring to his "cup," his "baptism," his "service," and his identity as the expendable one who is given as the "ransom for many."

The narrative of self-enslavement is found also in the parable in Luke 12:36–38: "Truly, I tell you, the master will dress himself for service and have his servants recline at table, and he will come and serve them." This is a very odd statement in the context. If it is left out, we get what would be expected if the social order were preserved, which is exactly what the narrative simile prepares us for: "like servants awaiting their master as he returns from a wedding feast, so that they can open the door for him quickly when he gets home." But the social order is upset: the master comes in tired after the party, and *he waits on the servants*.

Similarly also Jesus's washing of his disciples' feet in John 13. The servant doing that needed no special skill or knowledge and would be silent and nearly invisible. It was a task that, without anyone needing to think about it, identified the doer as the lowest in the relationship (John 1:27). Thus Jesus demonstrated what sort of "master" he was for his disciples in such a way that they could "understand" both that (13:12–13) and, consequently, how they are to be with each other (13:14–17).

Similarly also the parable about a different arena of social distinction, that among guests at a dinner party, in Luke 14:7–11. Jesus signals that he is talking here about the eschaton by using the words "wedding feast" (14:8) in a context that could otherwise be about any sort of feast. So he is not just giving advice about etiquette. But that does not mean that the Gospel-writer's introduction to the parable (14:7) is wrong. Eschatology and how we live are deeply interconnected, such that we can say "both-and" to the question of which the parable is about. Stepping down in honor was a strange thing to do then, and we are not altogether different now: we still want to get credit, to have our skills, knowledge, and position recognized, for some of us in no place more than in church. We generally take for granted the advice given by Sir Ruthven Murgatroyd:

> My boy, you may take it from me,
>   That of all the afflictions accurst
>   With which a man's saddled
>   And hampered and addled,
>   A diffident nature's the worst.
> Though clever as clever can be—
>   A Crichton of early romance—
>   You must stir it and stump it,
>   And blow your own trumpet,
>   Or, trust me, you haven't a chance![18]

Whose Slaves?

Here again we can ask: Of whom are Jesus and his disciples slaves? Or to whom do they enslave themselves?[19] Paul and Jesus both use persuasive, hortatory language and are therefore calling for *self*-enslavement, decision of the will not to assert the will, and the "to whom?" can again be answered with a broad "the other" or "the evil one," that is, whoever is asserting his or her or their own will. Kenosis allows the one who insists

---

18. Gilbert, "Ruddigore [1887]" Act I. Especially those of us who write books.
19. See the first subsection of chapter 9 above.

on his or her own way to have it but still—and in that way—carries on toward the goal of the triumph of God's rule.

The question is helpful to the degree that it is kept in contact with actual experiences. For instance, in Jesus's case, his much-criticized choice of whom to eat with (e.g., Luke 15:1–2), which went hand-in-hand with his teaching that his disciples should welcome, not condemn, repenters (e.g., Matt 20:1–16). In the parable of the prodigal, the elder son speaks for Jesus's critics (Luke 15:29–30), but those critics became much more dangerous as Jesus let them continue rather than calling down fire or angels. Jesus and his disciples took on the burden of the effects of kenosis as targets of that criticism. The disciples thus took on the kenotic pattern of God in creation, provision, and incarnation as they became people moving with redemption. So also Paul took seriously his own teaching of imitation of Christ as slave (Philippians 2) by giving up his rights and enslaving himself to "all" for the sake of evangelism (1 Cor 9:19; cf. 2:1–5; 2 Cor 11:7).

When we see how kenosis is characteristic of God, not just a description of the means of the incarnation,[20] then we see how the humility and self-sacrifice taught by Jesus is Godlikeness. Humility is submission not simply to God or to "God's will"[21] but to being like God, to accepting God's kenotic ways as one's own. The humble disciple is a servant because to become a servant is to follow God's humility.

FALSE ENDINGS

King Jesus

> I hope no reader imagines me so weak [as] to stand up in the defence of real Christianity, such as used in primitive times (if we may believe the authors of those ages) to have an influence upon men's belief and actions: To offer at the restoring of that would indeed be a wild project. It would be to dig up foundations; to destroy at one blow all the wit, and half the learning of the kingdom; to break the entire frame and constitution of things; to ruin trade, extinguish arts and sciences with the professors of them; in short, to turn our courts, exchanges, and shops into deserts; and would be full as absurd as the proposal of Horace, where he advises the Romans all in a body to leave their city, and

---

20. See chapter 2 above, under "The Kenosis of the Trinity."
21. See chapter 4 above, under "For Other Wills."

seek a new seat in some remote part of the world, by way of cure for the corruption of their manners.

Therefore I think this caution was in itself altogether unnecessary, (which I have inserted only to prevent all possibility of cavilling) since every candid reader will easily understand my discourse to be intended only in defence of nominal Christianity; the other having been for some time wholly laid aside by general consent, as utterly inconsistent with our present schemes of wealth and power.[22]

So Jonathan Swift in his time, and the task of anyone arguing for discipleship to Jesus today would be just as absurd or difficult except for two differences: identification as "Christian" is less normative now, and there is no legally enforced normative form of it (such as Swift's Restoration Anglicanism), so less is immediately at stake for society at large in how strange we make our Christianity.

To his credit, Swift was a satirist, for which reason, among others, I never know quite what he means. And I do not know if he mentally underlined "our present schemes of wealth and power," but, needless to say by this point, I hear it that way. "Our present schemes" are what I have called the normal story (chapter 2) and the lie of the powers (chapter 7), that which lures us away from the odd story of kenosis, even though that story determines the shape of our universe. Or our "schemes of wealth and power" might be identified with premature "false endings" of the story embraced by those who are eager to get past all the story's difficulties to some sort of happily-ever-after.[23]

But the shape of the universe is foreign to us, as we see in the reactions of Jesus's disciples to his predictions of the cross. They knew that Jesus was King Messiah, so Peter denied the possibility of the crucifixion, or the disciples were upset or baffled, or they kept acting and thinking in normal ways, as if crucifixion would be just a minor bump in the road. They were eager to get to the glorious end, the kingdom of Jesus: "kingdom now!"[24]

---

22. Swift, "Argument against Abolishing Christianity," 6–7.

23. See the first subsection of chapter 1 above on "false endings."

24. Early on, some Christians might have believed that Jesus having been resurrected meant that the resurrection had already happened for all of them as well (2 Tim 2:18), another false ending and an echo of the Zebedee brothers' "kingdom now!"

The emphasis some preachers and writers currently want to give to *King* Jesus[25] relies on a strong view of the difference resulting from being on the opposite side of Jesus's resurrection from where the disciples were when they made those mistakes and when Jesus called Peter "Satan" (Matt 16:23). There is, in fact, a difference. But, pondering what Jesus said to the disciples on their side of the resurrection, I have to wonder what sort of comeuppance might be coming for some "kingdom now!" preachers of today. In view of the erosion of Christian dominance of society and culture that has been going on for the last three centuries, it might be that "King Jesus" is merely a typical overbold assertion of a passing regime.[26] And it might also be a sign of dissatisfaction with pluralistic democracy.[27]

On this side of Jesus's resurrection "all authority in heaven and earth" has become his (Matt 28:18; also Rom 14:9; Eph 1:20–22; Col 2:10; Phil 2:9; 1 Pet 3:22), though in some sense he had it all already (Matt 11:27; John 13:3). But it is far from certain whether the nature and exercise of that authority is more captured or obscured by whatever Americans, whose founding fathers were rebels against monarchy, might mean by the title "king." At any rate, this one with "all authority," this *king* if you will, tells his followers (Matt 28:19) not "Therefore, go and *assert my authority*" but, in effect, "Therefore, go and *win them over*, appealing to their minds and using persuasion, not coercion."[28] Then the manner of life that Jesus tells them to teach is the same as what he taught before his crucifixion (Matt 28:20; cf. John 14:15, 21; 15:10), including "take up your cross." And those in succeeding generations who believe are, just as much as those original followers, "disciples" (as in the verb translated "make disciples," Matt 28:19, also in Acts 14:21).

---

25. The large number and broad variety of things that come under that title (try a Google search, but only if you are very curious) means that I could hardly be thinking here about all of them, and it would be impossible either to like or to dislike all of them together.

26. One of the clearest examples of this historical pattern is the nineteenth-century assertion of papal infallibility a few decades after the loss of most of the pope's temporal power. Others could be named.

27. Explicitly so with the "reconstuctionism" of Rushdoony and others, which assumes or hopes for the return of a state-church situation.

28. See further below, under "Persuasion." "'All power is given Me—go therefore and . . . subdue? Not so: the purpose of the Lord is to bring men to the knowledge of the truth—to work on and in their hearts, and lift them up to be partakers of the Divine Nature. And therefore it is not 'subdue,' but make disciples of" (Alford, *Greek Testament*, 1:283).

None of this is very king-like. What Jesus does can be called "kingdom," and he called it that himself. But it has to said almost tongue-in-cheek because in this kingdom "the evil one" is not resisted (Matt 5:39). This kingdom is like a tiny seed, which is effective by being invisible and which will grow impossibly and upset mountains that otherwise appear permanent (Matt 13:31–33; 17:20).

Ethics

In a sense (and not in all senses), Christians have no place left for discussion of ethics because they have already taken up the cross.[29] Discipleship to Jesus is what we have instead of ethics. In the Bible, as we have seen, most specifically in the early chapters of Genesis and in Jesus's teaching,

- people get into trouble for the first time for trying to get at "knowledge of good and evil,"
- sinners are accepted by God, the alienation from him having been resolved at God's initiative and expense,
- laws are considered a problem,
- people who are ostensibly righteous are rejected by God,
- despicable sinners are justified, and
- Christian ethics, if it is anything, would have to be an exploration of the counter-intuitive, the non-accepted, and the unknown, because sin has made obedience to God unknown and unnatural to us.

How, then, can we expect to construct an ethics on the basis of the Bible?

In biblical theology, there is no ethics, just obedience to the gospel. Ethics can be the attempt to uproot the tree of the knowledge of good and evil and transplant it out of God's garden and into our own, to make it our own. If we have ethics, we can think that we are independent of God. If we have ethics, we might know what to do, but then we *must* know what to do. The gain in the garden was knowledge of good and evil. The loss was the garden itself, that is, the place where people know God face-to-face.

---

29. Cf. Yoder, *War of the Lamb*, 40. Yoder's term is "corner" rather than "place."

The way in which God has made it again possible for us to know him is by becoming a human. This face-to-face relationship is essential and is the one thing we least want to do. Hear Dietrich Bonhoeffer:

> All ethical reflection then has the goal that I be good, and that the world—by my action—becomes good. If it turns out, however, that these realities, myself and the world, are themselves embedded in a wholly other ultimate reality, namely, the reality of God the Creator, Reconciler, and Redeemer, then the ethical problem takes on a whole new aspect. Of ultimate importance, then, is not that I become good, or that the condition of the world be improved by my efforts, but that the reality of God show itself everywhere to be the ultimate reality. Where God is known by faith to be the ultimate reality, the source of my ethical concern will be that God be known as the good, even at the risk that I and the world are revealed as not good, but as bad through and through.[30]

> The knowledge of good and evil appears to be the goal of all ethical reflection. The first task of Christian ethics is to supersede that knowledge. This attack on the presuppositions of all other ethics is so unique that it is questionable whether it even makes sense to speak of Christian ethics at all. If it is nevertheless done, then this can only mean that Christian ethics claims to articulate the origin of the whole ethical enterprise, and thus to be considered as an ethic only as the critique of all ethics.
>
> For Christian ethics, the mere possibility of knowing about good and evil is already a falling away from the origin. Living in the origin, human beings know nothing but God alone.[31]

Or Jacques Ellul: "There can be no Christian morality if we truly follow evangelical thinking."[32]

One of the shocks for Christians about living after Christendom is that people have found it possible to take bits of Christian belief (or what they think is Christian belief) and consciously leave aside other bits of Christian belief (or of what they think that is). There is no glue holding Christianity together in a cohesive, all-or-none package. What we can say to people who take this pick-and-choose approach must come ultimately

---

30. Bonhoeffer, *Ethics*, 48.

31. Bonhoeffer, *Ethics*, 299–300. Bonhoeffer does not, it should be noted, make a claim for any "uniqueness" of Christian ethics even while he speaks of its "attack on the presuppositions of all other ethics."

32. Ellul, *Anarchy and Christianity*, 7.

down to this: there is (not just was) a real person, the son of God, named Jesus; it is him with which we have to deal; and he refuses to be reduced to a set of ideals that he "represents."

> I don't want to talk about absolutes, I want to talk about Jesus Christ. The person of Jesus Christ is that ultimate reality to whom I am finally committed with a commitment which is not negotiable. At the end of the day you cannot translate that into any set of moral or philosophical principles. There is no doubt that these have their place, and you have to work at them, but it is this personal commitment to Jesus Christ that is essential.[33]

That real person Jesus plays a role in our universe that no one else does or could carry out. He is master and teacher. Those who are loyal to him know him, both on their own and as they are gathered together, as their master and teacher. A master calls for obedience, and a teacher calls for imitation. Both metaphors are necessary for us to understand what God wants from his people. We do what we do not because it is right according to some standard but because it is what Jesus does and tells us to do.

NEVERTHELESS

Persuasion

In a sense, what I have just said cuts us off from ethical discussion with the broader society. Christian ethics is, indeed, not directly communicable to society at large because it is discipleship to Jesus. I cannot bring what works in discussion among Christians into any broader discussion of right and wrong unless I am evangelizing, that is, unless I am trying to convince participants in that broader discussion that it is worthwhile to consider becoming disciples to Jesus.

Nevertheless, Christians can join in discussion of right and wrong with anyone around them on the basis of what we all share as a people with a shared history and, indeed, as humans in general trying to figure out how to live together, help each other, and not hurt each other. The people around us are our neighbors, those whom we love in those and other ways.

A greater difficulty in the way of Christians engaging in ethical discussion with the broader community (greater than our replacement of

---

33. Newbigin, "Face to Face."

ethics with discipleship to Jesus) is that people, including we ourselves, have given up on persuasion. In this our time, we do not believe in moral argument. Our first inclination is toward coercion, not persuasion. Indeed, we need not even persuade ourselves of any moral distinctions as long as we are able to impose our will. We are in that way rather Nietzschean (though that may not be quite fair to Nietzsche). For example, we can focus more on outlawing bad actions such as abortion and substitution of drug experiences for more positive participation in society than on persuading our people not to do those things. Persuasion requires patience, and our age has little of that. It requires a patience, in fact, that can wait and still not be fulfilled (the "even if not" of Dan 3:18), and it is hard to imagine how that waiting can be sustained apart from a hope ultimately and only for God to be glorified.

Indeed, that other difficulty, the differentness of being disciples of Jesus, might be just an excuse to hide our diffidence in regard to persuasion. If we were to speak more honestly, perhaps we would begin by admitting that diffidence and then go on to speak of our own confusion about how all of us as Americans or as humans in society can develop shared understandings of what is right sufficient to enable our living together.

Those who display such patience can become valuable models for believing in persuasion as a means by which Americans (and others) can love each other better than they have been accustomed to doing. If, for instance, we learn the arts of persuasion and speak to our society—our people—and say that it would benefit us not to practice abortion, then we show that we love and respect our neighbors more than we love laws.[34] And with that we will have also testified against the ethical agnosticism of postmodernism and in favor of the possibility of knowing and doing good—a possibility not of knowing and doing the perfect righteousness of God or of bringing about his kingdom but of developing shared understandings of what is good for us as humans who live together and of doing better on the basis of those understandings.

In that sort of interaction, we Christians can also give testimony in favor of a courage based on knowledge of forgiveness, which is our constant need, God's constant provision, and, as we imitate God in forgiving, that which will most enable our living together. This courage we certainly need as we imagine entering into the culture wars on the side of peace,

---

34. On persuasion versus coercion and respect as rhetorical strategy, see chapter 6 above, under "Power Games."

all the while knowing that we are not suited by nature to be advocates for that side any more than anyone else is. Persuasion is love, so our persuasion is characterized by a "rhetoric of nonviolence" or a "nonviolent epistemology,"[35] which again requires a patience that is not ours outside the lengthened perspective of faith in the kingdom of God.

It also requires a willingness to be persuaded. Think back again to Joe, Bob, and the chairs.[36] According to Emmanuel Levinas, Joe need not think of Bob's entry as a threat or a diminishment of himself, even if it entails him changing his position to make room for this *other*. Joe might, rather, understand this encounter with the other as a privilege. Bob's entry alters things for Joe, no doubt, but it thus creates an opportunity, bringing the possibility that Joe becomes more by the encounter. More what? More *human*, because being human is something one does with others, not in isolation. That is not a statement of fuzzy-warm ethics but a simple fact of what we are. The isolated human is abnormal, perhaps less than human, whether isolation is chosen or imposed.[37]

But Joe also becomes more *wise* when Bob walks in. Levinas speaks of philosophy as the "wisdom of love" rather than the "love of wisdom." Truth is not found apart from relationship. Knowledge comes only after the encounter with the *other*. So ethics is "first philosophy." When I was in college I witnessed a fellow evangelical convincing a chemistry major whom he had just met that God exists, which that chemistry major had not believed before. The chemist's response was "Yeah, so you've convinced me. So what." And he walked away. That was a moment Levinas could have spoken to. Once I have established an "objective truth" by argument and logic, I have not really arrived at truth because truth is only realizable in relationship. Argument, even convincing argument, is no substitute for relationship, and in relationship even the evangelist risks undergoing change. Even the evangelist, as certain of truth as possible, can think about truth and knowledge as shaped in relationship. A person may gain knowledge alone, but it may not be a sort of knowledge any of us should want.

Love and knowledge are different things, and knowledge without that love is pretty near worthless (1 Cor 8:1–2; 13:1–2). If we want to

---

35. The phrase "rhetoric of nonviolence" was used at least as early as Yinger, *Cesar Chavez*. For "nonviolent epistemology," see Yoder, *Pacifist Way of Knowing*. See also Gorsevski, *Peaceful Persuasion*.

36. In chapter 4, under "For Other Wills," and chapter 6, under "Power Games."

37. See also chapter 3 above, under "The Image of God."

possess truth, then we can be like Eve responding to the snake's temptation, gaining knowledge to become like God. But Jesus set aside even divine knowledge to serve us (Matt 24:36).[38] This is kenosis: God not overwhelming creation but allowing it to exist (see chapter 4 above), then not overwhelming humanity but becoming "the servant of all," and then the disciples of Jesus not overwhelming others with argument but admitting them into relationship and conversation.

Personalism

Thus we set a variety of personalism in the middle of our understanding of what it looks like to follow Jesus. Philosophical "personalism" is a multifarious thing and has been the basis of a wide variety of political positions. Here it boils down to saying that any individual human is worth more than any number of ideals, ideologies, institutions, nations, corporations, oil wells, or what-have-yous.[39] Speaking positively, God is personal and a personalist, so love is foundational to what exists.[40] Speaking negatively, personalism includes critique or neutralization or at least demotion of those ideologies, institutions, and the rest. The love command (Matt 22:39) is central.

Those human collectivities go beyond being human (and therefore can be called transhuman and demonic) in that they are greater than the sum of their human parts. They not only include humans but also order humans around. But any individual human is worth more than any of them, and redemption frees humans from them. That is hard to

---

38. Similarly Isa 42:1–4, quoted in Matt 12:18–21: It is *justice* that the servant brings, not his own vindication. Therefore, he will not shout out the truth loudly and publicly (Isa 42:2), and, even as he "brings forth justice," he is careful that that does not amount to beating up his enemies with his words (v. 3). Winning the argument is not the goal because "bringing forth justice" includes (or simply *is*) loving those to whom he must speak.

39. That is roughly what it has meant for the Catholic Worker movement (including Peter Maurin, Dorothy Day, and Katherine Temple), Jacques Ellul, and William Stringfellow. See, e.g., Zwick and Zwick, "Emmanuel Mounier." Martin Luther King Jr. in particular linked the identification of God as personal (see chapter 3 above, under "God Is Personal") with "the dignity and worth of all human personality" (see "Personalism" in the bibliography below). And behind all that is Søren Kierkegaard's placing of the individual over the "numerous masses," e.g., Kierkegaard, *Works of Love*, 80. See also, e.g., Ellul, *Violence*, 31, 34, 86, 112; and, with his typical polar pigeonholing, C. S. Lewis, "Man or Rabbit?" (Lewis, *God in the Dock*, 108–14).

40. See chapter 3 above, under "The Universe."

understand because, apart from redemption, we are so defined by, dependent on, and subservient to those powers that we cannot even imagine what "human" means apart from them.

And we love and utilize our depersonalization of each other because it protects us from relationship. But that means that it also protects us from growth toward anything better. Heywood Broun Jr. said about the failures of the League of Nations meetings after World War I: "Beer and light wines can settle subjects which defy all the subtleties possible to ink." There is something serious here: among fellow drinkers or fellow whateverers, conflicts are dealt with more honestly and optimistically and with more concern for usable outcomes. Diplomats are forced to have too much formality, too little conversation, too few permissible outcomes, too many agendas of institutional pride, hate, and selfishness, and too much personal one-upmanship to do anything meaningful. They are easily deprived of being fellow anythings with each other. Broun goes on: "What the world needs, then, is not so much a league as an international beer night to be held at regular intervals by representatives of the nations. Good beer and enough of it would have settled the whole problem of the covenants which were going to be open and did not turn out that way" (witness World War II). This is not about drunkenness but about realization of our shared humanness, about our greater beauty when not hidden behind institutions, or simply about shared positive experiences.[41]

The "person" of personalism is not to be confused with or reduced to "humanity." Loving humanity is not the same as loving my neighbor. It is of no use to love humanity because humanity is an abstraction. My neighbor is a person, not an abstraction.

The person is also not to be confused with the autonomous individual of Descartes, Leibniz, and Rousseau. To understand what a human being is, those philosophers had to hang a human being in space, so to speak, to isolate him (the default human in their time being male) from other humans. We have not correctly spoken about ourselves if we leave out the fact that we live all over each other, affect many "each others" with every action (so much for "victimless crimes"), need each other in complex ways (sorry, Rousseau, and maybe Thoreau), and do everything we do in connection with each other.

So this personalism is not about "humanity" or "individualism" and is not the democracy of what is best for the most people. It is not about

---

41. Broun, "With a Stein on the Table," chapter 31 in *Pieces of Hate*.

improving society but about making life possible for this one person.[42] If I get in a crowd, I point randomly and go to that person, and then I have found the "neighbor" I am supposed to love.[43] I am not directed to love either humankind in general or the autonomous individual, which is good because neither exist in any practical sense, and personalism is practical.

This personalism makes it more difficult to have universal moral standards and impossible to enforce them. It is not anti-moral, but the point of loving one's neighbor as oneself (Lev 19:18) is not a specifiable universal moral code but both receiving and offering the will of God, salvation, forgiveness, sanctification, and discipleship. Moral rules enter in only as part of an attempt to express part of what God's will is.

This personalism also means that we do not separate ends and means. We hear it from a very different direction when Emma Goldman speaks of the "perversion of the ethical values," of, that is, the ideals of socialist revolution, in the Soviet Union of the 1920s:

> This perversion of the ethical values soon crystallized into the all-dominating slogan of the Communist Party: The end Justifies all means. Similarly in the past the Inquisition and the Jesuits adopted this motto and subordinated to it all morality. It avenged itself upon the Jesuits as it did upon the Russian Revolution. In the wake of this slogan followed lying, deceit, hypocrisy and treachery, murder, open and secret. . . .
>
> There is no greater fallacy than the belief that aims and purposes are one thing, while methods and tactics are another. This conception is a potent menace to social regeneration. All human experience teaches that methods and means cannot be separated from the ultimate aim. The means employed become, through individual habit and social practice, part and parcel of the final purpose; they influence it, modify it, and presently the aims and means become identical.[44]

---

42. I wish I could find somewhere other than in memory a song, recorded by one of the male "folk music" quartets of the late 1950s and early 1960s about the building of the Tennessee Valley Authority (a fine historical example of a transhuman institution/authority!) in which a crisis is raised because one woman refuses to leave her home. A similar thing happened when a neighborhood near where I live was demolished for a state university's parking lot, but without the song's silly happy ending. On "transhuman," see note 10 in chapter 7 above.

43. See further Kierkegaard, *Works of Love*, e.g., 37–39, 79, 89.

44. Goldman, *My Further Disillusionment in Russia*, 260. Whether Goldman was being fair to Jesuits or Communists of any particular time or place might be questioned.

If the revolution (or some other finely engineered public work on behalf of the people) is everything, then some people will have to be sacrificed to it. "We are causing much impure blood to flow, but it is our duty to do so, it is for humanity's sake."[45] Abstract humanity is served at the cost of the individual human, and ends triumph over means. We could find examples that are closer to home, perhaps abortion of children expected to be subject to Downs syndrome or any other setting where we distinguish who matters most. In contrast to that sort of commitment to efficiency, God has given value to the humanness of each human, and therefore the Christian heaven is a crowded and diverse city.

Nietzsche understood that Christianity teaches, through identification with Christ, valuing of the victim. That is what he rejected. So his system of valuing power is a baldly-stated opposite of Christian ethics. He hated the "slave morality" that elevates every person, even the humblest, and that speaks of the equality of all. Evolution toward the "superman" requires sacrifice of the weak individuals that are in the way and can make no contribution to the goal. Every value, be it nation, ideology, power, or *volk*, that stands against the individual will tend this way.

Personalism affirms the opposite: nothing can stand against the value of one person. No one can be hurt for the greater good of the greater number. It is impractical[46] and raises countless questions, but it is as such demonstration of how far the limited range of the possible as we imagine it is from God's kenosis and the way of Jesus.

Perfection

Imitation of Jesus in his kenosis and cross is the unmistakable path for every Christian. It is the way we are Christians. It is how our faith lives. But there have been several bases in Christian theology from which it has been argued that this following of Jesus is not exactly what we are about as Christians, or not for Christians of today, or at least not for all Christians, some as antinomian popularizations of the Reformed tradition.[47]

---

45. Joseph Fouché, duc d'Otrante, justifying mass executions in Lyons in 1793–94, quoted in Schom, *Napoleon Bonaparte*, 255. Similarly, Chesterton, *Ball and the Cross*, 320–21: "Life is sacred—but lives are not sacred. We are improving Life by removing lives." "Life, yes, Life is indeed sacred! . . . but new lives for old! Good lives for bad!"

46. In a way different from the practicality mentioned four paragraphs back.

47. And of the broader Augustinian tradition, including Lutheran theology. The Reformed tradition itself speaks quite freely of self-denial and imitation of Jesus (e.g.,

For instance,[48] we must, it is sometimes said, make a sharp distinction between Jesus and what he does, on the one hand, and what we his followers do, on the other. The cross as example or model is secondary to its place in substitutionary atonement, and to emphasize the example aspect is likely to lead us into "legalism." We should avoid "legalism"; as soon as we speak of human efforts toward being holy we have departed from the gospel of God's grace.[49] It is the "heart" that God cares about.[50]

Furthermore, biblical law, including Jesus's ethical teachings, is intended to lead us to repentance. That we are sinful means that we cannot hear what Jesus teaches as describing what we are to do or could do. This is especially seen in interpretations of the Sermon on the Mount: its unachievable demands require qualification, which we must supply rather than taking it all literally. They are, in fact, intended to lead us to despair in our own efforts and to seek salvation in Christ.[51]

But if we say that the demands of the Sermon are impossible, we have to qualify that by identifying the context in which they are so. If, for instance, we place limitations on love for enemies (Matt 5:44) out of regard for our own safety, we should be frank about letting the latter supersede Jesus's teaching at some points, rather than hunting out biblical qualifications to what he taught. Choosing to follow Jesus more closely is also served by such honesty since we thus identify the context of our discipleship, which is the fact of our having enemies and being afraid of what they might do to us, as a place where disciples of Jesus necessarily go against the grain. Going with the grain would be to treat our enemies with caution and violence; those who question such patterns for the sake

---

Calvin, *Institutes* 3.7). There has been a healthy move in much of American evangelicalism (except where it is just a matter of buzzwords) toward speaking of "discipleship" and away from the theological barriers that have been erected against such speech. Yoder's *Politics of Jesus* (1972) was a forerunner of that move, not so much by speaking out of the Anabaptist tradition as by careful examination of what Jesus said and a defense of its pertinence to Christian ethics.

48. For what follows, see Yoder, *To Hear the Word*, 52–53, 112–13; *Politics of Jesus*, 7–8, 18. Much of this group of statements amounts to an inability to say "both-and."

49. Perhaps an extreme and from near the edge of orthodoxy: "Legalism is the religious viewpoint that proposes that our performance of deeds enhances our relationship with God" (Plain Truth Ministries, "About").

50. "God cares about your heart being in the right place, everything else will catch up" (attributed to Joyce Meyers).

51. So, e.g., Morris, *Matthew*, 91–92; Carl Stange, quoted in Bauman, *Sermon on the Mount*, 177.

of following Jesus make themselves irritatingly irrelevant, seemingly disconnected from the realities others are willing to deal with.

That leads us into another strain of theological argument against discipleship: the need to be relevant trumps discipleship.[52] We derive our ethics from other places than the cross and Jesus's teaching of his disciples—for example, our responsibility to the social order. Or it is said that Jesus leads us away from reacting in kind to every provocation or assault, but does not intend to take away our right to defend ourselves and our property from attack. Or that God endorses the functioning of government for the sake of social order and enforced by violence (e.g., interpretations of Rom 13:1–5), and that Christians should take part in it. Or that Jesus taught his ethics for the brief period that he believed remained before the completion of God's kingdom, which is of no use to us in our long-surviving social order. Similarly, the kingdom of God, as understood by (at least some) dispensationalists, is for eschatological Israel, not for Christians in the present. Or, from a different direction, the difference in content between what we have in the Gospels and whatever Jesus taught (which we have no direct access to and can do little more than debate over) makes it futile to speak of following Jesus.

Similarly, Catholic understanding of different kinds of callings. We see an example where a statement of Christian life consisting of imitation of Christ is addressed specifically to the "religious," that is, to the small number of Christians who adopt a particular lifestyle, taking the "perfection" of Matthew 19:21 and the "obedience" of Philippians 2:8 as addressed to those especially committed Christians.[53] I want to be gentle to this part of the Catholic tradition because I know it only as an outsider and because it preserved the call to imitation of Jesus when the dominance of Christendom pointed in quite other directions. But what is given to the others, to non-heroic Christians? They are allowed to sink into relevance to self-protective concerns. Perhaps perfection has been misunderstood if it is regarded as unavailable to all of us Christians.

But being "perfect/complete/mature," *teleios*, is for everybody in at least some New Testament contexts. The courage to be irrelevant is

---

52. For the following examples see again Yoder, *To Hear the Word*, 52–53; *Politics of Jesus*, 5, 15–16, 18.

53. Aquinas, *Summa Theologiae* II.II.186.5. Here again interpretation of the Sermon on the Mount plays a part since therein Luther attacked the distinction between monks and ordinary Christians, to whom he extended the demands of the Sermon. See Schreiner, "Martin Luther."

available to all of us. Just as God the Father takes risks by loving both good and bad people, so Jesus calls on us to take the risks involved in loving our enemies, and so become "perfect/complete/mature, as your heavenly Father is perfect/complete/mature" (Matt 5:44-45, 48). Paul calls on the Corinthian Christians to be "perfect/complete/mature" in their thinking (1 Cor 14:20). The goal of the church's various ministries is the eschatological perfection of each person, as measured by Jesus (Eph 4:13; Col 1:28; 4:12),[54] the "complete" sanctification of each (1 Thess 5:23). Those who are "inexperienced in the word of righteousness" are contrasted with those who are "perfect/complete/mature," that is, "those who through habit have their judgment trained to distinguish good and evil" (Heb 5:13-14). "The testing of your faith produces endurance. Let that endurance have a perfect/complete/mature work so that you may be perfect/mature and complete,[55] lacking in nothing" (Jas 1:3-4). A sign of such maturity is care over what one says (3:2).

If we want the New Testament as a whole to, for instance, reject human efforts toward being holy as "legalism," it refuses to do so and instead harps on our need to put forth those efforts. For instance, 1 and 2 Timothy and Titus and passages in other parts of the New Testament use athletic and pedagogical metaphors for such efforts (including 1 Tim 4:6-10; 2 Tim 3:16-17: "training in righteousness"; Tit 2:11-12; 1 Cor 9:24-27). These metaphors are mainly directed to teachers, but to be a disciple is also to be at least a potential teacher (see the first section of this chapter). The athletic picture is particularly helpful because most of us can appreciate the difference between memorizing data and training muscles. The goal is not to take in information but to become changed people, those who have not just new knowledge but new habits.[56]

None of this submits to any desire to have the whole New Testament speak against "works-righteousness." It speaks, rather, of a movement toward completion. Movement is work (ask anyone who is busily neglecting their gym membership)—but more so to the degree that I do

---

54. Col 4:12 also includes ("fulfilled") a form of the verb *plēroō*, serving here as a near-synonym of *teleios*.

55. *Holoklēros*, another near-synonym of *teleios*.

56. One could keep going to different parts of the New Testament to speak of the discipleship imperative. Here, just a couple more suggestions of where to go: pull out all the terms Paul uses to name his goal in Phil 3:8-14; look at the interplay of indicative and imperative in Paul and 1 John and note how they resist disentangling (particularly in 1 John 3:2-3) and how, lacking either indicative or imperative, our purification/conformation to Christ does not occur (see also Rom 8:29-30; Eph 1:4).

not love that toward which I am moving. It would be logical here to introduce some spiritual disciplines, but I hope, rather, to simply remove that theological fear that can be used as an excuse for not engaging in the disciplines.

11

Witness to Freedom

FREE NOT TO GOVERN

The Odd King

> The devil put Jesus on the top of a high mountain and pointed out all the great kingdoms spread out below them. He said "I'll give you all that if you bow down and honor me." Jesus said "Go back to your hell, Satan. The Bible tells us to worship and serve only God." So the devil left. (Matt 4:8–11)[1]

DOES THIS TEMPTATION NARRATIVE assume that the devil really had all that authority at his disposal,[2] or that he was lying or exaggerating?[3] And is what the devil claims the same as what Jesus would claim later: Did the devil's "all the kingdoms of the world" become Jesus's "all authority in heaven and on earth" (Matt 28:18) after a transfer of authority accomplished by Jesus's victory on the cross,[4] or earlier (perhaps the day before

---

1. This temptation is stated differently and placed differently in Luke 4:5–8. On the temptations of Jesus in general see chapter 8 above, under "Staying on His Own Course" and "Staying on the Human Course."

2. E.g., Illich, "Educational Enterprise." Note "since it has been given to me, and I give it to whomever I want" in Luke's version, Luke 4:6.

3. Jerome, according to Aquinas, *Catena Aurea*, 1:127, tried to deal with the question whether the devil truly had control of "all the world's kingdoms and their glory" in simple fashion: "An arrogant and vain vaunt; for he hath not the power to bestow all kingdoms, since many of the saints have, we know, been made kings of [i.e., by] God."

4. See John 12:31; 16:11; Col 2:15; Heb 2:14. See also chapter 8 above, under "Jesus, Warrior and Son" and "Tying Up the Strong Man."

Matt 11:27: "all things")?[5] But if that similarity of expression from one end of Matthew's Gospel to the other—"all kingdoms," "all authority"—is something we are supposed to notice, it is ironic. The authority offered by the devil resides *in* "the kingdoms of the world," but Jesus has his authority because he has triumphed *over* the kingdoms (Col 2:15).

What Jesus was to receive is not what the devil offered, but if the devil could confuse Jesus on that point, perhaps the alternate course of action the devil laid out would not seem so drastically different from what Jesus was setting out on. Perhaps it could look like a means to the same end, a way for Jesus to accomplish his mission without the cross. Perhaps it might even look like the only possible means to that end so that, if Jesus refused it, he would be giving up on achieving anything at all.

But Jesus's response put the focus entirely on the means and said nothing about the end. Or better, it made the means—loyalty to God—the end in itself. "Achieving" drops out of view altogether. Jesus ignored questions of whether the devil really had anything to offer or whether saying no to the devil would limit his own effectiveness. He did not worry over what the devil did or did not have but only said what he himself would do, which was to reject the devil's whole line of talk in favor of worshiping and serving only God, regardless of consequences.

Jesus thus took that question about the devil's power and reconstructed it for us as a matter not of what the devil has but of what Jesus will give recognition to by his response, and of what we give recognition to by our responses. If I, for instance, agree with the devil's claims to power, then, by that very response, I make his claims true. I give him that power by giving it my recognition. But Jesus's response gives recognition and honor only to God and God's word. The devil and what he claims, legitimately or not, simply do not matter.[6]

Similarly, the transhuman powers have power only over those who give it to them, who agree with their claim to authority.[7] Those who do not acknowledge that authority are freed from it. That is the freedom that Jesus has brought us. The most the powers can do is kill us (Matt 10:28).

---

5. Or a little before Luke 10:17–18.

6. This is one reason that interpreting the temptation accounts as meaningful for faith does not require belief in the devil's existence in a traditional sense and that core statements of Christian doctrine have often not bothered to mention the devil.

7. As I said in a similar context in chapter 7 above (under "Who Are They?"), "believing it was true made it true." On my use of "transhuman," see note 10 in chapter 7 above.

Whether they do that, or whatever vain action they take to assert their authority over us (like Pilate's threat, John 19:10, or the accusations of the chief priests and elders, Matt 27:13), is not the final issue, because of resurrection (John 10:17–18).

Jesus decided on that high mountain to accept the path of kenosis, worshiping only God and submitting to whatever the powers can do. He rejected any means to authority quicker or easier than the one that included his own crucifixion. He has defeated the kingdoms and has done so by his own apparent defeat in death, by, that is, by God's means, kenosis.[8] Another portrayal of the same thing is in Revelation 5: "Who is worthy to open the scroll?" Or, we might say, Who can crack the code? (5:2). The one who is worthy is a conquering lion (v. 5) who turns out to be a dead, but upright, lamb (vv. 6–7). Attempting to translate Jesus into our understanding makes him seem thus to be his own opposite, but the problem is not with him but with our understanding, which does not readily comprehend kenosis. He is the one who is strong by being weak and who conquers by dying. He could have called on legions of angels to rescue him and did not (cf. John 14:30–31) but submitted to the powers that tried, convicted, and executed him.

Like Jesus, the church has been tempted by power, but it has often failed to follow his lead by repeating his "No" to that temptation. In fact, Christians more often than not have been seekers and holders of power, those who have believed the stories of effectiveness by force and have lived them out.[9] The alliance of church with government that has characterized much of the history of Christianity has, in both theory and practice, run counter to the way followed and taught by Jesus, our kenotic redeemer. Much of that history has been one of saying "Yes, that sounds like a good idea" to the devil when he has offered alternatives to patiently waiting for and following Jesus.

How do we deal with that past? We might choose from it exceptional church leaders who refused to use coercive power and say that we identify with them and not the others. There has, in fact, been a long historiographical tradition in believers-church denominations tracing a succession of parentage through various groups through church history, often from those considered heretical or schismatic in their own times.[10]

---

8. Jesus came to destroy the devil's works (1 John 3:8; Rev 12:9).

9. See chapter 2 above, under "The Oddness of the Story."

10. The issues have been baptism and other ecclesiological issues more often than possession or use of coercive power. See, e.g., Duvall, "Successionism View." For an

At best, what those historical groups represent is the ability of the Bible to break through the functioning of faith as social glue into its functioning in creating communities of free and therefore socially aberrant disciples of Jesus.

Taking that traditional historiographical route would not serve us well. If we believe that God's grace is available in the name of Jesus, then we cannot simply deny that past Christian generations had faith in Jesus, no matter what we might identify as their failings. Nor can we afford to be selective about whom in the past we identify with. We stand on the whole Christian experience and, while we might recognize centuries-long mistakes, we cannot choose our parents any more than we can choose among those who claim the name of Christian today. Neatly categorizing Christians of the past and present in such ways makes no allowance for limitations in, for instance, my understanding of the way of Jesus or of the actions of people in different circumstances than mine. And critique of past generations is not the same as hearing the word of God.[11] Perhaps the best place to begin is with some new images of our Christian communities.

Pictures of the Church

For example, we might hear Isaiah 2:2–4 as describing prophetically the origin, growth, and nature of the church. People from "every tribe, tongue, people, and nation" (Rev 5:9) will join in the worship of the God of Israel and will want to learn his ways. Through his teaching (*torah*, Isa 2:3) God settles arguments among members of this worldwide community, and therefore they no longer have any need for implements of war or training for battle.[12]

---

example (less doctrinaire than others), see Broadbent, *Pilgrim Church*. Some reflections of this tradition are seen in more recent works. For example, a recitation of lists of groups similar to those in Broadbent is in Yoder, *War of the Lamb*, 49–51.

11. Here I am cutting through past a number of questions that could be asked. For instance, what difference does what Christian tradition, with what sort of past, that we stand in make in how we hear God's word on these issues? What assumptions about how faithfulness is expressed are we bringing to our hearing? How is that affected by current movements of thought or lack thereof we identify with or react against? And there are endless hermeneutical questions, including what parts of the Bible we favor, and the constantly necessary questions regarding how fair or unfair to whom, in the past or now, we are with our judgments.

12. Taking "tongue" in Rom 14:10–11's quotation of Isa 45:23 as meaning "language," we see there the same combination of ideas.

Can we imagine that as a description of ourselves as Christians instead of (or in addition to) something to be brought about in a yet-unreached eschatological future? That is perhaps outrageous or absurd given the antagonisms among Christians and churches' adherence to their national bellicosities. But still, might Isaiah 2:2–4 be an only partly-fulfilled description of the church as an international community of cooperation and of discipleship to Jesus?[13] Might our delaying it for the future be a way of giving up on the possibility of a more complete testimony to God's work among us? Granted that this vision leaves non-Christians out of the equation, augmented by our historical propensity toward labeling enemies as non-Christians despite their confession. But we should not worry ahead of time about the effects of a witness we have barely recognized through much of our history, let alone begun to give clearly.

Two other ways we might have of understanding and articulating this witness would be to see the Sermon on the Mount as describing the church[14] and to explore the possibilities of Ephesians 2:14–22. In the latter we read that the building of the church is how peace is brought about. The language does not restrict itself to Jew-Gentile issues in a first-century church but provides a broad opening for our ethical imagination: How might we bear witness to our membership in a worldwide community in which hostility has been erased and a new humanity has been made from the combination of all of us together? How might we testify to our freedom from any political words that would cause us to think of that peace as merely one idea competing with others for our attention?

Why We Obey Laws

Even Romans 13—"Let every person be subject to the governing authorities . . ."—can contribute to this inspired imagination.[15] It is usually heard as simply acknowledging an authority given by God and possessed by human governments, whether it is rejected or gladly claimed as such.[16] But

---

13. This is how it was understood by Twisck, *Peaceful Kingdom of Christ*. The millennium of Rev 20 is fulfilled in the church according to Twisck.

14. See chapter 10 above, under "Perfection." Twisck also wrote in *Peaceful Kingdom* of the Sermon on the Mount as that which is fulfilled in the Christian community.

15. "One must transcribe almost the whole New Testament to collect all the Proofs it affords us of that Gentleness and Long-suffering, which constitute the distinguishing and essential Character of the Gospel" (Bayle, *Philosophical Commentary*, 84).

16. Rom 13:1–7 is a text that calls for interpreters to pay attention to their own

it is set in the context of Christian love, both mutual love in the Christian community and love for neighbors, including persecutors, and efforts to live at peace with all (12:9–14, 15–21; 13:8–10). So what Paul calls for is not just a submission compelled by fear of punishment (though he does allow for that in 13:3) but a submission that arises from specifically Christian motivations, not just love for neighbor and enemy but also knowledge of our freedom from the very institutions that we submit to, the governments. We have seen them for what they are, not what they describe themselves as—whether the divine Augustus, the all-fixing welfare state, or the unfailing enforcer of righteousness—but at the best merely "God's servant," holding authority only from God (13:1–2, 4, 6). Our pattern for this new kind of law keeping is Jesus, who triumphed over evil by good (cf. 12:21), that is, by his chosen submission to the governments that opposed him "as far as death, even death by crucifixion" (Phil 2:8). "His submission is one of love."[17] It is this complete love (Matt 5:48) that expels fear and provides a different motivation for submission than fear of punishment (1 John 4:18).

This different motivation works even for taxpaying. The rhythm of Romans 13:7 recalls Jesus's "to Caesar what belongs to Caesar, to God what belongs to God" (Matt 22:21). Even there, we miss some of the meaning if we take it as affirmation of our tendency to divide our obligations into separate domains, as if Caesar and God had agreed never to demand what belongs to each other. The church of the first three centuries received much of its shaping of thought from the fact of such trespassing of God and Caesar onto each other's claims. The freedom we receive from the Son of God (John 8:36) enables us both to find reasons to pay taxes that are based not on fear or on unfreedom but on our freedom as God's children (Matt 17:24–27) and to distinguish between God's claims on us and what we can afford to give to Caesar.

That distinction between obeying and paying out of obligation or fear and obeying and paying as those who follow Jesus in submitting enables us to think clearly when the habit is otherwise to assume that there is nothing to think about. For example, it is *necessary*, or so the institutions tell us to believe, to dispense justice and for everyone to assist

---

contexts as much as the text's historical context. Our knowledge of the latter is slim enough to have been called on in support of a wide range of interpretations. See Käsemann, "Principles of the Interpretation of Romans 13," or, more briefly, *Romans*, 351.

17. Illich, "Educational Enterprise."

in the dispensing of justice.[18] That is, if you are a fugitive from the law, it is *necessary* that I assist the police in apprehending you, because if we do not all (unthinkingly) retain our belief in that necessity and act on it, society will not function properly, criminals will be running loose, and we will not be safe. Those are the sorts of things the institutions as powers tell us. But in our freedom and in our knowledge of the God who laughs at horses and chariots[19] we can afford to be aware of the falsehood of such necessities, even the necessity of paying taxes, which we do for other reasons than the government's compulsion.

Behind all this, and just as much in need of thought by those who can afford to think, is the necessity of power if one is to accomplish things. When we follow the institutions in speaking in terms of this "necessity," we thereby acknowledge the institutions as powers, agree with them, and give them power over us. And we also thereby acknowledge the normal human story of or belief in power as the means to accomplish things rather than God's way of kenosis.[20] By, on the other hand, skipping over "necessity" we break that power. We debunk the "necessary"-ness, the lies of the powers. We do this, even as we are "subject to the governing authorities" for reasons other than their authority or their ability to punish. Our reasons arise from our knowledge of God and his way of kenosis.

A False Ending: Differentiating "Forms of Government"

Governments exist to manage sin. That is, first, they are the sum and institutionalization of the compromises we make to contain our competitiveness and the resulting chaos. And second, they are a way to focus and justify our actions against outside enemies and internal enemies, that is, those nonconformists and disrupters we call "criminals." So we have given up our freedom for the sake of our safety, and this loss of our freedom also takes away use of our ethical imagination.[21]

Then we hear God's laughter at the puniness of our power over each other, we see the necessity and grandiosity of our authorities debunked,

---

18. Augustine was aware of the difficulties of conscience and ambiguities of evidence that come with the judicial responsibilities of the ordinary citizen, but still he regarded those duties as necessary for the Christian (*City of God* 19.5-6).

19. See chapter 7 above, under "Fear Not."

20. See chapter 2 above, under "The Oddness of the Story."

21. See chapter 7 above, under "Freedom and Captivity," particularly under "Who Are They?"

and we obey laws for a reason that does not arise from the structures and compulsions of government.[22] Then, once we have seen all that, we begin avoiding as much as we can using those structures, particularly the civil courts, in disputes. Instead we do the hard work of dealing with others directly and loving them, knowing that the greatest personal loss would be inability to carry out that love of neighbor and enemy (Lev 19:18; Prov 24:29; Matt 5:39-41; Rom 12:16-21; 1 Cor 6:1-8; 1 Thess 5:15), which reaches far beyond what is lawful (1 Cor 6:12) or deserved (1 Cor 9:1-15).

The Bible does speak about God setting up and tearing down specific governments, but we should not expand that into a belief that every rise or fall of a government is orchestrated by God. He may be involved, but not because of any political preferences on his part. If he does that sort of thing, it is only in aid of his own movement of creation and redemption. He lets governments continue that he dislikes intensely. He is not very interested in the small battles and temporary victories that can be won or lost by governments. He is interested in the grand movement of creation-redemption.

Because the Bible as canon is committed to that grand movement, it does not give advice to the managers of sin or concern itself with temporary remedies. Some of its parts, extracted from the whole, can be made to do so,[23] but as canon it does not. Even when a government voice reads the Bible more carefully, a government finding counsel in the Bible is still not that far from applying "a house divided against itself cannot stand" to itself (so Lincoln's Gettysburg Address, quoting Mark 3:24), which is laughable. For government to care what the Bible says, the Bible would have to be considerably more practical and immediate than it is and therefore of more fleeting value. It exists, rather, for those who know how small are the great concerns of the moment.

So if we hear the Bible telling something to those who are not committed to God's grand movement of creation-redemption other than that they should be committed to it, we hear it wrongly. If we hear it telling

---

22. It might be true, as Girard and others have said, that government is always Satanic (*I See Satan Fall*, 44), but I avoid saying that because it makes government sound bigger than it is. "Satanic" might, by its grandiosity, lead us away from recognizing the prosaicness and ordinariness both of sin and of human efforts to contain sin, i.e., government. See again chapter 7 above, under "What Are We Afraid of?" on the humanness of institutions and sin.

23. Particularly what can be found in Proverbs and similar samples of general wisdom, which are only peripherally connected with the creation-redemption story.

the managers of sin what their job is, we fail to see that it calls all of us to repentance and away from belief that the small battles matter and from faith in what humans can do.

Furthermore, government cannot subject itself to anything outside itself, such as God, and remain what it is. It must ultimately answer to sin. It is there to manage sin and it consists of sinners. Redemption is too large for even something so grand as a government to contemplate. If government sets great goals, those goals must still remain nothing before redemption. So if redemption is set forth before a government and that government has been in the habit of speaking with grandiosity about its aims, then it must regard redemption as an enemy. Redemption is too large a distraction. It outshines the grand goals and hopes of government too much.[24]

In the meantime, we cannot construct much of a politics, in the limited sense of a platform to put forward or a program to work for in the democratic give-and-take of politics, on faith in God and his creation and redemption of us.[25] This is especially so because democracy, that recognition that "what I think to be just is tainted by my own self-interest" and that therefore "someone has to stand against me, and declare his different conviction,"[26] is a tiny, barely discernible component in the big picture understanding that we give testimony to in our confession of Jesus.

It is possible—indeed, it is done—to think that we live in a situation in which God and our government (over which there is, after all, no Caesar) do not have conflicting claims, that sorting out those claims is not something we have to tend to as the early church did. But the distinctions between those claims are only more subtle, not absent.

All this should direct us away from allying Christianity with whatever ideology or political program is in fashion or that we prefer.[27] There is no form of government that has not been excused or rationalized or even sanctified by being labeled "Christian." That in itself should tell us to avoid connecting faith too closely with political questions. Our imitation

---

24. I am, of course, speaking abstractly and not about any necessary lack of faith or insight on the part of any person involved in government. In that abstract way, see again, as in note 38 in chapter 6 above, Dostoevsky's "Grand Inquisitor," who is offended at Jesus's return because the church (it could as well be a government) is taking care of human happiness (Dostoevsky, *Brothers Karamazov* 5.5).

25. So Ellingsen, *Blessed Are the Cynical*, 40.

26. Niebuhr, *Justice and Mercy*, 44.

27. Jacques Ellul was particularly insistent on this (e.g., *Anarchy and Christianity*, 5). And one can certainly think of the Barmen Declaration (1934) in this regard.

of God in using persuasion rather than coercion or deception might be compatible with an *ideal* of democracy, but barely so with democracy as it is practiced anywhere today on national levels. Putting too much faith in any particular government can be another false ending to the story of humanity.[28]

"It Shall Not Be So among You"

We have seen in chapter 10 how Jesus attaches teachings on discipleship to predictions of his trial, death, and resurrection. The teaching segments following the second and third predictions use the figures of a child and a slave as social-class metaphors for kenotic discipleship.[29] In Matthew 20:20–28, the teaching comes in the course of an incident involving Jesus and his disciples, and how that story is told emphasizes the contrast between two worlds, the world of "rulers" and "great men," which the disciples assume as they speak to Jesus and argue among themselves, and the very different world of "slaves."[30]

The disciples' acclamation of Jesus as a king, led by Peter (Matt 16:16, 20), was backed by Peter's readiness to take up arms on behalf of Jesus (v. 22). But, Jesus said then, Peter was thus "setting [his] mind not on divine things but on human things" (v. 23). And it becomes clear that the disciples do not understand that the storming of gates (v. 18) comes by way of suffering, death, and resurrection. The irony of their misunderstanding, which began earlier in the Gospel, will reach its peak in chapter 26:

> Jesus told them, "Tonight all of you will give up. . . ."
> Peter and all the rest of them said, "Even if we follow you to death, we'll *never* desert you!" (vv. 31–35)

> Jesus prayed in agony: "Father, if possible, take this cup away from me. But not my will, but yours alone."
> Then he saw that his disciples were sleeping. (vv. 36–40)

---

28. See above, the first subsection of chapter 1 and under "False Endings" in both chapter 7 and chapter 10.

29. See chapter 10 above, under "The Child and the Slave."

30. Richard Horsley understands the contrast more in terms of political domination and subservience, with "servant" being a term for a lesser ruler or official in relation to one acknowledged as superior (Horsley, *Jesus and the Spiral of Violence*, 243). But there is no such political relationship in which Jesus is the "slave."

> Right after Jesus had been arrested and taken away,
> > all the disciples deserted him and ran off. (vv. 50–56)

> Peter was hanging out in the courtyard, and people started saying "You're one of them, aren't you?"
> > He answered, "Nope. Never even met him." (vv. 69–74)

The disciples were merely following the normal understanding of power in the wider human world and therefore understood Jesus's "kingdom" as implying both the unsuitability of him experiencing defeat, suffering, and death and the possession of rank and power by his closest followers. A broader assumption is also present, that there is such a thing as legitimate power or authority, which goes beyond simple ability to coerce and includes some rightness in its actions.

Jesus's teachings in Matthew 20 are constructed in relation to this set of assumptions about power and about his own power. The disciples speak of his "*kingdom*" (20:21), *but*, he says, he "came not to be served but to serve" (v. 28); the disciples "*know*" how things work in this world (v. 25), *but* they "don't know" how things will work out for Jesus and his closest followers (v. 22); the disciples *know* that "*great men*," which is what they want to be, "exercise authority" (v. 25), "*but*," Jesus says, "it shall not be so among you" (v. 26); and the disciples aspire to be "*great*" and "*first*" (vv. 25–26), *but* Jesus is a "slave" and his disciples are called to be slaves (vv. 26–28).

What Jesus teaches in vv. 25–27 has, I believe, been softened to mush by most interpreters. His response to James and John is a call to repentance: "Whoever wants to be great should, *instead of seeking that*, be a slave." Jesus rejects the human activity of self-magnification rather than redefining or redirecting it: "If you want to be a leader, then you need to repent of that and be a slave instead." The commentators generally disagree with this understanding and thus miss out on the contrast driving the story. Ulrich Luz is an exception: Jesus is not teaching against excessive ambition but against any ambition to be great/first. He is not giving the church "a new way of becoming great" but teaching his disciples to give up the desire to be "great" altogether.[31]

---

31. Luz, *Matthew 8–20*, 545. The papering over of Matt 20:26–27 (and 23:11) seem to be focused on the term "great" in 20:26 (similarly "first" or "preeminent" in v. 27):
- taking it as a positive term rather than allowing it to remain the (negative) opposite of the paradoxically positive "slave,"
- taking Jesus's "whoever wants to be great/preeminent" as meaning that the way to preeminence among the disciples should be by way of being a servant,

Augustine's words about desire for honor as both "the occasion of destruction" and "the instrument of good works"[32] exemplify what is perhaps behind some of the typical readings of Jesus's teaching here, namely a sense that striving for honor is inevitable. That supposed inevitability might have to be attributed to something other than "honor" in our day, perhaps "competition" or "ambition." Be that as it may, we have here another assumed necessity that Jesus allows us to challenge, a necessity that could, in Augustine's day, function only for the upper side of society while remaining blind both to the impracticality of honor ideals for those at the bottom (and for women) and to Jesus's rejection of such ideals.

It could also be said that Jesus is not rejecting the validity of government but merely describing relationships among his disciples as quite different from those among fellow politicians.[33] But that makes Jesus' teaching here no easier to swallow. To challenge the validity of the visible power structures is one thing, but to challenge Christians' assumptions about the finality of power may be even more difficult.[34]

So disciples of Jesus are to steer clear of anything that places them in authority over each other: "It shall not be so among you." No matter the form of government, politicians compete with each other, and that is a problem for followers of Jesus. He responds to his disciples' squabbling not with teaching on kindness or tolerance but with teaching on

- saying that, in contrast to everyone else, Jesus "defines greatness in an entirely opposite way" (Hagner, *Matthew 14–28*, 580–83, as one example; another is Montefiore, *Synoptic Gospels*, 1:252: "He who serves best is by that very fact the greatest"), or
- reading positive uses of "great" from elsewhere (e.g., Matt 18:4; 23:11) into interpretation of 20:26 (most explicitly Bruner, *Church Book*, 332, though now with some uncertainty in view of what Luz has written).

18:4 might argue for humility as a path to "greatness in the kingdom of heaven," but it can cut both ways because the child remains a child. Jesus does "redefine greatness" there, but in doing so rejects the category and ridicules the disciples, who themselves have brought up that term "greatest," which refers to the ruling class (18:1). He points to the child and thus contradicts the world of their assumptions, because a child in that day was obviously not "great." Born at that time, Mozart would have been an embarrassment to his father. "Whoever humbles himself like a child" is a direct contradiction of the disciples' aspirations for upward mobility and power.

32. *Sermon* 22(72).4.333 in Bruner, *Church Book*, 333.

33. This view is explicitly opposed by Horsley, *Jesus and the Spiral of Violence*, 243–44. Part of what is involved here is the meaning of *katakyrieuein*, whether "lord it over" or simply "rule," in verse 25. See further Clark, "Meaning of [Kata]kyrieuein."

34. See chapter 6 above, under "Legality and Other Means of Justification," for what William Stringfellow has written on "justification by works" in activist American Protestantism.

government, because that is what they are interested in. His way to church unity is for his disciples to set aside any idea of government and authority among themselves in favor of becoming servants and slaves. Government is something done by "Gentiles" (Matt 20:25), that is, by outsiders. "Gentiles" echoes v. 19 ("the chief priests . . . will hand over [Jesus] to the Gentiles to mock, whip, and crucify him") and thus refers to those who have the authority to carry out judicial killing (cf. John 18:31) and who are outside the people of God.

There is still some amount of metaphor in Jesus's language: he is not telling his disciples in Matthew 20:26–27 to sell themselves into slavery, something often done at that time but not without the compulsion of circumstances. But recognizing that non-literalness is not an invitation to trivialize what he says into "an attitude of servanthood." Jesus on the cross is the best proof that he had in mind more than an attitude adjustment. Or with the term "servant leadership"[35] the gap between "ruler/great/leader" and "servant" is narrowed to the vanishing point and Jesus's words are moved completely out of social class structure into—what?—management models? It would have been difficult for the disciples to understand Jesus's metaphorical language as that far removed from the literal, since in the questions, requests, and avowals they brought to Jesus, social class and political power were not metaphors at all. As a contradiction of the values of ambition, the metaphor of self-enslavement resists use in any context tolerant of those values.

BEARING WITNESS

The Manner of Our Churchliness

Knowing that we are freed from the power of sin and having heard the powers and institutions of this world laughed at by the creator, we are freed for ethical imagination and creativity. We can imagine what "as in heaven, so on earth" might look like and then can take creative steps toward that imagination. So the blessing of freedom becomes a freedom of

---

35. The term is used in exposition of this story in Bruner, *Church Book*, 332 (citing C. L. Blomberg) and in countless sermons. Commentators go to some length to soften the passage, but seldom as far as the Jesus Seminar went to remove it from Jesus: "During Jesus' lifetime, the organization of the movement was probably so minimal that such competition probably did not exist" (Funk et al., *Five Gospels*, 227). That is quite naive: Have none of the Seminar members ever been a member of a small church? A low level of organization is hardly incompatible with competitive tempests in teacups.

motion that others might envy (cf. Rom 11:11, 14). We can give our focus to the one story of creation and redemption so that it can be the backdrop for whatever we do, displacing merely political concerns and conflicts.

In this age, before Jesus has returned and longer before he has laid the kingdom down before the Father (1 Cor 15:24), our steps toward that vision have the quality of testimony. They are, that is, means by which we tell of our freedom and how it has been won. We bear witness to our having become convinced that things can be done differently, and that they can because Jesus has debunked and disarmed the powers and because the Holy Spirit gives us the ability to follow Jesus.

We can hear Matthew 20:25–27 as a teaching about church (non)government, and Paul shows us that Jesus's "servant" instructions took hold in the church (1 Cor 9:19; 2 Cor 4:5; Gal 5:13). Once we have an understanding of "church" derived from "It shall not be so among you," we realize the presence of some oxymorons in our history, such as "church politics," "church law," or "church trial," that is, occasions on which churches have followed, and continue to follow, governmental models. But, again, we need most to identify the contradictions in our actual church lives, not in the past or in somebody else's life. For instance,

- it does us no good to know what is wrong with a hierarchical denominational structure if our church is congregational in governance,
- we are unlikely to know well what is good or bad about that structure or any other we do not work within,
- we are also unlikely to know how much such a structure is shaped or even contradicted by the personalities involved so that "It shall not be so among you" really works there, and
- if the failures to follow "It shall not be so among you" in our own church setting are less structural and more subtle than in others, then we have a harder task of discernment.

That is only an example, and the point is not to define ourselves positively against anyone else but to apply ourselves seriously to the spiritual task of *self*-knowledge.

It is probably best for most of us to apply that kind of thinking to the local congregation because that is where we are in a position to encourage changes[36] and because structural changes toward "It shall not be so

---

36. The ecumenical movement has included much heartfelt concern for this witness. It seems to me, however, that it has often missed the point by wanting to effect *institutional* unity.

among you" that come from upper levels of a denomination might well be another oxymoron. Bearing testimony may seem beside the point when everybody in the room is a member of the administrative committee or whatever you call it. It is more likely to be weekly worship that a stranger wanders into (1 Cor 14:16), but that committee meeting is just as much a place where we shape ourselves, our community's ways of doing things, and therefore our witness to the presence of the Holy Spirit.

Here are some questions we might ask about our ways of doing things:

- How are decisions made? Is there a sense of finding a consensus, an "It seems good to us, having come to one accord" and an "It seemed right to us and to the Holy Spirit" (Acts 15:25, 28)?

- Do we hunt out the alternate voices? Then, do we take the time to work through things? Going a step more personal, do we think of the alternate voices as something to overcome on the way to a goal that we have already mapped out, or has our spirituality advanced beyond that?

- If we have a decision-making group of leaders, are we willing to think critically about how we might be shaping that group in such a way as to accomplish some kind of exclusion and also willing then to shape it to accomplish inclusion?

- Do we approach prayer as another step on the way toward goals we have already defined (whether we have said so out loud or not), or do we allow prayer time to shape our thinking? Are we willing to be honest about our hopes and goals and to describe them before we have finished shaping them?

- Are we willing to accept whomever we consider "the weak" and to give up judging each other (Rom 14:1–4)? Are we able to let the rules take a distant second place after the rule of love?

- The giving and taking of money in church obscures the message for some hearers. Might we better communicate what faith in God's provision is about if we find ways to leave out some of the money talk? What things do we do without money? How can we reduce our dependence on the two things that seem most to tie our congregations to money-gathering, namely, real estate and professionalism?

Jesus is not bound by what is practical or what works. At every point, he looks in love to the individual. He does not withdraw from that personalist perspective in the interest of getting something done. Giving up our fixation on effectiveness and action is probably the hardest part of all this. But even an ethic of valuing the individual and the victim can be used for power. Every handle we get on the way of the cross can be, indeed is, used in the quest for power. Witness the use of the language of the civil rights movement on behalf of entitlement, victimism, and political correctness.[37] "Often we believe we are imitating the true God, but we are really imitating only false models of the independent self that cannot be wounded or defeated. Far from making ourselves independent [of the contagion of scandal] and autonomous, we give ourselves to never ending rivalries."[38]

Understanding sin as expressing a power struggle helps us to understand sanctification.[39] Sanctification is a renunciation of power struggles, of the struggle against God and all the other fights as well. Church is where the power struggles do not take place. Again, "it shall not be so among you."

Our witness extends to how we deal with conflict within a congregation. Jesus has given us ways of doing that that do not follow a judicial or governmental model but seek reconciliation by way of forgiveness. The church uses no normal coercive enforcement, that is, what a government uses (Matt 18:15–17). It can treat offenders as what they want to be—as government officials (18:17), and it can also cancel the bond of brotherhood (18:18–20; cf. 16:19). Even so, the last word is forgiveness (18:21–22, reinforced by the parable in vv. 23–35). Jesus sets aside usual notions of what is just and fair for a standard that is quite different (20:1–16). Discipleship is expressed not in power games but in being like and caring for little children (18:1–14). And in case anyone missed the lesson, Jesus receives and blesses children (19:13–15).

Leading the Way Out of Fear

Christians are different from other people. We await the completion of our salvation and the full accomplishment of God's rule. In the meantime,

---

37. So James G. Williams in Girard, *I See Satan*, xxii.
38. Girard, *I See Satan*, 14.
39. See chapter 6 above, under "Sin as Power Struggle."

we are not alarmed by what alarms others (Isa 8:11–12; Jer 51:46; Matt 24:6), and we know that the "necessary" things, the assumptions that the institutions want us to take for granted, can be challenged. And the point of departure for our way of life is the setting aside of power, which comes prior to any arguments for use of force and makes it impossible to apply them to us.

We are, therefore, set us against some of the fundamental beliefs and rituals of our people, nation, and culture, just as Christians of the first centuries had to set aside the customary sacrifices to Caesar and to Victoria/Nikē. Jesus does not take into account either the *pax Romana* or any American mission when he tells us how his disciples are to live. Rather, we love our enemies (Matt 5:44), we seek reconciliation even before worship (vv. 23–24), and we fear God's judgment rather than what others fear (10:28). We live out God's redemption of us by imitating him in his kenosis.

All this places American Christians in both a difficult position and an interesting place in history. We are protected by the largest and most powerful military organization in human history. Many of us are grateful for that and also regard that military institution as, on balance, what it claims to be, namely, a force for good.[40] But we also have available to us God's word about his laughter at human power and institutions and about our freedom to stand aloof from any obligation to believe arguments for our acceptance of institutions or to be alarmed by what others are alarmed by. Therefore we are free to acknowledge that protection by the American military comes at an unacceptable price. And there is also, again, God's judgment, which takes the measure of what the American military promises and accomplishes far more accurately than any of us could.

Judgment is historical as well as eschatological. We cannot know the long-term outcomes of our military excursions any better than those of actions within our immediate relationships. Even outcomes of past actions fail to be obvious, or at least easy to overlook: we can argue away the outcomes of our parents' oppression of Native Americans and African Americans, though they stare us in the face. So we are protected from thoughts of judgment on our and our parents' actions by ignorance of our

---

40. The language of American patriotism identifies protection of the American people as the primary function of the American military. That is, of course, regularly questioned, but since I am talking about means more than aims (see chapter 10 above, under "Personalism") we can let it slide.

history and by misunderstanding of our present difficulties with people on the other sides of the world.

Along with that there are the historical and therefore predictable effects of militarization of a society, magnified by the vast extent of our militarization, including

- spiritual depletion, as we rely on that vast military power for safety rather than on God and teach ourselves to regard violence as necessary,
- the mental ill-health effects for those trained for and sent to war,[41] and
- violation of our mission among "all peoples," which is that they learn the way of Jesus (Matt 28:19–20).

Bear with me, then, as I engage in an impractical thought exercise about our place in history. It seems that we have an opportunity to give a startling testimony to the one story of creation and redemption and that we are in our kenotic discipleship to Jesus exactly what our people needs as we show the way out of fear and those "necessary" assumptions.

After September 11, 2001, I thought, but did not hope, that President Bush could lead us in (1) seeking to understand why Americans are so hated by some people and (2) finding ways we could make life better for people outside our borders. If that had happened, our enemies might not have received it or been impressed by it. But if our generosity were sufficient and sustained, they would have lost considerable moral traction. That would have posed a great temptation for Americans since we easily think that we are better and more generous than other people, but such generosity, small in consideration of our wealth, would carry a great moral example. As it was, President Bush led us in quite different directions, squandering what goodwill was gained after the attacks, fostering growth of our fears, and sinking us deeper in our militarism. But the only surprising thing about it was the severity of some of his rhetoric. Otherwise, he could have hardly done otherwise, given his position.

When I refer to the opportunity we have even now, I am thinking not of what a president could do but of what Americans can do, and American Christians bring far more to that opportunity than others. If,

---

41. "Standing calmly at attention while the man abreast of you is disemboweled by a cannon ball is an acquired skill and not a natural act" (Ellis, *His Excellency*, 117). See Pols and Oak, "War and Military Mental Health," for some military perspectives, and "Physical and Mental Health Costs," on longer-term outcomes.

for instance, the Department of Defense were led by "we the people," so many of whom are Christians, to beat swords into plowshares (Isa 2:4),[42] perhaps no one in the world would go hungry. No one would live outdoors unless they wanted to. There would be a great multiplication of fig trees for people to sit under (1 Kgs 4:25; Micah 4:4). This may be a childishly simplistic vision, but perhaps we fail to have confidence in the power of persuasion (2 Cor 10:4)[43] and to understand the oddness of the story we bear witness to if we reject the vision for that reason.

As so often when we look at some version of the big picture, the inclination is to ask rhetorically "What could we possibly do?" When that question means "What can we *accomplish*?" it can be disheartening. But if what we do is to give our testimony, perhaps telling our leaders a simple "We do not want this supposed protection," then the question is shifted away from accomplishment and back to faithful doing. Testifying is what we always do.[44]

I am (obviously) bypassing countless practical questions. How *do* we guard against potential skyjackers? I do not know. But just as asking pacifists to have answers for situations brought about by wars, hot and cold, is hardly a good test of their faith, so also expecting the testimony to Jesus to make sense within the constraints of a world dominated by human sin and unredemption will not work. We love our enemies not because it "works" but because Jesus told us to. Furthermore, part of the testimony to Jesus is willingness to suffer loss, to die, and to await the resurrection. All that is, of course, quite impractical except as measured against the far broader context of how God has shaped our universe, which is according to kenosis.

If it is beyond us to give this testimony, the account of Gideon shows that, to accomplish his purposes, including preserving his people so that his purposes with them can go forward, God prefers to work through the weak and the few, those who, at the end of the day, can give even clearer testimony that it is God who has saved, not they themselves (see particularly Judg 6:11, 15, 27; 7:2–7; 8:23).

---

42. What would that mean? Perhaps realizing that tanks make dandy tractors? But armor plating would increase soil compaction to unacceptable levels. It would have to go.

43. See chapter 10 above, under "Persuasion."

44. The testimony would be similar to that of Martin of Tours: "I am the soldier of Christ. It is not lawful for me to fight." And, if necessary to prove the point, "I will take my stand unarmed before the line of battle" (Sulpicius Severus, *Life of St. Martin* 4).

> The call comes to our Protestant church, just one like many others in the world: You are to redeem Israel; you are to set the people free from the chains of fear and cowardice and evil that bind them. This call startles the church and troubles it profoundly, this church without influence, powerless, undistinguished in every way—why is it the one to be burdened with this call? It looks at the hopelessness of its proclamation; it looks at the apathy and the misery of those who are supposed to be listening and recognizes that it is not equal to the task. It looks upon its own inner emptiness and barrenness, and it says fearfully and reproachfully, with what am I supposed to redeem this people? How am I supposed to do this phenomenal thing?[45]

Through all this, we can keep before us that image of "testimony" that I began with, that of the personal testimony given at baptism or in the informal "testimony meeting." There each of us retells the story of our redemption by God in such a way that our belonging to the community of those with similar testimonies is affirmed. There we tell how God has freed us from fear, from hesitation, from cultural captivation. There we answer the question "What is Christianity?" and give evidence for our answer, not in doctrinal exposition or apologetics but in the credibility of our testimony about what God has done in changing our lives. There, in what we say, God asserts his uniqueness over against those who testify on behalf of idols (Isa 44:8–9).[46] And there we join ourselves with those whose testimony concerning Jesus rouses the enmity of the devil (Rev 12:17) and of the particular "Babylon" they face (17:5, 6) and who thereby risk exile or death (1:9; 2:13; 6:9; 11:7; 20:4) but also thereby defeat the devil (12:10–11).

---

45. Bonhoeffer, *Berlin 1932–1933*, 464.

46. See chapter 1 above, under "Narrative Theology," and chapter 9, under "Confession and Testimony."

Bibliography

Abe, Masao. "Kenotic God and Dynamic Sunyata." In *The Emptying God: A Buddhist-Jewish-Christian Conversation*, edited by John Cobb and Christopher Ives, 3–65. Maryknoll: Orbis, 1990.
Adler, Felix. *Creed and Deed: A Series of Discourses*. New York: Putnam, 1880.
Alford, Henry. *The Greek Testament: An Exegetical and Critical Commentary*. London: Rivingtons, 1849–1863.
Allen, Willoughby C. *A Critical and Exegetical Commentary on the Gospel according to St Matthew*. International Critical Commentary. Edinburgh: T&T Clark, 1907.
Anselm of Canterbury. *Proslogium; Monologium; An Appendix in Behalf of the Fool by Gaunilon; and Cur Deus Homo*. Chicago: Open Court, 1926.
Aquinas, Thomas. *Commentary on the Four Gospels Collected Out of the Works of the Fathers [Catena Aurea]*. Oxford: Parker, 1874.
———. *Summa contra Gentiles: Of God and His Creatures*. Translated by Joseph Rickaby. St. Louis: Herder, 1905.
Augustine. *The Confessions of Augustine*. Translated by William G. T. Shedd. New York: Wiley, 1860.
Aulén, Gustav. *Christus Victor: An Historical Study of the Three Main Types of the Idea of Atonement*. London: SPCK, 1931.
Baillie, D. M. *God Was in Christ: An Essay on Incarnation and Atonement*. New York: Scribner, 1948.
Bakunin, Mikhail. *God and the State*. New York: Mother Earth, 1883.
Barr, James. *Biblical Faith and Natural Theology*. Gifford Lectures. Oxford: Clarendon, 1994.
———. "The Image of God in the Book of Genesis: A Study of Terminology." *Bulletin of the John Rylands Library* 51 (1968) 11–26.
Barth, Karl. *Christ and Adam: Man and Humanity in Romans 5*. New York: Harper, 1956.
———. *Church Dogmatics*. Edinburgh: T&T Clark, 1969–1981.
———. *The Epistle to the Romans*. New York: Oxford University Press, 1968.
Barton, John. "Disclosing Human Possibilities: Revelation and Biblical Stories." In *Revelation and Story: Narrative Theology and the Centrality of Story*, edited by Gerhard Sauter and John Barton, 53–60. Aldershot: Ashgate, 2000.
Bauckham, Richard. "'Only the Suffering God Can Help': Divine Passibility in Modern Theology." *Themelios* 9.3 (1984) 6–12.

Bauman, Clarence. *The Sermon on the Mount: The Modern Quest for Its Meaning.* Macon: Mercer University Press, 1985.

Bavinck, Herman. *Created, Fallen, and Converted Humanity.* Vol. 1 of *Reformed Ethics.* Grand Rapids: Baker Academic, 2019.

Bayer, Oswald. *A Contemporary in Dissent: Johann Georg Hamann as a Radical Enlightener.* Grand Rapids: Eerdmans, 2012.

Bayle, Pierre. *A Philosophical Commentary on These Words of the Gospel according to St. Luke, Chap. XIV. ver. 23. And the Lord Said unto the Servant, Go Out into the Highways and Hedges, and Compel Them to Come In, That My House May Be Fill'd. Containing a Refutation of the Literal Sense of This Passage.* Indianapolis: Liberty Fund, 2005.

Beecher, Henry Ward. "Immortality." In *The World's Great Sermons*, edited by Grenville Kleiser, 6:3–25. New York: Funk and Wagnalls, 1908.

Berkhof, Hendrik. *Christ and the Powers.* Scottdale: Herald, 1962.

Bierce, Ambrose. *A Cynic Looks at Life.* New York: Neale, 1912.

Bonhoeffer, Dietrich. *Berlin 1932–1933.* Dietrich Bonhoeffer Works 12. Minneapolis: Fortress, 2009.

———. *Creation and Fall: A Theological Exposition of Genesis 1–3.* Dietrich Bonhoeffer Works 3. Minneapolis: Fortress, 1997.

———. *Discipleship.* Dietrich Bonhoeffer Works 4. Minneapolis: Fortress, 2003.

———. *Ethics.* Dietrich Bonhoeffer Works 6. Minneapolis: Fortress, 2005.

———. *Letters and Papers from Prison.* Enlarged ed. New York: Macmillan, 1971.

Braaten, Carl E., and Robert W. Jenson, eds. *Christian Dogmatics.* Philadelphia: Fortress, 1984.

Broadbent, E. H. *The Pilgrim Church: Being Some Account of the Continuance through Succeeding Centuries of Churches Practising the Principles Taught and Exemplified in the New Testament.* Glasgow: Pickering and Inglis, 1935.

Broun, Heywood, Jr. *Pieces of Hate and Other Enthusiasms.* New York: Doran, 1922.

Brown, Catrina, and Tod Augusta-Scott. *Narrative Therapy: Making Meaning, Making Lives.* Los Angeles: Sage, 2007.

Bruce, Alexander Balmain. *The Humiliation of Christ: In Its Physical, Ethical, and Official Aspects.* 2nd ed. New York: Armstrong, 1901.

Bruner, Frederick Dale. *The Church Book: Matthew 13–28.* Rev. ed. Grand Rapids: Eerdmans, 2004.

Brunner, Emil. *Dogmatics.* 3 vols. Philadelphia: Westminster, 1952–1962.

Brunner, Peter. "Die Freiheit Des Menschen in Gottes Heilsgeschichte." *Kerygma und Dogma* 5.3 (1959) 238–57.

Bulgakov, Sergei. *The Bride of the Lamb.* Grand Rapids: Eerdmans, 2002.

———. *The Comforter.* Grand Rapids: Eerdmans, 2004.

Bultmann, Rudolf, et al. *Kerygma and Myth: A Theological Debate.* New York: Putnam, 1953.

Burnet, John. *Early Greek Philosophy.* London: A&C Black, 1892.

Burrell, David D. "Can We Be Free without a Creator?" In *God, Truth, and Witness: Engaging Stanley Hauerwas*, edited by L. Gregory Jones et al., 35–52. Grand Rapids: Brazos, 2005.

Calvin, John. *Commentaries on the First Book of Moses Called Genesis.* Edinburgh: Calvin Translation Society, 1847.

———. *Commentary on the Book of Psalms.* Edinburgh: Calvin Translation Society, 1845–1849.

———. *Mosis libri V: cum Iohannis Caluini commentariis; Genesis seorsum, reliqui quatuor in formam harmoniae digesti*. Geneva: Stephanus, 1563.
Caputo, John, and Mark Yount. "Institutions, Normalization, and Power." In *Foucault and the Critique of Institutions*, edited by John Caputo and Mark Yount, 3–23. University Park: Pennsylvania State University Press, 1993.
Cather, Willa. *A Collection of Stories, Reviews and Essays*. Reprint, Frankfurt: Outlook, 2018.
———. "Four Letters: Escapism." In *Commonweal Confronts the Century: Liberal Convictions, Catholic Tradition*, edited by Patrick Jordan and Paul Baumann, 371–73. New York: Simon and Schuster, 1999.
Catholic Church. *Catechism of the Catholic Church*. Vatican: Libreria Editrice Vaticana, 1993. Online. https://www.vatican.va/archive/eng0015/_index.htm.
Chaddick, Tim, and Craig Borlase. *Better: How Jesus Satisfies the Search for Meaning*. Colorado Springs: Cook, 2013.
Chamfort, Nicolas. *Maximes, Pensées, Caractères, et Anecdotes*. Paris: Baylis, 1796.
Chesterton, G. K. *Alarms and Discursions*. New York: Dodd, Mead, 1911.
———. *The Ball and the Cross*. New York: John Lane, 1909.
———. *The Club of Queer Trades*. New York: Harper and Brothers, 1905.
———. *Heretics*. New York: Lane, 1905.
———. *Twelve Types*. London: Humphreys, 1902.
Clark, Kenneth Willis. "The Meaning of [Kata]kyrieuein." In *The Gentile Bias and Other Essays*, by Kenneth Willis Clark, 207–12. Leiden: Brill, 1980.
Clines, David J. A. "The Image of God in Man." *Tyndale Bulletin* 19 (1968) 53–103. Reprinted in *On the Way to the Postmodern: Old Testament Essays, 1967–1998*, by David J. A. Clines, 2:447–97. Sheffield: Sheffield Academic, 1998.
Coakley, Sarah. "Kenosis and Subversion: On the Repression of 'Vulnerability' in Christian Feminist Writing." In *Swallowing a Fishbone: Feminist Theologians Debate Christianity*, edited by Daphne Hampson, 82–111. London: SPCK, 1996.
Collange, Jean-François. *The Epistle of Saint Paul to the Philippians*. London: Epworth, 1979.
Colloquium on Violence and Religion. "What Is Mimetic Theory?" Online. https://violenceandreligion.com/mimetic-theory.
Craddock, Fred B. *Luke*. Interpretation. Louisville: John Knox, 1990.
Crossan, John Dominic, and Jonathan Reed. *In Search of Paul: How Jesus's Apostle Opposed Rome's Empire with God's Kingdom*. San Francisco: HarperSanFrancisco, 2004.
Cullmann, Oscar. *The Earliest Christian Confessions*. London: Lutterworth, 1949.
Dawn, Marva. *Powers, Weakness, and the Tabernacling of God*. Grand Rapids: Eerdmans, 2001.
Decker, Rodney J. "Philippians 2:5–11, The Kenosis." Unpublished paper, 1996. NT Resources (blog). Online. http://ntresources.com/blog/wpcontent/uploads/2013/05/kenosis.pdf.
Delitzsch, Franz. *A New Commentary on Genesis*. Edinburgh: T&T Clark, 1888.
Dorner, Isaak August. *The History of the Development of the Doctrine of the Person of Christ*. Edinburgh: T&T Clark, 1880.
Driver, Samuel Rolles. *The Book of Genesis*. 2nd ed. Westminster Commentaries. London: Methuen, 1904.
Drown, Edward S. "The Growth of the Incarnation." *Harvard Theological Review* 7 (1914) 507–25.

Duff, Patricia A., and Jill Sinclair Bell. "Narrative Inquiry: More Than Just Telling Stories." *TESOL Quarterly* 36 (2002) 207–13.
Dunn, James D. G. *The Theology of Paul the Apostle*. Grand Rapids: Eerdmans, 1998.
Duvall, James R. "The Successionism View of Baptist History." *Journal of Baptist Studies* 3 (2009) 3–15.
Ellingsen, Mark. *Blessed Are the Cynical: How Original Sin Can Make America a Better Place*. Grand Rapids: Brazos, 2003.
Ellis, Joseph J. *His Excellency: George Washington*. New York: Vintage, 2005.
Ellul, Jacques. *Anarchy and Christianity*. Grand Rapids: Eerdmans, 1991.
———. "Cain, the Theologian of 1969." *Katallagete* 2 (1968–1969) 4–7.
———. *The Ethics of Freedom*. Grand Rapids: Eerdmans, 1976.
———. *The Meaning of the City*. Grand Rapids: Eerdmans, 1970.
———. *On Freedom, Love, and Power*. Toronto: University of Toronto Press, 2010.
———. *The Subversion of Christianity*. Grand Rapids: Eerdmans, 1986.
———. *Violence: Reflections from a Christian Perspective*. New York: Seabury, 1969.
Fee, Gordon D. *Paul's Letter to the Philippians*. New International Commentary on the New Testament. Grand Rapids: Eerdmans, 1995.
———. "Philippians 2:5–11: Hymn or Exalted Pauline Prose?" *Bulletin for Biblical Research* 2 (1992) 29–46.
Fischer, John Martin. "Foreknowledge, Freedom, and the Fixity of the Past." *Philosophia* 39 (2011) 461–74.
Flanagan, Owen. *Consciousness Reconsidered*. Cambridge: MIT Press, 1992.
Ford, David F. *Barth and God's Story: Biblical Narrative and the Theological Method of Karl Barth in the Church Dogmatics*. Eugene: Wipf and Stock, 2008.
Forsyth, P. T. *The Creative Theology of P. T. Forsyth*. Edited by Samuel J. Mikolaski. Grand Rapids: Eerdmans, 1969.
———. *The Person and Place of Jesus Christ*. 1909. Reprint, Grand Rapids: Eerdmans, 1965.
Frankfurt, Harry. "Alternate Possibilities and Moral Responsibility." *Journal of Philosophy* 66 (1969) 829–39.
Frazer, J. G. *The Belief in Immortality and the Worship of the Dead*. Gifford Lectures. London: Macmillan, 1913.
Frede, Michael. "The Case for Pagan Monotheism in Greek and Graeco-Roman Antiquity." In *One God: Pagan Monotheism in the Roman Empire*, edited by Stephen Mitchell and Peter van Nuffelen, 53–81. New York: Cambridge University Press, 2010.
Frei, Hans W. *The Eclipse of Biblical Narrative: A Study in Eighteenth and Nineteenth Century Hermeneutics*. New Haven: Yale University Press, 1974.
Fukuyama, Francis. "The End of History?" *The National Interest* 16 (1989) 3–18.
———. *The End of History and the Last Man*. New York: Free Press, 1992.
Funk, Robert W., et al. *The Five Gospels: The Search for the Authentic Words of Jesus*. New York: Macmillan, 1993.
Gaylor, Annie Laurie. *Women without Superstition: No Gods—No Masters: The Collected Writings of Women Freethinkers of the Nineteenth and Twentieth Centuries*. Madison: Freedom from Religion Foundation, 1997.
Gilbert, W. S. "Ruddigore [1887]." In *The Complete Plays of Gilbert and Sullivan*, edited by David Reed and David Widger. Project Gutenberg, February 1, 1997. Online. https://www.gutenberg.org/cache/epub/808/pg808-images.html#link2H_4_0024.

Girard, René. *I Saw Satan Fall like Lightning*. Maryknoll: Orbis, 2001.
Goetz, Ronald. "The Suffering God: The Rise of a New Orthodoxy." *Christian Century*, April 16, 1986. 385.
Goldingay, John. "Biblical Narrative and Systematic Theology." In *Between Two Horizons: Spanning New Testament Studies and Systematic Theology*, edited by Joel B. Green and Max Turner, 123–42. Grand Rapids: Eerdmans, 2000.
Goldman, Emma. *Living My Life*. New York: Knopf, 1931.
———. *My Further Disillusionment in Russia*. Garden City: Doubleday, 1924.
Gore, Charles. *The Incarnation of the Son of God: Being the Bampton Lectures for the Year 1891*. London: Murray, 1891.
Gorman, Michael. *Inhabiting the Cruciform God: Kenosis, Justification, and Theosis in Paul's Narrative Soteriology*. Grand Rapids: Eerdmans, 2009.
Gorsevski, Ellen W. *Peaceful Persuasion: The Geopolitics of Nonviolent Rhetoric*. Albany: State University of New York Press, 2004.
Green, Garrett, ed. *Scriptural Authority and Narrative Interpretation*. Philadelphia: Fortress, 1989.
Greer, A. Rowan. "Sighing for the Love of Truth: Augustine's Quest." In *God, Truth, and Witness: Engaging Stanley Hauerwas*, edited by L. Gregory Jones et al., 13–34. Grand Rapids: Brazos, 2005.
Griffin, David Ray, ed. *The Reenchantment of Science: Postmodern Proposals*. SUNY Series in Constructive Postmodern Thought. Albany: State University of New York Press, 1988.
Gunton, Colin. "Barth, the Trinity, and Human Freedom." *Theology Today* 43 (1986) 316–30.
———. *Triune Creator: A Historical and Systematic Study*. Grand Rapids: Eerdmans, 1998.
Hadot, Pierre. *Philosophy as a Way of Life: Spiritual Exercises from Socrates to Foucault*. Oxford: Blackwell, 1995.
Hagner, Donald A. *Matthew 14–28*. Word Biblical Commentary. Dallas: Word, 1995.
Hamilton, Victor P. *The Book of Genesis Chapters 1–17*. New International Commentary on the Old Testament. Grand Rapids: Eerdmans, 1990.
Harnack, Adolf von. *The Mission and Expansion of Christianity in the First Three Centuries*. London: Williams & Norgate, 1908.
Hauerwas, Stanley. *Better Hope: Resources for a Church Confronting Capitalism, Democracy, and Postmodernity*. Grand Rapids: Brazos, 2000.
———. "The End Is in the Beginning." In *Approaching the End: Eschatological Reflections on Church, Politics, and Life*, by Stanley Hauerwas, 3–21. Grand Rapids: Eerdmans, 2014.
———. "Explaining Christian Nonviolence: Notes for a Conversation with John Milbank and John Howard Yoder." In *Performing the Faith: Bonhoeffer and the Practice of Nonviolence*, by Stanley Hauerwas, 169–83. Grand Rapids: Brazos, 2004.
Havel, Václav. *Letters to Olga*. New York: Knopf, 1988.
Hawthorne, Gerald F. *Philippians*. Word Biblical Commentary. Waco: Word, 1983.
Hazlitt, William. *The Spirit of the Age: Contemporary Portraits*. New York: Wiley, 1849.
Heim, S. Mark. *Saved from Sacrifice: A Theology of the Cross*. Grand Rapids: Eerdmans, 2006.

Heppe, Heinrich. *Reformed Dogmatics: Set Out and Illustrated from the Sources.* London: Allen and Unwin, 1950.

Hessert, Paul. *Christ and the End of Meaning: The Theology of Passion.* London: Element, 1993.

Hill, Wesley. *Paul and the Trinity: Persons, Relations, and the Pauline Letters.* Grand Rapids: Eerdmans, 2015.

Hodge, Charles. *Systematic Theology.* New York: Scribner, 1871.

Holland, Saba, and Sarah Austin. *A Memoir of the Reverend Sydney Smith by His Daughter, Lady Holland, with a Selection from His Letters, Edited by Mrs. Austin.* London: Longman, Brown, Green, and Longmans, 1855.

Holmes, Michael W. *The Apostolic Fathers: Greek Texts and English Translations.* 3rd ed. Grand Rapids: Baker Academic, 2007.

Holstein, James A., and Jaber F. Gubrium. *The Self We Live By: Narrative Identity in a Postmodern World.* London: Oxford University Press, 2012.

Holzinger, Heinrich. *Genesis Erklärt.* Kurzer Hand-Commentar zum Alten Testament. Freiburg: Mohr, 1898.

Hooker, Morna D. *The Gospel according to Saint Mark.* Black's New Testament Commentary. London: A&C Black, 1991.

———. "Letter to the Philippians." In *The New Interpreter's Bible*, edited by Leander E. Keck et al., 9:467–549. Nashville: Abingdon, 2000.

Hoover, Roy W. "The Harpagmos Enigma: A Philological Solution." *Harvard Theological Review* 64 (1971) 95–119.

Horsley, Richard A. *Jesus and the Spiral of Violence: Popular Jewish Resistance in Roman Palestine.* San Francisco: Harper and Row, 1987.

Huffman, Norman A. "Atypical Features in the Parables of Jesus." *Journal of Biblical Literature* 97 (1978) 207–20.

Hugo, Victor. *Les Misérables.* Translated by Isabel F. Hapgood. New York: Crowell, 1887.

Hühn, Peter, et al., eds. "The Living Handbook of Narratology." February 20, 2021. Online. http://www.lhn.uni-hamburg.de.

Illich, Ivan. "The Educational Enterprise in the Light of the Gospel." Manuscript for lecture delivered in Chicago, November 13, 1988. Edited by Lee Hoinacki. Online. https://www.davidtinapple.com/illich/1988_Educational.html.

Jacobs, Alan. *Looking Before and After: Testimony and the Christian Life.* Grand Rapids: Eerdmans, 2008.

Jahn, Manfred. "Narratology 2.3: A Guide to the Theory of Narrative." *University of Cologne*, June 2021. Online. https://www.uni-koeln.de/~ame02/pppn.pdf.

James, William. *A Pluralistic Universe: Hibbert Lectures at Manchester College on the Present Situation in Philosophy.* New York: Longmans, Green, 1909.

Jenson, Robert. *Systematic Theology.* New York: Oxford University Press, 1997.

Jewett, Paul K. *God, Creation, and Revelation: A Neo-Evangelical Theology.* Grand Rapids: Eerdmans, 1991.

Jones, L. Gregory. "Narrative Theology." In *The Blackwell Encyclopedia of Modern Christian Thought*, edited by Alister E. McGrath, 395–98. Oxford: Blackwell, 1993.

Jüngel, Eberhard. *The Doctrine of the Trinity: God's Being Is in Becoming.* Grand Rapids: Eerdmans, 1976.

———. *God as the Mystery of the World: On the Foundation of the Theology of the Crucified One in the Dispute between Theism and Atheism.* New York: Bloomsbury, 1983.

Kärkkäinen, Veli-Matti. *Christ and Reconciliation*. Vol. 1 of *A Constructive Christian Theology for the Pluralistic World*. Grand Rapids: Eerdmans, 2013.

Käsemann, Ernst. *Commentary on Romans*. Grand Rapids: Eerdmans, 1980.

———. "Principles of the Interpretation of Romans 13." In *New Testament Questions for Today*, by Ernst Käsemann, 196–216. Minneapolis: Fortress, 1969.

Keener, Craig S. *The Gospel of Matthew: A Socio-Rhetorical Commentary*. 2nd ed. Grand Rapids: Eerdmans, 2009.

Kierkegaard, Søren. *Concluding Unscientific Postscript*. Princeton: Princeton University Press, 1944.

———. *Fear and Trembling*. London: Penguin, 1985.

———. *Practice in Christianity*. Princeton: Princeton University Press, 1991.

———. *Purity of Heart Is to Will One Thing: Spiritual Preparation for the Feast of Confession*. New York: Harper and Row, 1967.

———. *Works of Love: Some Christian Reflections in the Form of Discourses*. New York: Harper and Row, 1962.

Knox, John. *The Humanity and Divinity of Christ*. Cambridge: Cambridge University Press, 1967.

Kowal, Emma, et al. "Indigenous Genomics." *Australasian Science* 37 (2016) 18–20. Online. https://www.researchgate.net/publication/305092405_Indigenous_Genomics.

Lewis, C. S. *Christian Reflections*. Grand Rapids: Eerdmans, 1967.

———. *God in the Dock: Essays on Theology and Ethics*. Grand Rapids: Eerdmans, 1970.

———. *Mere Christianity*. Rev. ed. New York: Collier, 1960.

———. *Perelandra: A Novel*. Scribner Classics. New York: Scribner, 1996.

Lowry, Eugene L. *The Homiletical Plot: The Sermon as Narrative*. Rev. ed. Atlanta: John Knox, 2001.

Luther, Martin. "Promotionsdisputation von Georg Major und Johannes Faber. 12. Dezember 1544." In *Disputationen 1539/45*, edited by G. Bebermeyer, 293. Vol. 39.2 of *D. Martin Luthers Werke*. Weimarer Ausgabe. Weimar: Hermann Böhlau, 1932.

———. *Selections from the Psalms*. Vol. 12 of *Luther's Works: The American Edition*. Saint Louis: Concordia, 1955.

Luz, Ulrich. *Matthew 8–20*. Hermeneia. Minneapolis: Fortress, 1989.

Maritain, Jacques. *Approaches to God*. New York: Harper and Brothers, 1954.

McDermott, Brian O. *Word Become Flesh: Dimensions of Christology*. New Theology Studies 9. Collegeville: Liturgical, 1993.

McKeown, James. *Genesis*. Two Horizons Old Testament Commentary. Grand Rapids: Eerdmans, 2008.

Middleton, J. Richard. "A New Heaven and a New Earth: The Case for a Holistic Reading of the Biblical Story of Redemption." *Journal for Christian Theological Research* 6 (2006) 73–97. Online. http://digitalcommons.luthersem.edu/jctr/vol6/iss2001/4.

Mieroop, Marc van de. *Cuneiform Texts and the Writing of History*. London: Routledge, 1999.

Milbank, John. *Theology and Social Theory: Beyond Secular Reason*. Malden: Blackwell, 2006.

Mill, John Stuart. *Three Essays on Religion*. New York: Holt, 1874.

Miller, J. C. *A Collection of Souls: Tales of Terror, Delight, and Magic*. Bloomington: iUniverse, 2012.

Mills, Paul. "A Brief Theology of Time." *Cambridge Papers* 7 (1998). Online. https://www.cambridgepapers.org/a-brief-theology-of-time.
Mitchell, Stephen, and Peter van Nuffelen, eds. *One God: Pagan Monotheism in the Roman Empire*. New York: Cambridge University Press, 2010.
Moltmann, Jürgen. *The Crucified God*. 40th ann. ed. Minneapolis: Fortress, 2015.
———. *God in Creation: A New Theology of Creation and the Spirit of God*. New York: Harper and Row, 1985.
Montefiore, C. G. *The Synoptic Gospels, Edited with an Introduction and a Commentary*. 2nd ed. London: Macmillan, 1927.
Morris, Leon. *The Gospel according to Matthew*. New International Commentary on the New Testament. Grand Rapids: Eerdmans, 1992.
Morson, Gary Saul. *Narrative and Freedom: The Shadows of Time*. New Haven: Yale University Press, 1994.
Mozley, J. K. *The Doctrine of God*. London: SPCK, 1933.
Murphy, Francesca Aran. *God Is Not a Story: Realism Revisited*. Oxford: Oxford University Press, 2007.
Murphy, Nancey C., and George F. R. Ellis. *On the Moral Nature of the Universe: Theology, Cosmology, and Ethics*. Minneapolis: Fortress, 1996.
Nash-Marshall, Siobhan. "Free Will, Evil, and Saint Anselm." *Saint Anselm Journal* 5 (2008) 24–46.
Neuner, J., and J. Dupuis, eds. *The Christian Faith in the Doctrinal Documents of the Catholic Church*. Dublin: Mercier, 1976.
Newbigin, Lesslie. "Face to Face with Ultimate Reality." *Third Way* 17 (1998).
Niebuhr, Reinhold. *Justice and Mercy*. Edited by Ursula M. Niebuhr. Reprint, Louisville: Westminster John Knox, 1991.
Norton, Andrews. *A Translation of the Gospels: With Notes*. Boston: Little, Brown, 1856.
Oden, Thomas C. *The Living God: Systematic Theology Volume One*. San Francisco: Harper and Row, 1987.
Paley, William. *Natural Theology or Evidences of the Existence and Attributes of the Deity; Collected from the Appearances of Nature*. London: Faulder; Philadelphia: Morgan, 1802.
Perry, Dennis R. *Hitchcock and Poe: The Legacy of Delight and Terror*. Lanham: Scarecrow, 2003.
"Personalism." *Martin Luther King Jr. Research and Education Institute*, n.d. Online. https://kinginstitute.stanford.edu/personalism.
Peterson, M. L. "C. S. Lewis on the Necessity of Gratuitous Evil." In *C. S. Lewis as Philosopher: Truth, Goodness and Beauty*, edited by David Baggett et al., 175–92. Downers Grove: IVP Academic, 2008.
Pinnock, Clark H. "From Augustine to Arminius: A Pilgrimage in Theology." In *The Grace of God, the Will of Man: A Case for Arminianism*, edited by Clark H. Pinnock, 15–30. Grand Rapids: Zondervan, 1989.
Placher, William C. *Narratives of a Vulnerable God: Christ, Theology, and Scripture*. Louisville: Westminster John Knox, 1994.
Plain Truth Ministries. "About." Online. https://www.ptm.org/about.
Plantinga, Alvin. "The Free Will Defense." In *The Analytic Theist: An Alvin Plantinga Reader*, edited by James F. Sennett, 22–49. Grand Rapids: Eerdmans, 1998.
Pols, Hans, and Stephanie Oak. "Physical and Mental Health Costs of Traumatic War Experiences among Civil War Veterans." *Archives of General Psychiatry* 63

(2006) 193–200. Online. https://jamanetwork.com/journals/jamapsychiatry/fullarticle/209288.

———. "War and Military Mental Health: The US Psychiatric Response in the Twentieth Century." *American Journal of Public Health* 97 (2007) 2132–42. Online. https://ajph.aphapublications.org/doi/10.2105/AJPH.2006.090910.

Pritchard, James B., ed. *Ancient Near Eastern Texts Relating to the Old Testament*. 3rd ed. Princeton: Princeton University Press, 1969.

Rad, Gerhard von. *Genesis: A Commentary*. Old Testament Library. Rev. ed. Philadelphia: Westminster, 1972.

Rahner, Karl. "On the Theology of the Incarnation." In *Theological Investigations*, by Karl Rahner, 4:112–16. Baltimore: Helicon, 1982–92.

Ratzinger, Joseph. *"In the Beginning . . .": A Catholic Understanding of the Story of the Creation and the Fall*. Grand Rapids: Eerdmans, 1995.

Rawls, Joe. "Bulgakov on the Incarnation." *Byzantine Anglo-Catholic* (blog), March 5, 2008. Online. https://thebyzantineanglocatholic.blogspot.com/2008/03/bulgakov-on-incarnation.html.

Rice, Richard. "Divine Foreknowledge and Free-Will Theism." In *The Grace of God, the Will of Man: A Case for Arminianism*, edited by Clark H. Pinnock, 121–39. Grand Rapids: Zondervan, 1989.

Rogers, Katherin A. "Anselm on God's Perfect Freedom." *Saint Anselm Journal* 1.1 (2003) 1–8. Online. https://www.anselm.edu/sites/default/files/documents/institute%20of%20sa%20studies/4.5.3.2j_11rogers.pdf.

Rousseau, Jean Jacques. *The Social Contract*. London: Dent, 1913.

Sands, Paul. "The *Imago Dei* as Vocation." *Evangelical Quarterly* 82 (2010) 28–41.

Schmid, Heinrich. *The Doctrinal Theology of the Evangelical Lutheran Church*. 3rd ed. Minneapolis: Augsburg, 1899.

Schmiechen, Peter. *Saving Power: Theories of Atonement and Forms of the Church*. Grand Rapids: Eerdmans, 2005.

Schom, Alan. *Napoleon Bonaparte*. New York: HarperCollins, 1997.

Schreiner, Susan E. "Martin Luther." In *The Sermon on the Mount through the Centuries: From the Early Church to John Paul II*, edited by Jeffrey P. Greenman et al., 109–27. Grand Rapids: Brazos, 2007.

Segal, Alan F. *Paul the Convert: The Apostolate and Apostasy of Saul the Pharisee*. New Haven: Yale University Press, 1990.

Segundo, Juan Luis. *Grace and the Human Condition*. Vol. 2 of *A Theology for Artisans of a New Humanity*. Maryknoll: Orbis, 1973.

Seuss, Dr. *The Butter Battle Book*. New York: Random House, 1984.

Shuster, Marguerite. "The Temptation, Sinlessness, and Sympathy of Jesus: Another Look at the Dilemma of Hebrews 4:15." In *Perspectives on Christology: Essays in Honor of Paul K. Jewett*, edited by Marguerite Shuster and Richard Muller, 197–209. Grand Rapids: Zondervan, 1991.

Simpson, John W., Jr. "Shaped by the Stories: Narrative in 1 Thessalonians." *Asbury Theological Journal* 53 (1998) 15–25.

Skinner, John. *A Critical and Exegetical Commentary on Genesis*. International Critical Commentary. 2nd ed. Edinburgh: T&T Clark, 1930.

Smit, Laura A., and Stephen E. Fowl. *Judges and Ruth*. Brazos Theological Commentary on the Bible. Grand Rapids: Brazos, 2018.

Snyder Belousek, Darrin W. *Atonement, Justice, and Peace: The Message of the Cross and the Mission of the Church*. Grand Rapids: Eerdmans, 2012.

———. "God, Jesus, and Nonviolence: A Response to J. Denny Weaver." *Mennonite*, July 1, 2010. Online. https://anabaptistworld.org/god-jesus-nonviolence-response-j-denny-weaver.

Sparks, Kenton L. *Sacred Word, Broken Word: Biblical Authority and the Dark Side of Scripture*. Grand Rapids: Eerdmans, 2012.

Stringfellow, William. *An Ethic for Christians and Other Aliens in a Strange Land*. Waco: Word, 1973.

———. *Free in Obedience*. New York: Seabury, 1964.

———. *A Keeper of the Word: Selected Writings of William Stringfellow*. Edited by Bill Wylie Kellerman. Grand Rapids: Eerdmans, 1994.

Strong, Augustus Hopkins. *Systematic Theology: A Compendium and Commonplace-Book Designed for the Use of Theological Students*. Old Tappan: Revell, 1907.

Stroup, George W. *The Promise of Narrative Theology: Recovering the Gospel in the Church*. Atlanta: John Knox, 1981.

Swartz, Norman. "Foreknowledge and Free Will." *Internet Encyclopedia of Philosophy*, 2004. Online. https://www.iep.utm.edu/foreknow.

Swift, Jonathan. "Argument against Abolishing Christianity" ('An Argument to Prove That the Abolishing of Christianity in England May, as Things Now Stand, Be Attended with Some Inconveniences, and Perhaps Not Produce Those Many Good Effects Proposed Thereby, Written in the Year 1708')." In *Swift's Writings on Religion and the Church 1*, edited by Temple Scott, 5–19. Vol. 3 of *The Prose Works of Jonathan Swift, DD*. London: George Bell, 1898.

Taylor, Barbara Brown. *The Luminous Web: Essays on Science and Religion*. New York: Cowley, 2000.

Thielicke, Helmut. *The Evangelical Faith*. 3 vols., Grand Rapids: Eerdmans, 1974–1977.

Thiemann, Ronald F. *Revelation and Theology: The Gospel as Narrated Promise*. Notre Dame: University of Notre Dame Press, 1985.

Thiselton, Anthony. *Systematic Theology*. Grand Rapids: Eerdmans, 2015.

Tiessen, Terrance. *Providence and Prayer: How Does God Work in the World?* Downers Grove: InterVarsity, 2000.

Tolstoy, Leo. *Ivan the Fool*. New York: Webster, 1891.

Toronto Baptist Seminary and Bible College. "Doctrinal Statement." Online. http://tbs.edu/about/doctrinal-statement.

Tsumura, David Toshio. "Genesis and Ancient Near Eastern Stories of Creation and Flood: An Introduction." In *I Studied Inscriptions from before the Flood: Ancient Near Eastern, Literary and Linguistic Approaches to Genesis 1–11*, edited by Richard A. Hess and David Toshio Tsumura, 27–57. Sources for Biblical and Theological Study 4. Winona Lake: Eisenbrauns, 1994.

Twain, Mark. "The Czar's Soliloquy." In *Life as I Find It: A Collection of Mark Twain Rarities*, edited by Charles Neider, 267–72. Garden City: Doubleday, 1961.

———. *The Mysterious Stranger*. New York: Harper and Brothers, 1916.

Twisck, Pieter Jansz. *The Peaceful Kingdom of Christ*. Elkhart: n.p., 1913.

Ullmann, Carl. *The Sinlessness of Jesus: An Evidence for Christianity*. Edinburgh: T&T Clark, 1858.

Valliere, Paul. *Modern Russian Theology: Bukharev, Soloviev, Bulgakov*. Grand Rapids: Eerdmans, 2000.

Ward, Pete. *Introducing Practical Theology: Mission, Ministry, and the Life of the Church.* Grand Rapids: Baker Academic, 2017.
Warfield, B. B. "Augustine and the Pelagian Controversy." In vol. 5 of *Nicene and Post-Nicene Fathers*, Series 1, edited by Philip Schaff, xiii–lxxi. Reprint, Grand Rapids, 1982.
———. "Person of Christ." In *International Standard Bible Encyclopedia*, edited by James Orr, 2338–48. 1st ed. Grand Rapids: Eerdmans, 1929.
Weaver, J. Denny. *The Nonviolent God.* 2nd ed. Grand Rapids: Eerdmans, 2011.
———. "The Peace Church as Worship of God." *Mennonite*, July 1, 2010. Online. https://anabaptistworld.org/peace-church-worship-god.
Weber, Otto. *Foundations of Dogmatics.* 2 vols., Grand Rapids: Eerdmans, 1981–1983.
Wenham, Gordon. *Genesis 1–15.* Word Biblical Commentary. Dallas: Word, 1987.
Wesley, John. *Directions for Renewing Our Covenant with God.* 2nd ed. London: Paramore, 1781.
Wesleyan Church. *The Discipline of the Wesleyan Church 2012.* Indianapolis: Wesleyan, 2012.
Westermann, Claus. *Genesis 1–11.* Continental Commentaries. Minneapolis: Fortress, 1994.
Wiedemann, Thomas. *Greek and Roman Slavery.* Baltimore: Johns Hopkins University Press, 1981.
Wilken, Robert. "The Resurrection of Jesus and the Doctrine of the Trinity." *Word and World* 1 (1982) 28.
William of Ockham. *Opera philosophica et theologica.* Edited by Gedeon Gál et al. St. Bonaventure: Franciscan Institute, 1967–1988.
Williams, Jay G. "Genesis 3." *Interpretation* 35 (1981) 274–79.
Williams, Rowan. *Arius: Heresy and Tradition.* Grand Rapids: Eerdmans, 2002.
Williamson, Ronald. "Hebrew 4:15 and the Sinlessness of Jesus." *Expository Times* 86 (1974) 4–8.
Wink, Walter. *Engaging the Powers.* Minneapolis: Fortress, 1992.
———. *Naming the Powers.* Minneapolis: Fortress, 1984.
———. "Stringfellow on the Powers." In *Radical Christian and Exemplary Lawyer: Honoring William Stringfellow*, edited by Andrew W. McThenia, 17–30. Grand Rapids: Eerdmans, 1995.
———. *Unmasking the Powers.* Minneapolis: Fortress, 1986.
Wojcik, Michal. "The Uses of Re-Enchantment: Fantasy and Postmodernism." *One Last Sketch* (blog), February 4, 2011. Online. https://onelastsketch.wordpress.com/2011/02/04/the-uses-of-re-enchantment-fantasy-and-postmodernism.
Wright, G. Ernest. *God Who Acts: Biblical Theology as Recital.* London: SCM, 1952.
Wright, N. T. *The Climax of the Covenant: Christ and the Law in Pauline Theology.* Minneapolis: Fortress, 1991.
Yinger, Winthrop. *Cesar Chavez: The Rhetoric of Nonviolence.* Hicksville: Exposition, 1975.
Yoder, John Howard. *Karl Barth and the Problem of War.* Nashville: Abingdon, 1970.
———. *Karl Barth and the Problem of War and Other Essays on Barth.* Edited by Mark Thiessen Nation. Eugene: Cascade, 2003.
———. *A Pacifist Way of Knowing: John Howard Yoder's Nonviolent Epistemology.* Edited by Christian E. Early and Ted G. Grimsrud. Eugene: Cascade, 2010.
———. *The Politics of Jesus: Vicit Agnus Noster.* 2nd ed. Grand Rapids: Eerdmans, 1994.

———. *To Hear the Word*. Eugene: Wipf & Stock, 2001.

———. "Trinity Versus Theodicy: Hebraic Realism and the Temptation to Judge God." Unpublished paper, 1996. Online. http://palni.contentdm.oclc.org/cdm/ref/collection/p15705coll18/id/3491.

———. *The War of the Lamb: The Ethics of Nonviolence and Peacemaking*. Grand Rapids: Brazos, 2009.

Zangwill, Israel. *Italian Fantasies*. London: Heinemann, 1910.

Zwick, Mark, and Louise Zwick. "Emmanuel Mounier, Personalism, and the Catholic Worker Movement." *Houston Catholic Worker*, August 1, 1999. Online. https://cjd.org/1999/08/01/emmanuel-mounier-personalism-and-the-catholic-worker-movement.

Index of Authors

Abe, Masao, 35–37
Adler, Felix, 48
Alford, Henry, 159, 184
Allen, Willoughby C., 179
Ambrose of Milan, 45
Andersen, Hans Christian, 97
Anselm of Canterbury, 39, 54, 66, 136, 137
Aquinas, Thomas. *See* Thomas Aquinas.
Aristotle, 1, 57
Athanasius of Alexandria, 45
Athenagoras of Athens, 17
Augusta-Scott, Tod, 2
Augustine of Hippo, 15–16, 45, 59, 60, 66, 71, 87–88, 99, 103, 117–20, 140, 144, 146, 163, 166, 177, 204, 209
Aulén, Gustav, 136

Baillie, D. M., 24
Bakunin, Mikhail, 5, 78, 84, 121
Barr, James, 45, 47
Barth, Karl, 9, 19, 22, 23, 24, 30, 36, 39–41, 43, 45, 51, 52, 54, 62–67, 78, 88, 99, 109–10, 114, 145, 146, 171, 172
Barton, John, 8, 13
Bauckham, Richard, 19
Bauman, Clarence, 194
Bavinck, Herman, 119
Bayer, Oswald, 31
Bayle, Pierre, 202
Beecher, Henry Ward, 48
Berkhof, Hendrik, 126

Bierce, Ambrose, 48
Bonhoeffer, Dietrich, 29, 47, 99, 114, 116, 154, 186, 217
Borlase, Craig, 154
Braaten, Carl E., 140, 145
Broadbent, E. H., 201
Brontë, Charlotte, 79
Broun, Heywood, Jr., 191
Brown, Catrina, 2
Bruce, Alexander Balmain, 24
Bruner, Frederick Dale, 209, 210
Brunner, Emil, 28, 59
Brunner, Peter, 20
Bulgakov, Sergei, 30–31, 35, 60, 61, 64, 77, 114
Bultmann, Rudolf, 12
Burnet, John, 18
Burnett, T Bone, 134
Burrell, David D., 51

Cafiero, Carlo, 121
Calvin, John, 18, 28, 37, 46, 47, 57, 71, 72, 76, 84, 112, 136, 137, 194
Caputo, John, 104
Cather, Willa, 91, 119
Catholic Church, 42
Celsus, 17
Chaddick, Tim, 154
Chalcedon, Council of, 21, 34
Chamfort, Nicolas, 3
Chesterton, G. K., 5, 40, 43, 62, 78–79, 91, 98, 105, 128, 152, 193
Clark, K. W., 209

231

Clines, David J. A., 45, 46
Coakley, Sarah, 8–9
Collange, Jean-François, 24, 27, 33
Craddock, Fred B., 159
Crossan, John Dominic, 32–33
Cullmann, Oscar, 23

Davidson, Arnold I., 18
Dawn, Marva, 126
Decker, Rodney J., 26
Delitzsch, Franz, 76
Descartes, René, 98
Dickens, Charles, 2–3, 111
Dorner, Isaak August, 140
Dostoevsky, Fyodor, 107, 206
Driver, Samuel Rolles, 46
Drown, Edward S., 20, 142
Duff, Patricia A., 3
Dunn, James D. G., 113
Duvall, James R., 200

Ellingsen, Mark, 206
Ellis, George F. R., 28, 42, 176
Ellis, Joseph J., 215
Ellul, Jacques, 18, 22, 75, 107, 126, 135, 186, 190, 206
Ephraim the Syrian, 46

Fee, Gordon D., 25, 33
Feuerbach, Ludwig, 5, 47, 98
Fischer, John Martin, 67
Flanagan, Owen, 2
Ford, David F., 22
Forsyth, P. T., 33–35
Foucault, Michel, 83, 104
Frankfurt, Harry, 88
Frazer, J. G., 48, 96
Frede, Michael, 17
Frei, Hans W., 9
Fukuyama, Francis, 109
Funk, Robert W., 210

Gaylor, Annie Laurie, 86
Gilbert, W. S., 181
Girard, René, 27, 75, 100, 105, 125, 177, 205, 213
Goetz, Ronald, 19
Goldingay, John, 7

Goldman, Emma, 86, 192
Gordon, George (Lord Byron), 3
Gore, Charles, 35
Gorman, Michael, 33
Gorsevski, Ellen W., 189
Green, Garrett, 9
Greer, A. Rowan, 118, 146
Gregory of Nyssa, 45, 141
Griffin, David Ray, 44
Gubrium, Jaber F., 2
Gunton, Colin, 30, 51, 52, 59, 60, 64, 67, 87, 89, 171

Hadot, Pierre, 173
Hagner, Donald A., 209
Hamann, Johann Georg, 31
Hamilton, Victor P., 77
Harnack, Adolf von, 18
Hauerwas, Stanley, 64, 67, 114
Havel, Václav, 94, 97
Hawthorne, Gerald F., 24, 27
Hazlitt, William, 111–12
Heidelberg Catechism, 65–66
Heim, S. Mark, 19
Heppe, Heinrich, 46, 63, 67
Hermas, 26
Hessert, Paul, 154
Hilary of Poitiers, 45
Hill, Wesley, 21
Hodge, Charles, 46, 138
Holmes, Michael, 155
Holstein, James A., 2
Holzinger, H., 46
Hooker, Morna D., 33, 149
Hoover, Roy W., 25
Horsley, Richard A., 207, 209
Huffman, Norman A., 159
Hugo, Victor, 49, 56
Hühn, Peter, et al., 2

Ignatius of Antioch, 144
Ignatius of Loyola, 173
Illich, Ivan, 169, 198, 203
Irenaeus of Lyon, 14, 17–18, 60, 136, 148, 175–76

Jacobs, Alan, 8, 168
Jahn, Manfred, 2

INDEX OF AUTHORS

James, William, 53, 55
Jenson, Robert W., 20, 67, 145
Jerome, 149, 198
Jewett, Paul K., 15, 54, 88
John Chrysostom, 42
John of Damascus, 17, 28–29, 36, 141
Jones, L. Gregory
Jüngel, Eberhard, 22, 33, 35
Justin Martyr, 17

Kant, Immanuel, 78
Kärkkäinen, Veli-Matti, 136
Käsemann, Ernst, 203
Keener, Craig S., 159
Kierkegaard, Søren, 65, 114, 116–18, 190, 192
Knox, John, 140, 141
Kowal, Emma, et al., 11

Levinas, Emmanuel, 189
Lewis, C. S., 5, 91, 98, 103, 190
Lindbeck, George, 9
Lowry, Eugene L., 6
Luther, Martin, 35, 42
Luz, Ulrich, 208

Maritain, Jacques, 98
McDermott, Brian O., 30
McKeown, James, 76
Middleton, J. Richard, 4
Mieroop, Marc van de, 3
Milbank, John, 50, 53, 64
Mill, John Stuart, 55
Miller, J. C., 91
Mills, Paul, 66, 67
Milton, John, 87
Moltmann, Jürgen, 28, 32, 41, 51, 55, 61, 66
Montefiore, C. G., 209
Morris, Leon, 194
Morson, Gary Saul, 3
Mozley, J. K., 49
Murphy, Francesca Aran, 9
Murphy, Nancey C., 28, 42, 176

Nash-Marshall, Siobhan, 88
Newbigin, Lesslie, 187

Niebuhr, Reinhold, 206
Norton, Andrews, 139–40

Oak, Stephanie, 215
Oden, Thomas C., 39
Origen, 18, 20, 66

Paley, William, 44
Perry, Dennis R., 91
Peterson, M. L., 63
Pinnock, Clark H., 65
Placher, William C., 14, 22, 177
Plantinga, Alvin, 44–45, 88
Pols, Hans, 215
Pritchard, James B., 56
pseudo-Clement, 42
pseudo-Dionysius, 22

Rad, Gerhard von, 113
Rahner, Karl, 35
Ratzinger, Joseph, 14, 59, 172, 175
Rawls, Joe, 30
Reclus, Elisée, 121
Reed, Jonathan, 32–33
Rice, Richard, 67
Rickaby, Joseph, 48, 54
Rogers, Katherin A., 39
Rousseau, Jean Jacques, 125

Sands, Paul, 45
Schmid, Heinrich, 41, 51, 97
Schmiechen, Peter, 136, 137
Schom, Alan, 193
Schreiner, Susan E., 195
Segal, Alan F., 168
Segundo, Juan Luis, 133
Seuss, Dr., 105
Shuster, Marguerite, 140, 141, 144
Simpson, John W., Jr., 23
Sinclair Bell, Jill, 3
Skinner, John, 46
Smit, Laura A., 19
Smith, Sydney, 124
Snyder Belousek, Darrin W., 37, 95
Sparks, Kenton L., 115
Stange, Carl, 194
Stringfellow, William, 107–8, 126, 127, 131, 164, 174, 190, 209

Strong, Augustus Hopkins, 41, 53, 55
Stroup, George W., 9
Sulpicius Severus, 216
Swartz, Norman, 67
Swift, Jonathan, 182–83

Taylor, Barbara Brown, 57, 59
Tertullian of Carthage, 72
Theodoret of Cyrrhus, 21
Theophilus of Antioch, 18
Thielicke, Helmut, 140
Thiemann, Ronald F., 9
Thiselton, Anthony, 88
Thomas Aquinas, 29, 39–40, 53, 54, 62, 87, 114–16, 139–41, 144, 149, 195, 198
Tiessen, Terrance, 62–63
Tolstoy, Leo, 94
Tsumura, David Toshio, 56
Twain, Mark, 93–94
Twisck, Pieter Jansz, 202

Ullmann, Carl, 141

Valliere, Paul, 30
Vatican Council I, 19

Ward, Pete, 8
Warfield, B. B., 25, 50

Weaver, J. Denny, 36
Weber, Otto, 15–16, 19, 22, 40–41
Wenham, Gordon, 46, 72, 76
Wesley, John, 110
Wesleyan Church, 8
Westermann, Claus, 72, 75–76, 113
Wiedemann, Thomas, 27
Wilken, Robert, 43
William of Ockham, 52
Williams, James G., 27, 213
Williams. Jay G., 88
Williams, Rowan, 18
Williamson, Ronald, 140, 141
Wink, Walter, 126
Wojcik, Michal, 44
Wright, G. Ernest, 41
Wright, N. T., 21, 25

Xenophanes, 18

Yinger, Winthrop, 189
Yoder, John Howard, 9, 51, 52, 65, 101, 114, 126–28, 130, 131, 142, 153, 154, 171, 185, 189, 194, 195, 201
Yount, Mark, 104

Zangwill, Israel, 120
Zwick, Louise, 190
Zwick, Mark, 190

Index of Biblical References

OLD TESTAMENT

Genesis

1–11	78, 81, 145
1–2	55, 89
1	68
1:2	56
1:6–7	55
1:9–10	55
1:10	82
1:12	82
1:18	82
1:20–25	55
1:25	82
1:26–28	81
1:26–27	45
1:26	45, 68
1:28	46, 60, 68
1:29–30	31, 68
1:31	82, 141
2–11	75
2	68, 85, 86
2:5–6	56
2:5	60, 81
2:7	73, 81
2:8–9	68
2:9	69, 113
2:15–17	81
2:15	60
2:16–17	165
2:16	31
2:17	69, 72, 73, 102, 113
2:19–20	46, 68
2:23–24	92
2:23	46
2:24	84
2:25	68, 84
3–11	70
3	74, 83, 85, 86, 96, 97, 99
3:1–6	68
3:1–3	99
3:1	68, 84, 85, 87
3:3	113
3:4–6	99
3:4	69, 84
3:5–7	113
3:5	69, 74, 102, 113, 146
3:6–12	165
3:6	69–71, 84, 146
3:7–11	76, 92
3:7–8	68, 92
3:7	95, 99, 164
3:8–10	99
3:8	85
3:9–13	164
3:9–12	68
3:10	92
3:11	113
3:12	99
3:13	99
3:16–24	68
3:16–19	72
3:16	46, 99
3:17–19	72
3:19	72
3:21	92, 95

Genesis (continued)

Reference	Page
3:21–24	165
3:22–24	72, 74
3:22	69, 73, 113
4–11	86
4	125
4:3–5	75
4:3–4	71
4:4b–8	69
4:5	71
4:6–8	75
4:8	96
4:9	75
4:10–14	75
4:11–12	75
4:14	75–76
4:15–17	75
4:15–16	70
4:17	70
4:23–24	70, 74, 76
5	73
5:1–2	81
6	83
6:1–4	73
6:1–2	70
6:3	73, 81
6:4	70, 71
6:5–7	73, 81
6:5	73
6:6	29
6:8	73, 77
6:11	70, 74
6:13	70, 74, 81
7:11	57
7:23	81
8:2	57
8:17	81
8:20–21	71
8:21–22	31, 57
8:22	31, 57
9:1–2	81
9:2	73
9:4–6	73
9:7	81
9:9–16	31
9:11–16	57
9:11	73
9:15	73
9:19	81
9:25–27	46
9:25	77
10:8–12	76
10:10	46
11	76, 83
11:1–9	74
11:1	81
11:4	70, 73, 81
11:6–7	73
11:6	74
11:8	73
11:9	81
12:1	81
12:3	81
14:19	85
20:7	72
26:11	72

Exodus

Reference	Page
14:9	129
14:21	56
14:23	129
15:1	129
15:8	56
15:19	129–30
15:21	129
15:24	70
16:2–3	70
16:3–4	146
16:3	147
17:7	146
20:2	67
20:17	177
32:1–6	146
32:10	170
34:28	147

Leviticus

Reference	Page
19:18	121, 192, 205

Numbers

Reference	Page
11:4–5	147
21:5	147
35:33	76

INDEX OF BIBLICAL REFERENCES

Deuteronomy
4:15–17	17
6:16	146
8:2	147
8:3	78, 146, 147
8:5	147
9:9	147
9:18	147
11:4	130
20:1	130

Joshua
24	8, 9

Judges
5:22	130
6:11	216
6:15	216
6:27	216
7:2–7	216
8:23	216
17:6	106
21:25	106

1 Samuel
14:44	72
22:16	72

2 Samuel
12	13, 158
24:1–2	86
24:1	74

1 Kings
2:37	72
4:25	216
19:10	179
19:14	179

1 Chronicles
21:1–2	86
21:1	74

2 Chronicles
9:25–26	129

Esther
4:11	180
5:1–8	180
7:2–4	180

Job	86, 101
1:6–12	74
2:1–7	74
3:3	70–71
9:13	56
26:12	56
38–39	36
42:2	74

Psalms
2:7	46
19:1–4	28, 29
19:3	29
20:7	129–30
33	72
33:17	130
35	29
72:1	46
76:6	130
78:2	87
78:40	29
89:9–10	56
95:8–9	146
96:5	17
104:5	57
104:27–30	72
104:29–30	73
106:14	146
106:21	146
121:2	15
139:13	85
145:4–7	41
147:10	130

Proverbs
1:7	165
17:13	121

Proverbs (continued)

17:25	29
20:22	121
21:31	130
24:29	121, 205

Ecclesiastes

3:11	91, 97

Wisdom

13–14	17

Isaiah

2:2–4	201, 202
2:3	201
2:4	216
2:7	129
8:11–12	214
31:1	130
31:3	130
40	15
40:27–28	15
40:28	85
42:1–4	190
42:2	190
42:3	190
43:17	130
44:6–20	17
44:8–9	8, 217
45:18	42
45:23	201
53:3	29
53:4–5	149
54:6	29
63:10	29

Jeremiah

3:20	179
4:13	129
4:23–26	57
6:23	129
8:16	129
10:2–16	17
50:42	129
51:21	130
51:46	214

Daniel

3:18	188
7–8	129
10:13	129

Hosea

6:6	165

Micah

4:4	216

Malachi

3:6	18

NEW TESTAMENT

Matthew

3:11–15	144
3:17	141, 150
4	117–18, 140, 146
4:1–2	139
4:1	149
4:3	78, 142, 149
4:4	147
4:5–6	142
4:6	149
4:8–11	198
4:8–9	116, 142
4:11	143
5–7	202
5:4	156
5:12	179
5:23–24	214
5:39–41	205
5:39	121, 157, 185
5:43–47	176
5:44–45	196
5:44	194, 214
5:48	116, 176, 196, 203

INDEX OF BIBLICAL REFERENCES 239

6	146, 162	16:23	184, 207
6:2	162	16:24–26	179
6:5	162	16:24	149, 178
6:13	143	16:25	178
6:16	162	16:28	178, 180
9:9–13	162	17:1–13	178
9:38	149	17:1	150
10:8	143	17:5	141, 150
10:24–25	174	17:12	143
10:25	129	17:16–17	143
10:27–28	171	17:20	143, 185
10:28	97, 199, 214	17:22–23	143, 179
10:32	167	17:23	179
10:38–39	179	17:24–27	203
10:39	156	18:1–14	213
11:27	23, 184, 199	18:1–5	179
12:18–21	190	18:1	143, 179, 209
12:18	150	18:3–4	179, 180
12:23	129	18:3	134
12:24–30	150	18:4	209
12:24–29	142	18:5	179
12:29	151	18:12	159
12:43–45	52	18:15–17	213
13:11–13	159	18:17	213
13:19	159	18:18–20	213
13:23	159	18:21–22	213
13:30	159	18:23–35	213
13:31–33	185	19:13–15	213
13:31–32	159	19:14	179, 180
13:35	87	19:21	195
13:38–43	159	19:28–30	180
13:44–46	159	19:30	155
13:49	159	20	208
15:17	160	20:1–16	182, 213
16	143	20:11–12	134
16:9	160	20:16	180
16:11	160	20:17–19	143
16:12–13	179	20:18–19	180
16:13–20	177, 178	20:19	210
16:16	178, 180, 207	20:20–28	180, 207
16:17	178	20:20–22	143
16:18	207	20:20–21	180
16:19	213	20:21	180, 208
16:20	178, 180, 207	20:22	208
16:21–23	142	20:24	180
16:21	143, 178, 179	20:25–27	208, 211
16:22–23	143, 150		
16:22	178, 207		

Matthew (continued)

20:25–26	208
20:25	208, 210
20:26–28	208
20:26–27	210
20:26	208, 209
20:27	208
20:28	208
21	177
21:23–27	180
22	143
22:11–13	93
22:21	203
22:39	190
23:11	208, 209
23:29–34	179
24:6	214
24:36	190
25:31–33	170
25:40	159
26	207
26:2	143
26:8–9	143
26:31–35	207
26:36–40	207
26:39	143
26:41	143
26:42	143
26:44	143
26:45	142
26:50–56	208
26:51–54	157–58
26:55	142
26:59–60	142
26:63	27, 143
26:69–74	208
27:3–4	142
27:12	27, 143
27:13	200
27:14	27, 143
27:18–19	142
27:23–25	142
27:39–44	143
27:40	142, 149
27:43	142, 149
28:18	184, 198
28:19–20	215
28:19	184
28:20	184

Mark

1:11	150
1:12	149
1:15	167
1:27	129
1:34	149
1:39	149
1:43	149
3:5	29
3:20–27	150
3:24–26	129
3:24	205
3:27	129, 151
4:13	160
8	143
8:27–30	177, 178
8:29	178
8:31	143, 178, 179
8:32–33	143, 150
8:32	178
8:34–37	179
8:34	149, 178
8:35	178
9:1	178
9:2	150
9:7	150
9:31	143, 179
9:32	179
9:33–37	179
9:33–34	143
9:35	179
10:14–15	179
10:14	180
10:15	180
10:29–31	180
10:32–34	143
10:33–34	180
10:35–45	180
10:35–39	143
10:35–37	180
10:41	180
10:45	27
11	177
11:27–33	180

INDEX OF BIBLICAL REFERENCES 241

12	143
13:24–25	57
14:35	143
14:36	143
14:38	143
14:39	143
14:61	143
15:5	143
15:29–32	143
15:34	30

Luke

1:37	74
3:22	147, 150
3:38–4:3	147
4	117–18, 140, 146
4:1–2	147
4:1	149
4:2	149–50
4:3–12	146
4:3	25, 149
4:4	147
4:5–8	198
4:6	198
4:9	25, 147, 149
6:27–30	132
6:32–34	132
6:35	132
6:36	133
6:40	174
7:36–50	165
9:18–21	178
9:18–20	177
9:20	178
9:22	178, 179
9:23–25	179
9:23	149, 178
9:24	178
9:27	178
9:35	150
9:44	143, 179
9:45	179, 180
9:46–48	179
9:46	143
9:52–55	157–58
9:62	91
10:13	170
10:17–18	199
10:18	130
10:19	151
10:22	23
11:4	143
11:11–12	133
11:14	126, 150
11:15–23	150
11:15	126, 150
11:16	142
11:17–18	150–51
11:19	150
11:20–22	130
11:20	151
11:21–22	151
11:23	151
12:8	167
12:36–38	180
12:48	170
14:7–11	181
14:7	181
14:8	181
14:11	155
14:26	178
14:27	179
14:33	156
15:1–2	182
15:7	162
15:8	99
15:11–32	31, 162
15:11–16	31
15:12	133
15:18–19	133
15:20	133
15:22–24	31
15:25–30	31
15:28–30	134
15:29–30	182
17:33	178, 179
18	164
18:2–7	163
18:10–14	160–62, 165–66
18:11–12	160
18:13	163, 165
18:14	160, 165, 180
18:15–17	6
18:16–17	179

Luke (continued)

18:16	180
18:17	180
18:29–30	180
18:31–33	180
18:34	160, 180
19	177
19:8–10	165
20:1–8	180
22:22	143
22:24–27	180
22:24	143
22:28	143
22:38	149
22:40	143
22:42	143
22:43	143
22:44	143
22:46	143
23:9	143
23:33–34	176
23:35	143
23:39	142, 143
24:21	135

John

	178
1:1	16
1:27	181
3:16	138, 172
4:34	144
5:26	23
5:37	150
5:39–40	23
6:15	129
6:27	150
8:18	23
8:19	23
8:36	203
8:44	69, 74
8:46	142
9:22	167
9:39	159–60
9:41	170
10:17–18	200
10:18	144
11:49–50	142, 153
12:23–25	150
12:27–28	150
12:28	150
12:31	102, 126, 130, 150, 172, 198
12:48	170
13	180–81
13:1	175
13:3	184
13:8	143
13:12–13	181
13:14–17	181
13:16	174
14:6–7	23
14:9–10	23
14:15	184
14:19	23
14:21	184
14:30–31	200
14:30	102
15:10	144, 184
15:20	174
15:22	170
15:24	170
15:25	212
15:28	212
16:11	130, 172, 198
17:5	43
17:23–24	43
18:14	153
18:31	210
19:9	143
19:10	200

Acts

1:8	8
1:22	8
2:24	8
2:32	8
3:26	159
14:21	184
16:31	167
17:1–4	23
26:23	176

Romans

1	31, 99

1:1	157
1:19–20	29
1:21–28	115
1:21–25	99
1:22	29
1:23	71, 99
1:24	31
1:26	31
1:28	31
1:32	97
3:10–12	82
3:19–20	165
3:20–4:8	161
3:23–24	161
4:16–17	15
4:24	167
5	96
5:6–8	133, 175
5:8	138, 171
5:14–18	149
5:14	145
7–8	156
7	177
7:7–25	106, 113
7:7–11	113
7:8	113
7:10–11	91
7:11	113
7:24	90
8:6	96
8:10	97
8:18	97
8:19–21	172
8:19	172
8:29–30	196
8:29	175
8:35	126
8:38–39	126
8:38	126–28
8:39	126
9:19	165
9:22	97
9:30–31	106
10:3	107, 162, 164
10:9	167
11:11	211
11:14	211
12:1–2	177
12:9–14	203
12:15–21	203
12:16–21	205
12:17	121, 153
12:21	203
13	202
13:1–7	128, 202–3
13:1–5	195
13:1–3	126
13:1–2	127, 203
13:3	203
13:4	203
13:6	127, 203
13:7	203
13:8–10	203
14:1–4	212
14:9	184
14:10–11	201

1 Corinthians

1	154, 159
1:17–18	154
1:18	135
1:20–21	135
1:21	154
1:23–24	27, 33, 154
1:23	54
1:24	110
1:25	154
1:26–29	174
2:1–5	182
2:6	128
2:8	126, 128
6:1–8	205
6:12	205
8:1–2	189
8:4–6	126
8:6	15, 23
9:1–15	205
9:1	8
9:19	157, 182, 211
9:24–27	196
11:27–28	135
13:1–2	189
13:2	160
13:8	160
13:12	145

1 Corinthians (continued)

14:16	212
14:20	196
15:3–8	8
15:12–14	8
15:24	126, 128, 211
15:45	146
15:49	61, 149

2 Corinthians

3:18	177
4:4	172, 175, 177
4:5	211
4:6	15, 23, 177
5:17	170
5:21	138, 142
8:9	26
10–13	174
10:1	135
10:4	216
10:10	135
11:3	69, 74
11:6	135
11:7	182
13:3	135

Galatians

3	162
4:9	161
4:19	177
5	175
5:1–4	161
5:13	211
5:16	177
5:22–23	175
5:25	177

Ephesians

1:4	196
1:9–11	15
1:10	148, 172
1:20–22	184
1:21	126, 128
2:1	96
2:2	126
2:8	158
2:14–22	202
3:2–5	15
3:8–11	15
3:10	126, 128
4:13	196
4:15	176
4:30	29
5:25	51
6:12	126, 128

Philippians

1:1	157
2	30, 182
2:3–4	157, 177
2:6	32, 156
2:6–8	25–27, 141–42, 175–77
2:6–11	21, 25, 32
2:7–8	24, 149
2:7	26, 157
2:8	195, 203
2:9–11	33
2:9	141, 184
2:11	167
3:7–14	177
3:7–11	156
3:8–14	196
3:8–10	165
3:9	165

Colossians

1:13	126
1:15	146, 175
1:16	15, 126–28
1:17	54
1:18	176
1:28	196
2:10	126, 184
2:15	126, 128, 198, 199
3:10	176
4:12	196

1 Thessalonians

1:1	23
1:3	23
1:9–10	17

2:15 179
3:11 23
3:13 23
5:3 57
5:15 121, 205
5:23 196

2 Thessalonians

1:9 97

1 Timothy 196

1:13 170
2:14 69, 73
4:6–10 196

2 Timothy 196

2:18 183
3:15–17 58
3:16–17 196

Titus 196

2:11–12 196
3:1 126, 128

Hebrews

1:2 15
1:9 150
2:10 141, 144, 147
2:11 144
2:14 144, 198
2:17 144
2:18 144, 149
4:15 138, 140, 142, 144, 149
5:2 149
5:7 143
5:8 141
5:9–10 141, 149
5:13–14 196
7:26–28 138
7:26–27 142
7:27 148
9:2 96
9:14 138, 142, 149
9:22b 95
9:26 148
10:26–27 170

James

1:3–4 196
1:13 85
1:14–15 139
1:22–25 116
3:2 196
4:1–2 64

1 Peter

1:18–19 149
1:19 142
1:21 167
1:22–23 142
2:19–20 144
2:22–24 138
2:22–23 27, 144
2:23–24 152
2:23 121, 174
3:9 121
3:22 126, 128, 184

2 Peter

1:17 150
2:21 170
3:3–7 90

1 John 196

1:5 85
2:13 23
2:16 117–18, 146
2:23 23
3:2–3 196
3:2 145
3:5 138, 142
3:8 200
3:12 75
3:16 175
4:9 23
4:10 165
4:15 167
4:18 203
4:19 165
5:19 102, 172

2 John

9	23

Revelation

	151
1:5	175
1:9	217
2:13	217
3:4–5	93
3:14	175
3:17–18	93
5	200
5:2	200
5:5	200
5:6–7	200
5:9	201
6:9	168, 217
9:1–11	126
11:7	168, 217
12:5	33
12:7–10	126
12:7–8	151
12:9	74, 172, 200
12:10–11	151, 217
12:11	33, 168
12:17	217
16:14–19	151
17:5–6	217
17:6	168
19:11–21	151
19:15	151–52
20	202
20:2	74
20:4	217
20:12	169
21:1	170
21:8	97